BURNT SNOW

My Years Living & Working with the Dene of the Northwest Territories

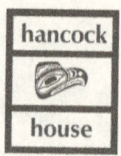

ISBN-13: 978-0-88839-309-8 [trade paperback]
ISBN-13: 978-0-88839-356-2 [trade hardcover]
ISBN-13: 978-0-88839-265-7 [epub]
Copyright © 2020 Kieran Moore

Library and Archives Canada Cataloguing in Publication

Title: Burnt snow : my years, living & working with the Dene of the Northwest Territories / Kieran Moore.
Names: Moore, Kieran, author.
Identifiers: Canadiana (print) 20200172816 | Canadiana (ebook) 20200172905 | ISBN 9780888393098 (softcover) | ISBN 9780888393562 (hardback) | ISBN 9780888392657 (EPUB)
Subjects: LCSH: Moore, Kieran. | LCSH: Indigenous peoples—Northwest Territories—Social life and customs—20th century. | LCSH: Moore, Kieran—Friends and associates. | CSH: Northwest Territories— Social conditions—1945-1999. | LCGFT: Autobiographies.
Classification: LCC E99.C59 M66 2020 | DDC 971.9/203092—dc232

All rights reserved. No part of this publication may be reproduced, stored in a retrieval system or transmitted, in any form or by any means, electronic, mechanical, audio, photocopying, recording, or otherwise (except for copying permitted by Sections 107 and 108 of the U.S. Copyright Law and except for book reviews for the public press), without the prior written permission of Hancock House Publishers. Permissions and licensing contribute to the book industry by helping to support writers and publishers through the purchase of authorized editions and exerpts.
Please visit www.accesscopyright.ca.

Illustrations and photographs are copyrighted by the artist or the Publisher.

Printed in the USA

PRODUCTION & DESIGN: M. Lamont & L. Raingam

EDITOR: D. MARTENS

We acknowledge the financial support of the Government of Canada through the Canada Book Fund and the Canada Council for the Arts, and of the Province of British Columbia through the British Columbia Arts Council and the Book Publishing Tax Credit.

Hancock House gratefully acknowledges the Halkomelem Speaking Peoples whose unceded traditional territories our offices reside upon
Published simultaneously in Canada and the United States by

HANCOCK HOUSE PUBLISHERS LTD.
19313 Zero Avenue, Surrey, B.C. Canada V3Z 9R9
#104-4550 Birch Bay-Lynden Rd, Blaine, WA, U.S.A. 98230-9436
(800) 938-1114   Fax (800) 983-2262
www.hancockhouse.com   sales@hancockhouse.com

BURNT SNOW

My Years, Living & Working with the Dene of the Northwest Territories

KIERAN MOORE

For my grandsons, Nakaiya and Jerhyn, also to my daughter Teya and son Braeden, in the hope that these stories will give them an understanding of the richness of the Dene culture that is part of their background and of the role it played in my life.

TABLE OF CONTENTS

Introduction 1

Heading to
the Northwest Territories 3

Tom Dornbross 7

Working at the Gold Mine 10

Founding of Rae Lakes: Gamètì 13

My First Days in Rae Lakes 17

Life in Rae Lakes 23

Rae Lakes: Memorable Individuals 27

Hislop Lake: K'Eàgotì 31

Put To the Test 37

Jimmy Lacorde: Teacher 41

Jimmy Lacorde: Survivor 45

The Ice Storm 47

Camping On the Hunt 59

Legends of Edzo 61

The Changeling 63

Hunting in the Barrenlands 65

A Gifted Story 69

The Joker: Dzèhkw'ii 71

Nàhga: The Bushman 77

Handball Game: Gohzìi 80

Cambridge Bay 82

Rae Lakes Community Hall 84

Rae Lakes Airport 87

Hottah Lake Yqhtsik'e 89

What Happened to Bear Lake Alexie? 99

Fort Franklin: Deline 107

Charlie Neyelle 111

Don't Burn the Snow 113

Fort Franklin to Rae Lakes 115

A Community Hunt and A Dog Called Jesus 127

Making Connections 136

Steel Space Industries 139

If Ravens Could Talk 143

Bear Lake Alexie Comes to Hay River 145

Chief Dan's Dilemma 152

Buffalo River 158

Hay River Reserve's Dream Bus 162

Raft Race 165

The Inquisitive One 169

Hay River to Fort Simpson 171

Fort Simpson and Hay River in 1977 191

The Horn Plateau Experience 193

Akaitcho 215

My Mother Saved My Life 219
Black Duck Camp: Whǫsìiwekǫ̀ǫ̀ 222
A Traditional Marriage 228
Dog Island 230
The Emergence of a Strong Leader 235
Brother Gosselin 240
Joseph Rabesca: K'aadee Susie 247
A New Beginning 257
Acknowledgements 259

BURNT SNOW

INTRODUCTION

The stories in this book begin in the early 1970s, when I was twenty years of age and facing impending layoffs at my construction job in Winnipeg. I was frustrated at the instability and purposelessness of my life at the time and, consequently, decided to head into the Northwest Territories in the hope of finding purpose and direction for myself there.

After a short time working in the Yellowknife area, I was asked to build a church in the Dene community of Rae Lakes, the Dene being one of the Indigenous groups that inhabit the northern boreal and Arctic region of Canada. That assignment led to my immersion in the world of the Dene throughout the 1970s and early '80s.

It was a time of dramatic change for their communities. I was a witness to both the richness of their traditional ways and to the confusion and suffering they were undergoing as the old ways came under threat from colonialism.

The tradition of storytelling was an integral part of the Dene way, and I learned a great deal by listening and sharing in that tradition. The stories I tell here reflect the level of my personal engagement with them. These stories are told in the spirit of the storytelling tradition of the Dene and that of my Irish ancestors.

Rae Lakes (Gamèti), and a little later Fort Franklin (Deline) were the jumping-off points for me. The elders I met in these communities were strong in their adherence to traditional ways and little influenced by outside forces. They were my teachers. They held fast to their traditions and legends and invited me to share in their storytelling culture. These individuals, male and female, fed my insatiable curiosity and welcomed me as one of their own.

Had I arrived in these communities ten years later, many of the enriching experiences I had would not have been available to me. I had the opportunity to participate in one of the last of a tradition of dog-sled hunting expeditions into the Barrenlands. That hunt served as a rite of passage for their young men, and it certainly served that purpose for me.

My travels in the region surrounding Great Slave Lake and Great Bear Lake led me into the heart of the traditional Dene world. There, I bonded with community members, elders, chiefs and medicine men. I worked alongside, ate, danced and hunted with them. One of the oldest of the elders, Bruno Mantla, took me under his wing when he saw my inquisitiveness and willingness to learn their ways. He saw something in me that prompted him to stop calling me by my name, Kieran, and instead referred to me as, Bruno sechi, or Bruno's younger brother.

Whatever strength of character I had when I arrived in Dene territory as a rudderless young man was enriched by my integration into the Dene world. In particular, I learned never to give up on whatever I set out to do, no matter how difficult the challenge. I learned, like the Dene, to persevere against great odds.

With the example they set, the challenges shared and the support provided, I found that sense of purpose I came north to find. I formed lifelong relationships with many of the Dene I met and who appear in my stories. I treasure the memory of those times we spent together and celebrate that connection in this book.

HEADING TO THE NORTHWEST TERRITORIES

I left Winnipeg in my beat-up Land Rover on the morning of the first of January, 1971. It was the first step on a journey I was undertaking to find myself somewhere in the remote reaches of the Northwest Territories.

The highway I chose to follow north was represented by a yellow line on a map mounted on the wall of my bedroom in Winnipeg, a line that led me into the NWT on my third day on the road.

I made one stop outside Hay River, at a Renewable Resources office, and told them that I was looking for work. I was advised that everything in the area was shut down for the winter and that I should go back to where I came from. This was not the answer I was hoping to hear after travelling 2,500 kilometres. However, I continued on.

I stopped in Enterprise to get gas and talked to the owner of the restaurant there, Bernie's Steak House. I asked Bernie if he thought I might find work farther north.

"What kind of work are you looking for?" he asked.

"A job maybe building log buildings."

"Do you know how to build log buildings?"

"No," I replied, "but I learn fast." He laughed at that.

"Don't waste your time; you've no idea what you're talking about. There aren't any logs big enough to build anything where you're headed. I'd advise you to go back to where you came from." More of the same advice. He was just being realistic and laughed at this young greenhorn with dreams of building log cabins as a career. Interestingly, I met this man close to ten years later, and we had a good laugh recalling that first meeting.

It was January 5, and a blizzard was blowing in close to -40C conditions as I got back on the road at about the 250-mile mark when I had my first sighting of a dog team in motion. They were travelling on a trail that intersected with the road and I watched in awe. It instantly reminded me of the time my grade 7 teacher asked me, what I wanted to do when I grow up and I answered "I want to deliver mail by dog team". This was the beginning of what I was looking for and, to my young eyes, a symbolic image of the true north. Little did I know that I would travel this trail to a Dogrib cabin named Blackduck Camp on frequent occasions a number of years later.

I was running low on gas, having trouble staying awake, and began to hit the snow banks along the sides of the road from time to time. I took a turnoff to find a place to rest and ended up at what looked like a large turnabout. I dropped into a deep sleep.

I didn't run the vehicle during the night, for fear of running out of gas. When I woke up, I got out and cranked up the engine, got it going and sat back in the driver's seat wrapped in my sleeping bag, waiting for the frosted window to clear up. When I next looked up, I saw that I was parked in the middle of a graveyard. I knew I must be close to Yellowknife because I remember thinking: When you're near the dead, it's a sure sign there's life nearby.

I left the graveyard, rounded a corner a mile away and descended into a beautiful valley with a small lake surrounded by Precambrian granite outcrops. It was a clear day, and in the distance I saw tall office buildings as the town arose like magic out of the wilderness. I felt warm satisfaction at having made it to this famous outpost of the north, Yellowknife.

I gassed up, ate breakfast at the Gold Range Restaurant and asked where I could find cheap lodging in town. They sent me next door to the Evergreen Hotel. It was cheap lodging and a welcome change from the cab of my truck. I washed up in the sink, fell into bed and slept. Around three o'clock in the afternoon, I was awakened by a loud banging on my door. I opened it to a bearded, professorial-looking man.

"Do you own the Land Rover outside?" he bellowed out.

"Yes."

"Welcome to Yellowknife. You're now officially a member of the Yellowknife Land Rover Club." I told him what I was doing in Yellowknife and asked how many members were in the club.

"Three, and you makes it four." Then he surprised me. "How about joining me and my family for supper tonight?" he asked. I accepted his invitation and shared a beautiful meal in the company of a local family who lived in the city that was to play such a large part in my future. I couldn't have asked for a warmer down-home welcome.

(Tjaart) Tom Dornbross
- credit –N.W.T. Archive/ McCall family

TOM DORNBROSS

I was in Yellowknife, looking for work, had a room, and was high in spirits— but low on money. I went to the library in the basement of the town hall, a warm place to hang around for a while. There were many empty chairs at the tables spread around the room. I picked a place to sit, hung my coat on the back of the chair, and was about to go looking for a book.

"Please move your stuff to another table," said the librarian. I looked around the empty room and was somewhat puzzled.

"Why?" I asked.

"There's a man who comes here every morning and he uses that chair."

"But there are dozens of other empty chairs around," I muttered.

"Suit yourself!" she said and walked away. I was disturbed by this curt exchange and so I decided not to move, got some books and sat down. An old man using a walking stick came down the stairs, walked up to my table, looked at the librarian and then looked at me. With one swipe of his walking stick, he sent everything I had put on the table tumbling to the floor. I got out of my chair to pick things up. I couldn't believe what I was seeing as he calmly took my place at the table and began to read his newspaper. I gathered up my stuff with as much dignity as the situation allowed and located the librarian.

"What was that all about?" I asked politely.

"Old Tom's an icon in the community, one of the first people to come to Yellowknife when it was just a tent city," she replied conclusively. I later found out that he was an immigrant from Holland and, while he never worked in the mines, he hauled water to the mine workers in pails hanging from a wooden yoke straddling his shoulders. The mine workers didn't want to take the time to cut through five-foot-thick ice to get water for cooking and washing, and consequently they depended on him. He performed this task for them for years and was rumored to have invested his money in properties in the area and become a rich man. Well, as fate would have it, that very same day I went to the local coffee shop. I hadn't been sitting for more than a few minutes when the owner asked me to move to another chair.

"Why?" I asked for the second time that day. He pointed at the doorway as Tom walked in. I moved right then and there, knowing the consequences of crossing this old-timer. Sure enough, he sat down in the chair I had occupied and ordered hot water. They gave it to him, along with an empty bowl. He poured the hot water into the bowl, took some ketchup packages from their container and emptied them into the bowl. He then crushed crackers into it, making his own tomato soup. He left without paying for anything. I checked with the owner.

"We've watched him do this for years. He's a town father, one of the oldest of the old-timers. Look up there on the wall—that's a picture of him from the old days." There on the wall was a picture inscribed with the name Tom Dornbross. It was a picture of him as a much younger man. He never married; had no friends to speak of, but he obviously commanded respect in town. My first impression had been that he behaved like a miserable old coot.

I was dissatisfied with bunkhouse living in Yellowknife and wanted a place of my own. I searched around the town and found a number of old abandoned buildings I thought might serve my purposes. I went to city hall to make enquiries in the Land Titles Department and was told that the buildings belonged to Tom Dornbross, my old nemesis.

I tried to find Tom. It was strange that everyone knew of him but no one knew where he lived. It took me two days to find that he had moved into the old folks' home. I located the place and knocked on his door. He opened it, looked at me and immediately slammed the door in my face. I knocked again and talked loudly to him through the door, thinking he might be partially deaf. He opened the door once again and gave me a chance to ask him about the properties. He denied owning any of the houses I was interested in renting and told me to go away. I left, but, being stubborn by nature, I took another tack.

I had heard that if a person did not pay their taxes on a piece of property and someone stepped in and paid them, then the properties would automatically be transferred to the person who paid the taxes. Even though I didn't verify the rumour, I went to the city hall offices to try my luck. I located the property department, spoke to the person behind the counter and told them I was willing to pay the taxes on a particular abandoned property. The secretary took the file to the town manager. A few more people were called in and they discussed the problem and said it was decided that they would not tell me how much was owed by way of taxes. It appeared that old Tom had the town's support, even though he had not paid his taxes.

I left the office still determined to get one of these houses, which could more accurately be described as shacks. I went back to Tom's place the next day and knocked on the door, which was ajar, but there was no answer. I peered in and talked loudly into the dark. There was a light on in a hallway off the room. I entered cautiously. There, in the middle of the room, were two neatly stacked piles of paper maybe three feet high. I called out Tom's name, and he appeared in a bathrobe and looked me in the eye.

"You again!" he exclaimed. He held up a sheet of paper in his hand. "Do you know what that is?" he asked rhetorically as he carefully oriented the page to place it on top of one of the stacks. "These are the stock exchange reports; I have to watch them closely. Somewhere in this pile there's a record of some stocks I bought in a company when it first started and the shares were just pennies at the time. You have to keep on top of these things. What do you want this time?" he asked.

I talked about the weather and other non-threatening things while trying to make heads or tails of the man and win his favour in the hope that he would rent one of his shacks to me. He didn't throw me out right away this time. He was actually sharing the moment with me. When I asked if he had any shacks for sale, he said he was not interested in selling any property, so that was the end of that; it was the last time I was to meet with him.

10 years later Tom died, I'm told, they tracked down a relative in Holland who inherited whatever he owned. Any discussion of the old days in Yellowknife would, in all likelihood, involve a reference to Tom with his yoke and two water pails. Everyone knew of him, but no one knew him.

WORKING AT THE GOLD MINE

I did some enquiring around Yellowknife and was told that the only place where work was available throughout the winter was at the mine. Reluctantly, I went to the head office of Giant Mines, a local goldmine, thinking I was scraping bottom to come all this way to end up working in a hole in the ground. I approached the mine's front office desk and asked if they were hiring.

"No," the lady behind the counter replied. "The mine cuts back in the winter. We'll be rehiring in March and April. If you're still around, we might find something for you." I sat back on the bench, looking in my wallet to see if I had enough to buy lunch. Then I remembered the business card I had been given by my former boss in Winnipeg. I pulled it out and read the note he had scribbled on the back of it.

"This guy is a real hustler," it read. So I approached the secretary with it.

"Would you give this card to the mine manager please?" She looked it over and saw what was written on it and smiled.

"What the heck, it's probably a waste of time, but okay, I'll do that." A minute or so passed and a man came out of the office area and, holding my card out, introduced himself and asked: "Who wrote this note on the card?"

"My boss." I replied.

"If I call him right now, will he vouch for what it says?" he asked.

"Call him." I said. Instead of doing that, he invited me into his office. He obviously took me at my word. We sat down and he asked me a question right off the top.

"Can you work in the cold?" he asked. I told him about my trip by way of an answer.

"You have a job, and you've got a week to prove yourself. The secretary will give you a bunkhouse key. You start tomorrow, and she'll show you where the cafeteria is." I picked up the key, and as I headed for the door, the office secretary looked at me and shook her head.

"Congratulations," she said with smile.

The next day I went to the carpentry shop, where I was introduced to a crew of carpenters and labourers from a wide range of ethnic backgrounds. The shop foreman was a Scotsman, the lead carpenter a Yugoslav and the workers in the timber shop were of Italian, Ukrainian and Chipewyan background. Here I was, about to add my Irish immigrant status to the mix.

At the mine, I became very good friends with two Indigenous workers, an Inuk named Lucky Dillon and a Yellowknife from N'Dilo, Philip Liske. They both worked in the mill at the most dangerous and unhealthy job there. The place they spent most of their working time was a glassed-in workroom called the Cottrell. They had to don special equipment before entering the room. Their job was to shovel arsenic out of bags into a vat. Toxic arsenic dust floated about in there, thick and heavy. Lucky and Philip were the only ones doing this work at the time I was there.

Philip told me the foreman arranged the shifts in the Cottrell so that when he and Lucky showed up for work they were scheduled to work there. Like many workers at the mine, they never argued about their assignment. They were just happy to have a paying job and didn't seem to consider the possible long-range consequences. This amounted to a form of exploitation of the Indigenous workers at the mine. I didn't realize the full implications of this advantage-taking practice, since this was my first brush with the darker side of life for the Indigenous people of the NWT.

When Lucky wasn't in the Cottrell, he worked at the blacksmith shop, where they fashioned special tools required at the mine and repaired tools. The blacksmith was an elderly Ukrainian immigrant who was a marvel to watch as he worked. I sat with him one evening in the bunkhouse, and he told me what a natural Lucky was as a smithy. He had never before met anyone who mastered the trade with such ease.

"All these skills that took me years to learn, Lucky grasps right away, but it's leading nowhere. It's a dying trade," he said with deep regret.

Lucky, Philip and I wandered the mine site in summer on one of our days off. They took me along the same path that the smoke from the stack took as it drifted with the prevailing winds. We came to a crystal-clear lake and went for a swim. I opened my eyes underwater and there was not a living thing in the lake. I got out wondering why a lake like this was not posted as being polluted. It didn't look polluted, but it certainly must have been. There wasn't a visible living organism in it. It wasn't a place in which I would swim again. Lucky, foolhardy as usual, swam in it to his heart's content.

In a very short time, I found that my comfort level was greater when I interacted with individuals from the Indigenous community. Those I met felt more like kindred spirits to me. Over time, these connections led to my involvement in a world and culture significantly different from that of my home community of Winnipeg. I didn't know it at the time, but I was entering that Indigenous world as it was undergoing one if the most significant transformations in the NWT since the years of first contact with the settler community.

Phillip, Lucky and I eventually went our separate ways. Philip became a game warden in Yellowknife and, as of 2004, was not showing any ill effects from his exposure to the arsenic. Lucky went back to Inuvik and, sadly died.

FOUNDING OF RAE LAKES: GAMÈTI

In early spring, I left Yellowknife after the breakup of a personal relationship. My truck was out of commission, and on impulse I hitchhiked on the dusty, gravel road leading to Fort Rae. I wandered into the town chapel there and sat quietly in a pew, feeling depressed and very much alone. A short while later, a priest came in. He approached me and asked if I needed to talk. I nodded, so he invited me to his office, where, without much urging, I explained my personal situation and how meaningless my life appeared to be.

"So why did you come up north?" he asked.

"To find a job in the bush and hopefully to do something purposeful."

"How?"

"I don't know, building things maybe!"

"Tell me a bit more about yourself," he said. I told him that I worked at the mine and hated the work there and knew I needed to do something different. I added that my truck had broken down and consequently couldn't go elsewhere to find work. He listened patiently and then summed up what I had told him.

"You like the bush. You're a carpenter in need of work. You want to help people. That's very interesting." What he went on to say floored me. "It just so happens that I got a call from the bishop telling me that our priest carpenter, who was getting ready to build a church, had an accident and cut two of his fingers off. I've been asked to find someone who could take his place and do the job. It doesn't pay much, and the location is a fly-in community, so no need for a truck. Do you want the job?" he asked.

"I'll do it for nothing. When do you need me?" I blurted out, flabbergasted.

"Tomorrow," he replied. "Get your belongings and go to the floatplane base in Yellowknife. The flight carrying the building materials leaves tomorrow for Rae Lakes. You'll take Father Duchassois' seat on that flight."

I can't remember how I got back to Yellowknife from Fort Rae, but I do remember how excited I was at the prospect of having my first experience of travelling by bush plane and looking forward to whatever came my way. I had no idea that I was about to take a flight into a future that would push me to my personal limits.

The following day, I got my toolbox and packsack to the float plane base, where a plane was sitting on the ice in the process of being loaded. There I met Father Amourous, the parish priest, and later, Father Duchassois. I became good friends with both of them during the time I spent in Rae Lakes. (As an aside, Father Duchassois once went to visit Vancouver, British Columbia. While there, he was approached by a woman after mass and asked if he had ever run into a man named Kieran Moore in the Northwest Territories. And of course he had. That woman was my sister, Deirdre.)

Father Amourous and Father Duchassois

Father Amourous was a northerner at heart, though he had come here straight from France. I told him that he and the Ayatollah Khomeini were look-alikes, he being a more pleasing version. He didn't appreciate the comparison. But otherwise, he had a melodious laugh and was an uncanny linguist. He had learned Dogrib before he learned English. He also spoke French, Swiss German and Italian.

After loading the plane, a single-engine Turbo Beaver, we taxied across the rough surface of the ice, splashing up water from standing pools, and took off. As we flew, Father Amourous gave me a rundown on what to expect when we landed. He spoke of Dogrib customs, their way of life and why the community was located where it was, and painted a picture of their economic and social circumstances. What follows is a summary, in my words, of what he had to say.

Some of the Dene who settled in Fort Rae in the early 1960s had gravitated there from other communities such as Fort Franklin and Fort Simpson (Liidli Kue). They intermarried with the Dogrib in Fort Rae. They were unhappy with the overcrowding and with their treatment in Fort Rae, in particular the difficulty they had in getting housing assigned to them. Their distinctive culture was being threatened, their language taken away, their children forced into residential schools. Along with that, disease was running rampant in Fort Simpson, Fort Rae and Fort Franklin. They met to discuss their situation and consulted their elders and medicine men on the matter of moving out of these communities. Three groups were formed to search for appropriate locations.

One of these went north to the Barrenlands, another east, and the third went west. All returned at an appointed time, saying that they had not found a place that would provide them with the essentials to support their families year-round. Discouraged, they all headed south. A storm came up. After they established camp, one of the men noticed the firelight reflecting on something in the trunk of a tree. It turned out to be the shaft of an arrow.

They discussed this finding amongst themselves and then shared what they knew of the region in which they were. Fish, moose and ducks were plentiful, and they were in close proximity to the caribou migration routes. They concluded from this, and the sign of the arrow in the tree, that this was a place where their ancestors had hunted, and so decided that this was where they would settle.

They returned to Fort Rae, and one group moved their families by boat that summer to their new location. They called it Gamèti (Rae Lakes), a traditional Dene settlement halfway between Great Bear and Great Slave lakes. Rae Lakes was founded about ten years before my arrival in the community. The other two groups created the settlements of Snare Lake (Wekweètì) and Wha Ti.

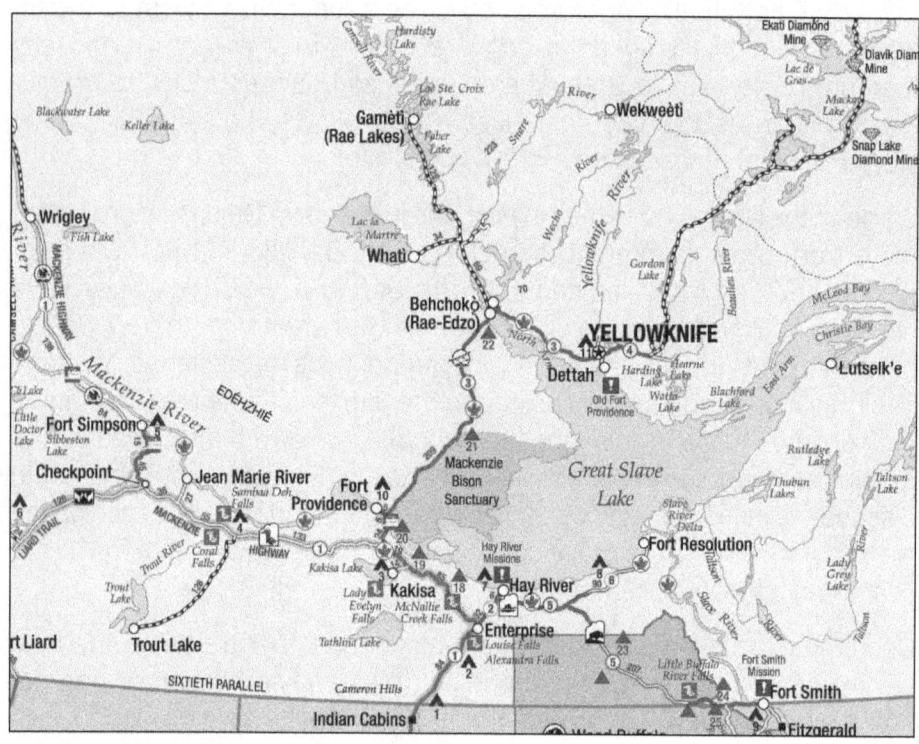

Location of Rae Lakes, Wekweètì and Wha Ti

MY FIRST DAYS IN RAE LAKES

After Father Amourous finished his detailed overview, I turned my attention to the landscape. The thousands of frozen lakes below had me wondering how it was possible to navigate and survive in such a sprawling wilderness. I was in disbelief at this stroke of good fortune that had me heading to work in a bush plane to do what I came north hoping to do, to give some concrete purpose to my life.

Whose God has a priest lose his fingers in answer to someone else's prayer? I wondered.

The plane circled the community, and down below I could see people coming out of their houses and heading for the dock. We landed on the ice and taxied up to the dock, exited the plane and started to unload right away. Over my shoulder, I saw a crowd, probably the entire population of the town, gathering on a hill by the shore. Father Amourous told me to stop what I was doing.

"Come; I'll introduce you to the community. They're expecting Father Duchassois and will be wondering who you are," he said.

Community members visiting with us at the priest's house

Approximately sixty people were gathered there, all dressed in bright colours. The women's scarves in red, blue and green presented a stark contrast to the background of ice and snow. The older women wore darker, full-length shawls and long dresses, and a number of the men wore blue or red kerchiefs like sweatbands around their foreheads. I stood out as pale as a sick ghost in the midst of people with such a dark and weathered complexion. Pride, self-confidence and unpretentiousness, masked by shyness, was a common characteristic of the men and women alike that I was to meet here.

Another mix of greeters

We climbed the embankment to join them. and Father Amourous proceeded to shake hands with every man, woman and child. He stopped and chatted, particularly with the elders. Their exchange was in Dogrib and laced with laughter, particularly when he addressed the women. The men, almost without exception, puffed on pipes, and the aroma of tobacco hung in the air. The arrival of a plane was a rare event here. The warm reception and my being the centre of so much attention was overwhelming.

I had gone from feeling like a person of little consequence to being the focus of an entire community. The building of the church took on a whole new meaning for me. I could see that it was so much more than just a job; it was an important contribution, the building of a significant symbol of a settled community.

With every step Father Amourous took along the line of people, shaking their hands, a young boy of about nine, the first to greet Father Amourous, followed behind him. He was nicknamed Shadow. Our luggage was carried ahead to a cabin on the shoreline, where we were to stay. All of the family who normally lived there, with the exception of the wife, were away at a sanatorium for TB treatment.

Typical log home at Rae Lakes

As we arrived, we found an elderly woman, Bruno Apple's wife, busy splitting firewood. She greeted us and ushered us into her spotlessly clean, one-room house, where we each had a two-by-four frame with planks to serve as a bed. In the centre of the house was a forty-five-gallon gas drum converted into a stove. Every home had a similar stove, except that in this case, the stove shone like stainless steel. The woman of the house scoured it daily with steel wool until it shone brilliantly.

We were invited to a feast, held that night in a cabin a little bigger than the one where we resided. Sheets of canvas were spread on the floor to form a large tablecloth. Piping hot pots, each filled with a selection of cooked caribou, moose meat or fish, steaming rice and raisins, were spread about on the canvas. Jars of jam, cubes of lard, heaps of bannock and bowls of boiled eggs were scattered amongst the pots, along with slabs of dry meat, pemmican and bone marrow. The house was lit by lanterns, and close to the ceiling was a grid of poles being used to dry meat.

Before going to the feast, I was told to bring a plate, a bowl, a cup, a knife and spoon wrapped in a tea towel—never a fork, which was regarded as the devil's tool by some. We sat on the floor, unwrapped the utensils and, once settled, someone walked down the middle of the tablecloth, serving tea. Others followed with rice and a soup of oatmeal and wild game. The men ate first, then the women, followed by the children. Any leftover food was shared out, to be taken home.

Youthful mothers visiting with us in the priest's kitchen

Once the house emptied out, it was cleaned and prepared for a drum dance. The drummers arrived and warmed the hand drums over the stove to tighten the hide, so as to achieve a certain timbre. Then, when all were ready, the drumming began, resounding in the room and deep inside my chest cavity as it took on the double beat of the heart: ba-boom, ba-boom. It was a mesmerizing first-time experience with a culture so uniquely different from my own. I was deeply moved by the whole experience.

Dancers formed a circle, and the drummers faced east. The tempo built, and soon people began to step forward to dance. No order was evident; men, women and children, married or unmarried, everyone from every corner joined in the line. The house resounded with the rhythm of the drums and a haunting chant. Those standing around were encouraged to join in or sometimes pushed involuntarily into the circle, as happened to me. It was a remarkably spirited event, a powerful ritual so obviously steeped in tradition, that had everyone moving as one. It was an entry point into another way of life for me.

During my first month in Rae Lakes, as I worked on the church I saw men from the settlement applying themselves to a special communal task nearby. They had a collection of handsaws, axes and knives and were working on wooden staves around them.

Preparing the gravesite fence

They would squat randomly and sit cross-legged, smoking pipes or cigarettes and chatting as they whittled away on the small staves. I was curious as to what had drawn them together with such common purpose and was told that they were making a cross for a child's grave and a picket fence to surround it. I was surprised to find that this was only the second gravesite to be set up in the community, a fact indicative of just how new the settlement actually was. The first grave was also quite recent. It was that of an elderly woman, the wife of David Quitte, otherwise known as Eight and a Half Times Right David. More about him later.

This second grave was for a stillborn child. This child, who had not even drawn breath, received the same dedicated attention given to anyone else who died. Playing out before my eyes was a demonstration of the profound respect this community had for the individual and for life itself, all expressed in this simple act of preparing a gravesite. There were no signs of outward mourning; they just worked away with an unspoken regard for a life lost.

Once finished, they formed a procession and walked single file toward the plot of land set aside as the graveyard, each carrying staves. The one leading the group carried the cross. Once at the gravesite, the cross was planted and the fence staked in place.

To me, this seemed fitting—that the first grave dug here was for an elder who had lived a long, productive life, and located beside her gravesite was the resting place of a stillborn child, prepared with equal respect. Someone said it was a way of giving a child to the old woman, so she would not be lonely in the spirit world.

This small experience prompted me to look at life from a different perspective. I'm not stretching it to say that it left me feeling attuned to the heartbeat of the planet. I had come north to give meaning to my life, and I believe it began to happen right here.

Log home, tipi smoke tent and my prospector's tent

John Bekali's brother (Michael) with staked-out dog team

LIFE IN RAE LAKES

I found myself losing track of time because of the almost twenty-four hours of daylight. The community of Rae Lakes was active well past midnight. There was no set time for people to go to bed; any time was proper, depending on how tired you felt. I was the only one on a conscious time schedule in the entire community. It was frustrating at first, when those who were working with me turned up at different times. I slowly adjusted, as did they. I was aware that, not only were they building the church, but they had families and dogs to feed, wood to cut, nets to check and repair, dog sleds to build, canoes and snowshoes to make or repair.

All of this was so very new to me. After work hours, I was engaged in many ways, such as checking fish nets. I learned how to remove fish from a net efficiently, to distinguish fresh from drowned fish, to avoid the spines on pickerel, and, hardest of all, how to untangle a four-foot jackfish that had spun a 150-foot net into a single rope. Fish needed to be caught by the hundreds to feed the many dogs in the settlement during the winter months. Most of the families had two dog teams; seven per team was the standard, and some were decked out with beaded blankets and bells.

I had a difficult time adjusting to the diet, primarily because they didn't eat vegetables. Theirs was a steady diet of meat of various kinds, since every part of the animals they hunted was used. Nothing was wasted. While my taste buds were adjusting, I resorted to using the HP sauce I had brought with me, the use of which was an old habit of my father's, to spice up the meat and fish diet. No one seemed to suffer from diet-related illnesses. It may be due to the fact that they ate every part of the animal: sausages made with the intestines, and soups made with the bones and the blood of the animals. The organs were regarded as a delicacy, and even the contents of the second stomach in the caribou, which is usually filled with caribou moss and lichen, was an item sought-after by the old-timers. What

I would have called the choice pieces of meat, such as steaks and roasts, were made into dried meat, while meat close to the bone was boiled or cooked on an open fire. Rice mixed with raisins was a favourite dish, and rolled oats were thrown in with fish soup or meat stews. Bannock was ever present, either baked or fried.

After I had worked for a few months, the meat supply ran low because the caribou had not arrived as expected. During this time, we ate fish almost exclusively. I grew tired of eating the soft-textured flesh daily and craved something tough to chew. In response to this wish, one of the elders took a large jackfish, cut the stomach out, washed it, and stuck it onto a stick, which he thrust into the fire. The stomach became seared and partially shriveled. He presented me with a piece and insisted I try it. Smiling, I insisted that he take the first bite, to be sure he wasn't playing a cruel joke. He did that and then passed it to me. It was hard to chew, but it was delicious. I had occasion to apply this particular lesson when I ran out of food in dire circumstances some years later.

The buildings in the community were of log construction, with the exception of the new church, which was built of milled lumber. I wasn't realizing my dream of becoming a log builder yet. The community had no land-based airport, just a dock for float planes to use when the lake was open. In winter, a runway was marked out on the ice with short trees stuck in the snow. As far as other mechanized transportation was concerned, there were only two snowmobiles in the community at the time, and they were forever breaking down.

The community store was opened once or twice a week, if the person with the key wasn't out hunting. Most of the purchasing there was done on a credit basis. There were few radios around, and the signal was unreliable. High-frequency radios, SBX-11s, were used for emergency calls.

Every residence had a smoke tent where daily chores took place, such as cooking, making dry and pounded meat, harvesting bone marrow, smoking meat or tanning hides. The tent was a tipi made of untreated canvas draped around thirteen long poles. The bottom edge of the canvas was left about two inches off the ground, which allowed for ventilation. While the women went about their tasks, their babies were often kept nearby in hammocks, always within reach.

When it came to having children, most of the women preferred to give birth at home rather than be flown to a hospital. One young woman made the decision to come back to Rae Lakes from the city one winter. She wanted to have her baby with her mother at her side and in the tent where they lived. Her name was Georgina Mantla. Her brother, John Mantla, was to be the best man at my wedding in Fort Rae years later.

On the matter of structures, apart from the tipi and smoke tent, there was the bush or house tent. It came in various sizes, but most had five-foot-high walls. Tent floors were deeply carpeted with spruce boughs laid out in one direction, which provided a uniform thickness to the floor covering. A drying pole was placed across the center of the tent at ceiling height for drying muskrat and beaver hides. Dried caribou hides were spread on top of the spruce boughs to provide more comfortable seating. Outside, they built elevated platform tents for secure storage purposes.

Handmade packsacks lined the outside walls, filled with all the tools or materials required for use in the tent or on the trap line. Fabrics were stashed in containers, waiting to be sewn into articles of clothing on hand-cranked Singer sewing machines. Knives, always razor sharp, were neatly wrapped in a canvas apron, with specific compartments for the different sizes. Most of these knives were prized possessions, many often obtained from Brother Gosselin, an Oblate brother who lived in Fort Rae.

It was common to see women out splitting wood in front of their houses, young girls packing babies and standing around chatting, and men squatting in the chief's house while playing checkers and smoking their pipes or cigarettes. Others sat outside, repairing fish nets strung between two trees. Women could be seen gathered around a large moose hide, stretching and scraping it with handmade bone tools. Young boys hauled water up from the shore or, in winter, chipped at the ice to make holes for people to set fish nets under the ice. Others dried fish over a smudge, fixed canoes or shaped paddles. There was a calmness and serenity in the middle of all of this activity, with no one appearing to be in a hurry; they got things done according to nature's clock and the circle of the seasons.

Staked dogs and platform storage tents

There was little money in circulation. This was a society rich in other ways, one in which people looked after one another. They worked as one when it was necessary, but no one commanded what needed to be done; it was suggested. The interaction I observed between the elders and the young people was a model of intergenerational relationships marked by respect. In this environment, no one yelled or got mad when someone wasn't pulling their weight, but rather, through example, the offending person caught on to what was expected.

On an average day I saw numerous dog teams come and go as they hauled firewood, fish and spruce boughs. The dogs were staked out around the community and were well looked after, to better serve the community during the winter hunting season.

The children in the community did have some toys, but I don't recall ever seeing a mass-produced toy during my time in Rae Lakes. What toys they had were made of local materials and ingeniously constructed, such as this float plane, its body made of gathered pieces of wood, with a propeller made of metal cut from a pop can.

Children playing with toy float plane

RAE LAKES: MEMORABLE INDIVIDUALS

My next-door neighbour in Rae Lakes was an elder named Eight and a Half Times Right David. He was a community character, a happy-go-lucky, colorful man, the picture of an old woodsman with a strong, muscular build, dark, weathered skin and deeply carved features, and was almost toothless. He had chewing tobacco or a pipe on the go at all times. I saw him frequently around the community, and he was always busy.

Eight and a Half Times Right David

I was surprised, on one occasion, as he came out of the woods and headed towards his house carrying a substantial, sixteen-foot log on his shoulder. He was in his late seventies at the time. He put the log down, gestured for me to sit on it and sat down beside me. He proceeded to tell me a story of one kind or another for close to half an hour. I hadn't yet begun to pick up the language and couldn't understand what he had to say, but I sat respectfully and listened. It was like listening to a lilting song of many verses; it was the way he strung his words together that held my attention.

I asked his daughter, Ya' Bai, how he came to have such an odd name, and, with her son translating, I learned that he was given this name because of a speech habit he had when he was engaged in conversation. If he was being told a story, he acknowledged what was being said by using an expression similar to the English acknowledgement, "Uh-huh." In Dogrib, this expression would translate to "Heh-eh." David had a habit of using this expression exactly eight times, and on the ninth repetition, he would half finish the expression with an abbreviated, "Eh!" Thus originated the nickname Eight and a Half Times Right David. After getting to know him, I heard this response pattern of his on numerous occasions, a sort of background accompaniment to any exchange we had.

One of the elders, Harry Simpson, became central to my involvement with the Dogrib culture in the Rae Lakes area. He was my non-English-speaking advisor, my mentor and teacher. In later life, he learned to speak English and became one of the most important historians of his people. His father, who came to the area from Fort Simpson and adopted the name Simpson as the family name, was a man rich in the knowledge of the ancestors. He taught Harry the legends of the Slavey and Dogrib Dene. Harry, who had no formal schooling, absorbed all of this lore and became a wise, knowledgeable, traditional Dene.

Harry Simpson and his wife, Elise

Harry taught me many things: values and skills, respect, observation, ambition in the sense of reaching beyond your own expectations, understanding fear and how not to fear fear itself. He taught me to believe in myself, to respect nature, the local customs and beliefs; and he helped put beliefs such as that of Nàhga, the Bushman, in context for me.

Harry later worked hand in hand with John B. Zoe, the chief land claims negotiator for the Treaty 11 Council. He revisited the places and legends of his father with Zoe, passing that knowledge on to him in turn. With attention to the oral history and legends, they were able to identify and geographically locate places of significance to the Dene culture. They identified places where arrows and spearheads were made and traded, and they recorded the traditional techniques of hunting and herding caribou. All things that, without their attention, might well have been lost to future generations.

Any time I came to Rae Lakes in later years, Harry's home was my first destination. It was always with Harry that I travelled to the Barrenlands. Elise, his warm-hearted wife, who was Chief Andrew Gon's daughter, always had the welcome mat out for me. She and Harry raised many children, all of whom were adopted. I saw Harry and his best friend Philip Zoe lead hunting parties and break trail for days in deep snow. They both were medicine men and assisted the man who played the part of The Joker at a traditional event in the community.

About three or four weeks after I arrived in Rae Lakes, I was getting to know those who spoke English and those who didn't. I picked up some of the local language, Dogrib, and those who taught me also wanted to learn some English in return. I was introduced to a blind fellow, Johnny Arrowmaker, who was about twenty, and spent many evenings with him. He had just returned from Camsell Hospital in Edmonton, where he had become fluent in English and served as a translator. He was homebound, and loved having me visit. He was very patient as he taught me how to curl my tongue around some of the more difficult Dogrib words.

Another local man, Charlie Tailbone, lived close to where I was staying. He was a man forever on the go, had a great sense of humour, teased me often and taught me a lot of risqué words in his language. He was an interesting twenty-five-year-old, a peer who knew the legends well. He must have been very attentive as a child. When I asked him questions, he gave detailed explanations as to why things were the way they were in the community and how their ways differed from white culture. He was a knowledgeable Dene who became proficient in English and yet had very little formal schooling.

Charlie had many brothers and sisters. One had special needs, a huge hulk of a lad who laughed and played like a child. His older sisters cared for him twenty-four hours a day. It was a daunting task, because he was exceedingly mischievous and unfortunately became very violent if he was upset. I admired the family's dedication in caring for him. In my hometown of Winnipeg, he might well have been placed in an institution, but here he was part of the family and the community, no matter how serious the difficulties he presented.

On the medical side, I learned that many who suffered from cancer had lived near a uranium mine, Rayrock Mine. Some of them had taken jobs there, and their dogs were also put to work underground, hauling ore. The priest told me that when he arrived on the scene and saw how the Dene were treated underground and found out that the lake where they got their water was a polluted tailings pond, he was appalled. He refused to say mass for the mine workers until the working conditions were improved. Charlie's brother, Armond, was one of the last to work at the mine, and he paid the price. He died at a young age.

HISLOP LAKE: K'EÀGOTÌ

I saw Charlie Tailbone readying his dogs in harness one evening after work. I asked him where he was planning to go. He said that he and three other dog teams were going to try to make it to Hislop Lake that night and be back the following day. That's about seventy-five miles each way.

"What's the reason for the trip?" I asked.

"Someone just came from Hislop Lake last night, sent by the families there, to plead with us to come to their rescue. He was sent by the village elder because they're worried about their food supply. They didn't get to the caribou hunting grounds and haven't seen any moose, but more importantly, they're not going to be able to catch any fish in their nets," he replied. I was puzzled by this last statement.

"Why can't they catch any fish?" I asked.

"Because they sent a boy to check his nets and he caught lots of fish, but when he took them from the net he didn't clean the blood from the ice, and during the night the wolves ate the blood. Because of this they say that they will not be able to catch any more fish. A week has passed and no one has caught fish. So we're going there to help them to move along with all of their belongings. They only have two dog teams for two large families, and one very old lady," Charlie said.

I was intrigued by this errand of mercy and asked if I could join them, but I was told that wouldn't be possible because they needed all the room they had on the sleds for the people and their belongings. Charlie suggested I ask the other guys if they had an extra team of dogs. I scurried around and asked, but without success.

"It's too dangerous; you've never run a team," I was told. "The dogs won't listen to you. If you don't know what you're doing and fall among the dogs, they could maul you." I was disappointed, to say the least. They were all set to go when Charlie came up to me.

"Go see my brother," he said. "Tell him to hook up the rest of my dogs for you." As he said this, he pointed to an old sled nearby. "Take that sled over there. There's no lead dog, but your dogs will follow us. Get ready in a hurry. You'll have to catch up; we're leaving right now." With that he yelled, "Hup-high!" to his dogs and was gone. I was left standing there in an excited panic.

I ran to his brother's place, pulling the sled behind me, and told him what Charlie had said. He hooked up five dogs quickly.

I had nothing packed, no matches, teapot, axe, nothing. I gave no thought to the fact that I was taking off on a whim from my church building responsibilities. The last dog was harnessed and the rest yelped and jumped excitedly. I had hold of the knot on the stake to restrain them. Suddenly, Charlie's brother yelled.

"Okay, let them go."

"What the hell am I doing?" I asked myself as I let go of the knot. Whooooosh! Off we went, with the dogs making a beeline towards the lake. So much for taking anything by way of gear or food along! The empty sled swung wildly and tipped. I scrambled to anchor the dogs as Charlie's brother ran to me.

"You have to hang on tight, Kieran," he yelled. I climbed back onto the sled, feeling like the total amateur that I was, and we were off once again and onto the lake surface. I was travelling into the twilight at full speed, an inexperienced and panicky novice. I felt I had no control over this twelve-foot, bent plank of a sled with canvas walls attached. All I could see of the other dog teams was three small specks in the distance, and they were fading fast into the twilight.

"The guys ahead of me are on a rescue mission, and pretty soon I may need the same service," I thought. "That would be embarrassing. This is nuts! I've got to get my shit together."

I struggled with the sled and at mastering the dogs. I didn't know what I was doing. On we went, and eventually the team slowed to a manageable pace. By then, there was no sign of the other teams, and I was dependent on the dogs to keep to the trail. Night came, and the temperature dropped. I sat backwards at the rear of the sled at times to warm my face and hands, all the while concerned about falling off. This was my first experience running a dog team. Doing it on impulse had not been in my plans, at least not like this.

The dogs seemed to know where they were going, thank goodness. As we entered a portage, I ran alongside or behind, always hanging onto the rope like a lifeline. Through an opening in the forest flanking the portage I saw a lake ahead. Out and onto the ice we went once more. I stopped the dogs and stared into the emptiness, looking for a sign of the other teams, but saw nothing and heard nothing. It was more than a bit unnerving. I drew assurance from Charlie's promise that the dogs would follow the scent of the teams. I gave them their head.

We travelled for the longest time down the length of Faber Lake. There were many islands on the left shore, and the dogs took me in that direction. With only ice and hard-packed snow under me, there was not much of a trail to follow, only the odd scrape of sled runners to indicate the others were ahead.

Then something caught my eye in the distance; it appeared to be a small campfire, likely where the others had stopped. I was relieved to know that I wasn't lost in these wide-open spaces. I looked forward to warming up beside the fire shortly, but my judgment was way off. I travelled for close to an hour before I pulled my dog team onto the shoreline where the other teams had stopped.

"We didn't know for sure if you were coming or not, Kieran. But just in case you were, we made a fire to let you know where we were," one of the men commented.

"Thanks, I saw it in the distance quite a while ago but couldn't figure out why it took so long to get here."

"Look over there," said the person who greeted me, pointing at the tree that had been set on fire. Not knowing how far behind I may have been, they had set an entire twenty-five-foot spruce tree alight. This was what I had thought was the small campfire in the distance. My sense of scale was way off.

"Have some tea and catch up," they urged. There was no time for socializing here; they were all business. So off they went again. I downed the tea right away and made damn sure I caught up quickly this time. We crossed a series of small lakes with a great deal of ankle-deep surface water. If I were alone, I would have been worried about going through the ice, but I was confident the teams ahead knew what they were doing and so followed close behind. At three o'clock in the morning, we arrived at our destination, a small cluster of cabins halfway up a hill. I felt a great sense of relief at having made it in one piece, considering this was my first-ever dog team run.

We were welcomed graciously and given something to eat and drink. I was exhausted beyond anything I expected. While we took a break in the cabin, our sleds were loaded and it was announced that we would be leaving in a few hours. They made a fire outside to dry our moccasins and told us to get some sleep. I crawled under someone's blanket and fell into a deep sleep.

Jimmy Lacorde after plugging the chimney

When we were awakened, I saw there was nothing left in the cabin and someone was busy on the roof, plugging the chimney so no animals would break in.

I walked out the door into the early dawn and an amazing northern wilderness scene, one I had not taken note of on our arrival in the darkness. The rolling hills of Rayrock Mine could be seen in the distance, and the wide span of the valley below. When I got to my sled I noticed I had a passenger.

A nine year old girl tucked under the blanket in my sled

Two dog teams were already well underway down the hill and struggling not to overrun one another, their sleds packed to overflowing. I had my dry moccasins on, and my sled was ready and loaded. There was none of the panic of yesterday's start.

There was another sled in front of mine, hauling a twenty-two-foot, canvas freighter canoe, loaded to the gunnels. It was quite the sight. A community elder, Jimmy Lacorde, who later became a friend and powerful influence in my life, was in the process of tying down the canoe. In front of Jimmy was his friend, Philip Zoë, also ready to go, with his family tucked up in his sled. By then, our dogs were howling and lunging, ready to go.

Down the embankment went Jimmy, fighting to control his sled with the loaded boat perched on it. I watched in amazement as he shifted his weight from side to side so as not to run over his own dogs. He manoeuvred the huge cargo with remarkable skill. As I watched, I had this thought about my cargo: They trust me; they've placed this young child in my sled. I took this as a vote of confidence, something of great importance to my mental state at that moment.

Packed and ready to go

I was a true rookie, but at no time in the journey, no matter how much I struggled, was I ever made to feel inadequate. We hit the ice moving at a steady pace. We passed by the storied fishing spot that gave no fish because of the wolves. When we hit the winter road, we found it had three feet of water on it. Consequently, the teams were forced to travel in single file on the top edge of the snow banks that lined the sides. It was a marvel to watch Jimmy navigate this ridge with that boat tied to his sled.

Our first stop was at a place called Squirrel Hill. It was a portage for the uranium trucks, and our travel there was complicated by raw ore spilled from the trucks because of the steep incline. To get Jimmy's load up the hill, we tied three dog teams together, twenty-one dogs in all, hauling his load. It was an awesome sight and a marvel of teamwork between dogs and men.

Resting the dogs and readjusting loads

We stopped to readjust the loads at one point. Also, the little girl in my sled was transferred to another, and a frail-looking older woman, Jimmy's sister, got into mine, and away we went. When we stopped to rest the dogs periodically, she got out of the sled and walked on ahead of the dog teams. She covered a lot of ground before we got going. When my team caught up with her, she simply climbed aboard. This relay of woman and sled happened repeatedly as we travelled.

The old woman who broke trail for us made me a beautiful dry meat bag as a gesture of thanks for my helping them out. Many years later, she and I met at a hunting camp site while I was on a lone dogsled run, and that small gift served as a talking point, a symbol of a friendship formed in a unique circumstance.

PUT TO THE TEST

I acquired a strong interest in dog teams. As a result, I found myself looking to travel with anybody planning to go on a hunt. One day, Chief Andrew Gon's son, Joe, came to see me. He was about my age and spoke English quite well. He told me that he was going to the end of the lake by dog team to shoot ducks in the rapids and asked if I wanted to accompany him.

"Definitely," I responded. I got my gun and jean jacket, and borrowed a team of four dogs from Charlie Tailbone. Once again, I had no leader dog. Charlie's brother, George, joined us.

Spring had arrived, the snow was melting and the ice was several yards from shore, floating free and starting to candle. We followed Joe and his dog team as he pulled up to where he had a canoe tied up. A young fellow came by and held the dogs while we got into the canoe and paddled to the edge of the ice pack, while pulling a long rope attached to Joe's lead dog. We clambered onto the ice, pulled the canoe out of the water and signaled to the young lad to let the dogs go, and they swam directly to us. Once the sled and dogs were on the ice, we tied the canoe on top of Joe's sled.

Joe and George took off, with me following. It was late evening and the temperature was dropping. I was hoping we would get back about midnight with a small clutch of ducks. On we travelled, slipping and sliding over the surface of the glare ice. We could see pools of water scattered here and there, mostly around rock outcrops that jutted through the lake surface. In some places, the dogs scooted through the pooled water without hesitation, but at other times skirted around them. As evening came, we approached the rapids, and fog began to set in.

When we halted within hearing distance of the rapids, Joe untied the canoe. We climbed aboard, paddled to shore and, with the tow rope in hand, we hauled the dogs into the water and they swam to shore. We walked the teams farther downriver, staked them to trees, made beds of spruce boughs for them and carried on downriver, where we set up a blind close to the rapids and waited for ducks. We waited for several hours before a small flock came, and we bagged a few. I had not eaten before we left, and by this time my stomach was growling. I thought it was about time to cook some ducks and then head home. I was wrong. When I suggested this to Joe, he reminded me of traditional practice related to eating on a hunt.

"These ducks are not for us to eat. We're hunting for our families. The ducks we have, we bring home. Besides, we've bagged so few as it is. If we eat some, we'll end up going home almost empty-handed, and we don't want to do that, do we?" He didn't expect an answer; message received. It turned very cold as night closed in on us.

Joe and George asleep in the rain

"Let's spend the night here," Joe said. We'll get more ducks in the morning." I mentioned how cold I felt, and he replied, "I thought you wanted to learn how to be a Dogrib. Well, tonight we'll show you what life is like on the trail, then you decide for yourself if you still want to learn our ways." He laughed and continued, "It's not an easy life; you have to be tough, travel light, don't eat much, and bring lots of food home." When he said travel light, he was not kidding. We had nothing but a gun, an empty sled and a bunch of hungry dogs. We built a large fire, warmed up and cut spruce boughs to serve as our bedding. We lay down close to the fire and fell asleep in no time. The fire died down, and I woke up shivering with the cold. It started to rain, and we had nothing with us to create a shelter. Joe and George stayed curled up and fast asleep.

What the hell, if they can do this, so can I, I convinced myself. With that, I curled up and went back to sleep. I woke up colder than ever, and looked again at Joe and George, who were still fast asleep. I managed to get a decent fire going. Joe woke up.

"How'd you like it so far?" he asked. I said nothing, keeping my thoughts to myself as I continued to warm up by the fire. He went back to sleep once again. As I put more wood on the fire, I heard the sound of a snowmobile approaching. I woke Joe.

"Build up that fire so they'll spot where we are," Joe said as he got up. The snowmobile came directly towards us through the fog. We caught sight of them about thirty feet away, going full tilt. They were heading for a wide, water-filled gap in the ice. We gasped as the snowmobile hit the water at full speed. It might have made it over the gap, but for the heavy sled they were pulling. The two guys launched themselves off the machine onto the ice, where they sat dumbfounded as they watched their machine sink into the icy depths, followed by the sled. The pair found an ice bridge to shore and joined us to warm up by the now-blazing fire.

Joe, George and I left them with their problem, lay down and went back to sleep, knowing we would have to wait for morning to do anything about the snowmobile anyway. This was to be a night of interrupted sleep. An hour or so later, I woke up to see the two snowmobilers had made it back out onto the ice. They had rigged up an ingenious tripod over the water-filled gap and, using this contraption, managed to get the rope around part of the machine. We helped hoist it out of the water and pulled them ashore. Seeing that there was nothing for us to do to help at this point, we resumed our interrupted sleep.

Some time later, we were awakened by the sound of an explosion, followed by screaming and yelling. The snowmobile was on fire. They managed to get the fire out as we rushed over to help. The hood of the snowmobile had partially melted, taking on the shape of the motor. It seems that one of the men had tried to check if water had gotten into the gas tank and did so using his cigarette lighter to look into it. The gas fumes ignited, the tank exploded, and fortunately, all he suffered was singed eyebrows. We left them to work on the damaged machine, and since there was nothing more we could do to help, we went back to sleep once more.

I woke up to the sound of the snowmobile engine firing. I quickly went to have a look at how they had managed to do this. They had hooked up a jerry can to the engine to replace the blown gas tank. Ingenious! These remarkably inventive young guys managed to get the machine up and running and left for home.

After warming up once more by the fire, we walked the portage in search of ducks. We got a few, but all in all, it was a disappointing hunt. The dogs were hungry, and so were we.

"Let's go feed the dogs," Joe said.

"With what?" I asked, somewhat grumpily.

"I'll show you," Joe said, and we walked out onto some large rocks sticking out of the water nearby, which was from a foot to six feet deep. He stopped, pointed to a big jackfish slithering among the rocks, and took his .22 rifle in hand, saying, "They come into the shallower water in the spring and they're easy to catch this way." He aimed the gun, discharged it into the water close to the fish and yelled to me. "Grab it before it wakes up." I grabbed the fish and threw it on the shore. "The concussion knocks them out for a few seconds," he explained. In a short time, sure enough, the fish was flapping around. We caught about twelve this way, one being about three and half feet long. We fed the dogs and had a feed of fish ourselves, then headed home.

I reflected on the trip later and suspected that the chief may have put his son up to taking me along on the duck hunt, by way of putting me to the test.

Some time later, the chief, old Andrew Gon, invited me to his house for some bear meat, an unusual meat to eat for a Dene. He joked with me about the trip with his son. He had obviously been well informed about our experiences on the hunt and how I had handled it. He suggested that I find a wife and settle in Rae Lakes for good.

"You're just like one of us," he said. "The people here all like you. You should stay." Those few spontaneous words meant such a great deal to me at this time and in this place.

JIMMY LACORDE: TEACHER

After we returned from Hislop Lake, people expressed their appreciation for what I had done. The story got around that this had been my first time running a dog team and that I had been on my own for much of the journey and, added to that, my dog team didn't have a lead. I began to be invited into people's homes regularly to share food and conversation.

A short time after we arrived back, two of the elders from the Hislop Lake group, Jimmy Lacorde and Philip Zoe, set up tents for their families on the south shore, beside Francis Williah's tent. It was the beginning of establishing an encampment and the usual activity that came with that. The flooring of spruce boughs was constantly changed by the women and children. Firewood needed to be hauled before the rains came and rotted the ice. Hides from the winter hunts were being tanned as they thawed out. The encampment was a beehive of traditional activity.

One of those activities involved splitting caribou bones. It was common practice to collect and keep certain bones from the caribou, the front lower leg bone in particular. On one occasion, I stopped by Jimmy Lacorde's tent and found him splitting these leg bones. I watched with great interest. Then he handed me a bone and asked me to split it as he had done. I managed to split it and proudly showed it to him. He shook his head and muttered a form of disapproval. So I recruited the help of a nine-year-old girl, Nora, Francis Williah's daughter, as translator.

She described in detail how Jimmy wanted me to split the bones. After wasting six of them, I got it right. I told him that I felt badly about wasting the bones, but he assured me that wasn't a problem and that he was very happy I had learned how to split them to create that razor-sharp edge. These bones were used for scraping hides; they were considered better for that purpose than steel knives and less likely to nick the hide. Other bone tools and game pieces are fashioned by the Dene in this manner.

Jimmy was a skilled traditional craftsman when it came to canoe building. He cut down some trees in the nearby woods and made a long, flat workbench beside the tent. Then he took poles about four inches thick, some twelve feet long and others three feet long. He laid the poles on the workbench and proceeded to split them from end to end with a knife and an axe. He got about four narrow wood strips from each of these poles. Using a small hand plane, he shaved strips down to three-eighths of an inch thick. These were the components required for the frame of a ten-foot rat canoe he intended to use for the spring hunt. I watched him with the greatest of interest. Then one day he took me into the forest.

We entered a small grove of trees, each tree about the same diameter. He directed me to watch what he did. He ran his hand down the trunks of the trees. I could see he was looking for the straighter ones and those that had fewer branches, which meant a reduced number of knots. This looked easy, I thought. So I cut down the perfect tree. He came over, shook his head to indicate that it was not what he wanted, peeled some bark off and indicated that mine had a twist in it like a barber pole.

He next brought me to a tree stump from a tree felled about a year before. He dug down and exposed the large root, took his axe, split the stump and removed part of the trunk, along with the root. He then split this piece of wood in half and took the two halves to his bench, where he shaped them to form the bow and stern segments of the canoe. He said that the root was the perfect shape and strength for its intended purpose. Its grain flowed through the ninety-degree turn required and would resist impact more effectively than other parts of the tree. He used small, green saplings to make the rib components for the canoe and bent them over his knee. When they didn't bend enough, he bundled them all together and soaked them in water overnight for use in the morning. He was the master craftsman and I was his keen apprentice.

While I visited with him as he built his canoe, he told me legends and stories of the old days again with the help of young Nora. There were times when I managed without her, and Jimmy would demonstrate things with the occasional Dogrib words that I was now beginning to understand thrown in. One day, as he was washing up, he had his shirt open. I noticed a large scar in his stomach area shaped like a capital T. I asked if he would tell me what happened. We sat down and he told me the story.

When he was thirteen years old and living at Hislop Lake, his dad told him that he was old enough to have his own trap line. On a very cold day in January, Jimmy started cutting the path through the bush that would become his own trap line. His dad told him to cut the trail in the direction of Fort Rae, so that they could use the trail when they returned there. A few days into building the trail, he said, he got a bit careless, wanting to finish it quickly. He decided to slash the trees down with his axe at snow-level instead of at ground-level. He covered a lot more ground doing that. When he returned to camp, he found that his mother was deathly ill, and so his father urged him to leave right away for Fort Rae to get help.

He hooked up his dogs and took off. He had a young, powerful dog team, so they hurtled along at a fast pace. At one corner in the trail he fell off the sled as it turned sharply. He managed to hold on to the sled rope. When he fell, he landed on one of the razor-sharp tree stumps he had axed earlier. It pierced his stomach and, as the dogs continued to pull, he was dragged forward and off the stump, resulting in more physical damage.

He managed to stop the team and stood up to find that his intestines were spilling out. He dug into his packsack, got his harness needle and thread, pushed the intestines back into his stomach cavity and sewed himself up. Fortunately, there was very little blood. He crawled onto his sled, covered himself, and made it to Fort Rae. There they cleaned him up and treated his wound at the mission hospital and sent help for his mom in Hislop Lake.

Kieran Moore sitting in front of finished church in Rae Lakes

JIMMY LACORDE: SURVIVOR

I was just beginning to understand how the traditional Dene used legends and stories of life experiences to relay principles of safety and responsibility. Mistakes in judgment became lessons, such as the story of Jimmy and the slashed sapling that almost cost him his life at the age of thirteen. Another such story, told to me by a neighbour of Jimmy's, pointed to the fact that even a hardened woodsman like Jimmy could make mistakes.

One time, Philip, Jimmy and a few other hunters went on a caribou hunt. They travelled for days, tracking a small herd of caribou, ran out of food and had gone much farther than they had planned. The decision was made to turn back, with the exception of Jimmy, who felt confident of success and decided to continue tracking the herd and hopefully shoot some caribou and catch up to them later that night with meat for everyone and their dogs.

He travelled quite a distance without success and was contemplating heading back when he stepped away from his sled to relieve himself. His dogs caught the scent of something and took off, leaving him behind with nothing, not even his gloves, which were sitting on the sled. He followed their trail for two days and, along the way, found his gloves, snowshoes and axe. With those in hand he headed cross-country on a shorter route back.

Meanwhile, his companions grew concerned about Jimmy. After four days had passed, they set out to search for him, taking the trail they had travelled earlier, with the exception of Phillip Zoe. He suspected that Jimmy would try to take a shorter route back and headed into the bush on his own search. He came upon fresh snowshoe tracks and within two hours located Jimmy. That story gets passed on now, along with the key lesson from it. Sled travellers, experienced and inexperienced alike, should at all times be in full control of their sled and never leave it unsecured.

I stayed in contact with Jimmy up to the time of his passing in the late 1990s. He and his wife moved from Rae Lakes to Fort Rae. Around that time, he was diagnosed with stomach cancer and shipped to Edmonton's Camsell Hospital. I was in constant contact with Father Pochat, who acted as the link between Jimmy's family and the doctors. They had removed most of his stomach and gave him three weeks to a month to live.

Jimmy was returned to the Yellowknife hospital, where we visited him after hearing that the priest was going to administer the last rites. Jimmy continued to insist that it was not his time. One month passed, and the hospital allowed him to go home at his request. Months passed, and every day he grew stronger. Father phoned the doctor to update him on Jimmy, and the doctor asked, "How is he getting nourishment if he's not on intravenous?" To answer this question, Father went to visit Jimmy at his home and observed his wife preparing pounded caribou meat. She put portions of the meat in her mouth, chewed it for a long time, swallowed and regurgitated it, then gave it to Jimmy to ingest. She also made blood soup for him daily. He continued to get stronger and became well enough to be seen splitting wood not long after.

After Jimmy had been home for a good length of time, I paid him a visit. When I arrived, he was standing in water up to his belly, lifting rocks bigger than his head, in the process of building a boat dock. He went on to travel the lake, cutting and hauling logs and eventually building a beautiful log cabin for his wife, sister and her adopted daughter. He lived there for many years, and he and his sister eventually died in their own home, just as Jimmy had wanted. He was a proud Dene, a role model, a close friend who was wise in the ways of his people and in the manner in which he chose to live his own unique and rich life.

THE ICE STORM

*Joseph Rabesca on the left,
Jimmy Lacorde on the right*

There is one particular experience I had in the company of Jimmy Lacorde that is so permanently etched in my brain that I would not be surprised if, on my deathbed, it became my final vision. For me, as a young man coming of age, it was nothing short of extraordinary.

I had finished working on the church in Rae Lakes and heard that the community was planning the annual fall caribou hunt on the Barrenlands. I was asked by Harry Simpson and Phillip Zoe if I would like to join them and was told that it would probably be a three-week journey there and back. I was elated, because the offer was in keeping with my keenness to take on new challenges. I spent much of my spare time at Harry's place enquiring about the hunt and determining what I needed to do to prepare for it.

Once I found out what I needed, I went around town and asked the women to make some of the items. In return, I promised to bring back meat in payment. This promise was great currency. I had a packsack made, canvas bags for storing sugar and tea bags, a gun case, a utensil wrap for knives and files, shell bags, and most importantly, a tumpline and a pair of moccasins made to size.

A woman by the name of Ya'Bai made most of the things I needed. She was single, had a thirteen-year-old son and was taking care of her father. She had no one to hunt for her. There was something very special about having all of the things I required tailor-made for me. I was being equipped in the traditional way to go on this age-old hunt and understood that there was no better way for me to gain firsthand experience with one of the unique cultural events undertaken by the community.

Early one morning, the word was passed around that we were leaving. Everything was brought to the lakeshore. I was cautioned by the young guys, and they could not stress the point enough, "travel light. Only bring the absolute basics. Nothing heavy, keep in mind that we all share each other's loads on the portages. Some of the portages are as long as three miles." Once at the shore we placed the re-canvased, freshly painted canoes in the water. There were five freighter canoes, each capable of carrying seven people. Four of the others were about nineteen feet long; the largest was twenty-five feet in length. I was assigned to the twenty-five-foot canoe. There was some discussion before we left that this canoe was much too big and heavy. But a lighter boat could not be freed up because the women needed the boat to check the nets and to haul firewood while the men were gone.

In traditional dramatic fashion, a volley of gunfire announced our departure. Then, one by one, we fell in behind each other and moved off in silence through calm waters and into a beautiful sunrise. We journeyed in a north-easterly direction within sight of the shoreline, which was draped in a canopy of yellowing birch leaves that provided a stark contrast to the reds and greys of the granite below them.

One of the first things I noted was that there were no markings to indicate the entry to the portages. I later learned that the Dogrib passed on this tradition to each succeeding generation of never marking portages. The historical origin of this practice was rooted in the not-so-distant past, when the Dene were hunted down by the Yellowknife and Chipewyan tribes and their women taken as slaves. When they fled these attacks, it was important that their trail to a place of safety not be marked. We entered lakes with dozens of bays on this journey, and there was always someone who knew where the portage entry point was, and we arrived at our daily destination as if we had travelled on a sign-posted highway.

After a few portages, it was noted that some packs were proving to be too heavy, so we stopped for tea and an inventory was taken of what each of us had brought along. One of the weighty items identified was canned fruit. It was decided that it had to go. The individual who packed this opened a can to eat, and it was passed around. There were not too many takers and, as I went to take some, I was warned that it was from the trading post store and was likely stale-dated and years old.

"They only ship us what they can't sell in Fort Rae," I was told. I couldn't resist something sweet and so had a spoonful or two. I paid for this later on, in a fit of vomiting that depleted my strength and was to cause me grief on the portages the following day. As we searched through our packs, some of the young fellows noticed the chocolate I'd packed that Father Amourous had given to me and that I intended to use as a treat for myself over the duration of the trip. However, now that it was noticed, I felt obliged to offer it around. I was careful not to make this mistake again, should I choose to bring myself a special treat, keeping in mind the adage, 'Only offer what you intend to part with.'

While we were still sitting around, one of the elders approached me, looked me over head to foot, shook his head and kicked my boots. A young fellow nearby, who had seen what had happened, came over to speak to me.

"You mean nobody told you? You can't wear white man's boots to hunt in the Barrenlands."

"So what will I do? They're my only good work boots."

I was told to tie them in a tree close by and to put on my moccasins. I was assured the boots would be picked up on the way back. As I tied them up, I couldn't help thinking that I was likely seeing the last of them.

As we travelled, legends and stories were told with great regularity. Many a hill had an historic event or story connected to it. If you remembered these, you knew where you were. We carried no maps. Their maps were the stories and places of people's recollections, and each one served as a connection to the next destination point. We passed a place where there was a long, flat rock very high up, forming a slide down to the shore. The story associated with it was that it was used to tell how long you would live. To do that you cut a spruce bough, climbed to the top of the rock slide and slid down while seated on the bough. How far you slid indicated how long you would live. We didn't stop to try it out that day because of bad weather, so I guess I'll never know my life expectancy. That image of sliding down this particular rock turned it into an easily identifiable landmark for future reference.

We travelled to another lake that had a strange story attached to it. Our boat crew refused to travel on the leeward side of the lake, even though it was much calmer there, and in answer to my query as to why, I was told the background story. That many years back a group of hunters returning from the Barrenlands arrived at this lake. They were wind-bound for many days, and during this time, while considering what route to take, one of the men had a dream and warned the others that they should not consider crossing on the north side of the lake. A number of the hunters disregarded the warning and went anyway. The story goes that when they got to the north side, the lake opened up under them and the canoes and men were swallowed up, never to be heard from again.

I later retold this curious story to Father Amourous. He had heard it some time back and, not giving it much credence, asked for the names of the missing people. He checked the names in the parish register and found their births recorded and yet couldn't find any record of their deaths.

"There must be some element of truth to that story of their curious disappearances," he said. "Something unusual happened out there."

We tried to navigate one of the shallow rivers and the boats were at risk of getting damaged. So, being young and enthusiastic, I jumped out of the boat and started to move some of the rocks likely to cause problems. Some young crew members who were watching me began pointing to other rocks and urging me to pull them out of the way. After a while, Louie Zoe leaned out of the boat and caught my attention.

"Stop what you're doing, Kieran," he said quietly.

"Why?" I asked.

"I don't like what those guys are doing. They're taking advantage of your good nature; they're making fun of you," he replied. I pulled myself together, thanked him and climbed back into the boat, surprised a bit at my gullibility. It was somewhat humbling, I must say.

We had arrived at one of the portages and were busy unloading when Bruno Mantla, one of the highly respected elders, asked someone to come and get me. I went to where he stood on shore, and he proceeded to instruct me on how to identify rat root, a traditional medicine, where to find it and how to harvest it. He explained how it's dried so that it could be stored for long periods of time. Bruno took great interest in teaching me at every chance he got. On numerous occasions at drum dances back in Rae Lakes he not only encouraged me to participate. If I didn't dance correctly, he stopped the drummers, instructed me and did a solo dance, urging me to follow along till I got it right.

We began running short of food after a few days and had only managed to shoot about seven ducks, with little meat on them. South of the NWT's border the fall ducks are fat from feeding off the pea and grain fields in Alberta, whereas in the NWT they're skin and bone. We set a net and caught a few fish. This meant meagre eating for thirty-five people. Each evening, we congregated in one of the tents for drumming and chanting, all of which fed the feeling of belonging and of being immersed in a deeply traditional undertaking.

One other interesting point I recall about my Dene companions was how differently they handled touchy issues. They were dealt with in a non-confrontational way. On the first day of the trip, we found out that the man who was assigned to bring a tent and stove had forgotten to bring them. This was the tent I was to sleep in with some of the crew. I was noticeably put off about this oversight, and one of the men quietly gave me some words of advice.

"Kieran, that's not how we do things. We don't stay angry. We see the problem, realize something needs to be done about it and move on. Getting mad won't fix it. All of us have to work together, solve the problem, and it doesn't get mentioned again." He said this in a manner that didn't leave me feeling put down. It was the essence of common sense and a lesson learned. We solved this problem by spreading ourselves among the other tents. The importance of this advice was realized many times over as we continued our journey. I understood its importance, given that we were living together in the close confines of both boats and tents.

Finally we arrived at the entrance to the longest portage we were to face. To our left, in the distance, was an old raft. I asked how it got there. I was told that it belonged to a number of white trappers who came north from Edmonton some years back. The fact that the raft was not used for the return journey was seen as a sign that they never returned. It was suggested I take note of what else was discarded along the portage, once we got over the steep incline we had yet to tackle. I was told I would see cast-iron stoves discarded piece by piece every few hundred yards along the length of this three-mile stretch of tundra we were about to portage.

I was feeling hunger pangs at this point, as were others, and was reassured that beyond this monster of a portage were the hunting grounds where we would find caribou. Right now, we stood staring upwards at a long, steep, sandy incline that led onto the portage. Harry Simpson looked at the hill and then turned to me and, not having the English, signed to ask if I wanted to carry the large canoe over this portage. He noticed I was not quite understanding what he was saying, so he asked one of the young men to tell me that he had noticed that I'd already carried the canoe over every portage so far and consequently, he wasn't expecting me to do this one, suggesting that someone else take a turn. I looked at Harry, who was about forty years of age at the time, and let him know I was up to it. The young guys warned me that there would be little stopping until we got to the end of the portage. But first, we had to scale the steep incline with the twenty-five-foot freighter canoe on our backs. This was obviously going to be a Herculean task.

The entire trip was taken at a feverish pace. It was one thing to keep the pace, but it was another to set the pace, and those who did were not the young men; they were the oldest of the thirty-five of us.

We congregated at the bottom of the incline. Four guys lifted the large boat, and the others assigned to it climbed under, resting the weight on our shoulders. Harry turned his head and smiled at me as we got set to go, likely thinking one of two things: Kieran doesn't know what he's got himself into, or, I'm glad he rose to the challenge. It may well have been a bit of both. He went to the front, I to the back. We had stacked the paddles inside and had jackets wrapped around our shoulders for padding against the pressure. I took one last look at the extreme gradient and could hear my heart already pounding.

Off we went, up and up slowly, with faces bent towards the ground, starring straight at the embankment. I had the urge to use my hands to grab the ground, but there was no letting go. The weight of the canoe was not only on the shoulders, but was also pushing backwards and forcing us to fight gravity with both our legs and arms.

I began to feel that I had nothing left to give when we were only halfway to the top. I remember Harry calling out in Dogrib asking if I was okay. I could see from my position at the back that his knees were shaking under the strain and he knew that mine were doing the same thing. Through his question, I understood everything he was trying to say by asking it.

"Please, don't say that you want to quit; tell me yes, you're okay so that we can take another step." I took a step; he took a step and so it went. I called out the same question to him with the same intent. Suddenly, Harry was over the top and the weight at the rear increased dramatically, pushing me beyond my limits, yet we made it over and onto level ground. Contrary to what I believed would be impossible, we continued on steadily until we reached the end of the portage. The relief to be out from under that crushing weight made the trip back to pick up our other gear seem like a walk in the country. I clipped along, feeling light on my feet, energized but hungry. I gave the hunger little thought, because after all we were in God's kitchen now. We were now in the Barrenlands, the traditional hunting grounds beyond the tree line.

I looked back the way we had come; it was like looking at a landscape of enormous rice paddies. The lakes we had travelled over were terraced below us and we could see them spread out for miles. It was as if we had passed through a gate, with the forest left behind us and now in front of us was an immense treeless, barren land, we were now above the treeline. We had arrived here without compass or map, just with the traditional knowledge and wisdom of elders and the Dene capacity for endurance.

We came to some gravesites. They were marked by small, decaying crosses stuck in the sandy ground, indications of hard times in days gone by. Some were the graves of women who died in childbirth, some of elders. It was moving to see the time and respect our hunting party gave to each of these graves we encountered. We stopped and paid respects to the dead each time and, in some cases, made a small fire and "paid" the fire in their memory. I was moved by that simple custom that spoke to the values held within the Dene culture.

We got to the end of the long portage and set out on the next lake. It is known to geographers as Lake Rawalpindi, but is named Hhtso Ti in Dogrib, meaning stove, likely a reference to the cast-iron stove parts scattered along the portage. This was a huge lake, and the treeless shoreline was a clear reminder that we were in the Barrenlands. The wind picked up, making lake travel difficult, and there was some deep discussion as to whether we should travel on or not. There were signs of snow squalls on the horizon. They decided that we were better off to be weather-bound farther into the hunting grounds. We had brought polyethylene vapour barrier, and we wrapped ourselves in it and headed out. I had the only pair of binoculars in the group and pulled them out once we got going.

There wasn't a sign of anything as I scanned the bare hillsides. I was told not get too anxious, because sometimes the hunting party has to travel on the Coppermine River into Inuit country to get to the caribou. That made me more determined to spot caribou. About fifteen minutes later, Jimmy lifted his head from under the poly, scanned the horizon and pointed.

"Caribou there," he said. As quick as he poked his head out, he drew it back under cover. I looked through the binoculars to where he had pointed and saw nothing. We travelled on for almost a half hour to the end of the lake, and I still could not see any sign of caribou. As we approached the shore, everyone loaded their guns, getting ready for the hunt. I still saw nothing.

"Where's this caribou?" I asked, straining to see it through my binoculars.

"It? No, not one. There are thousands out there. Look at that hill." I did as directed. I focused the binoculars on the hillside and, as hard as looked, all I saw was rocky tundra. "Don't look for one caribou; look for moving rocks," I was told. Once I focused on looking at the rocks, I could see that the whole surface of the hill was on the move, shifting in slow motion. The caribou blended remarkably into the surrounding landscape. Their rear ends look like Barrenland rock and the antlers like shrubs. When they are grazing they are hard to detect from a distance or by an untrained eye, like mine was, as they move slowly among boulders scattered throughout the landscape. I have since developed a very good eye and no longer have need of binoculars to spot the caribou, thanks to hunting with people like Jimmy.

We got ashore as the last of the caribou crested the hill, which was still miles away. Designated teams dispersed, and the group I was with travelled to a spot selected to serve as the group campsite. As we hiked, the stories and legends continued to flow. The area triggered references to tales of the past, back to the time of creation. Some of us set up the camp, while others set a net. By the time we were done setting up camp, there was freshly netted trout and one of the hunting parties returned with two caribou. The others came back empty-handed. We settled down to a well-earned break and a full meal of fish and game.

The spot chosen for the camp was selected with the intention that Jimmy Lacorde and Bruno Mantla could take me to a place of great significance to the Dogrib people. We were camped in a low valley, edged in on all sides by high hills. There were signs of many other campsites set up here in the past. It is worth noting that we never came across garbage as we travelled. Those who traveled this route before us largely followed the traditional way, in which almost everything carried or worn was biodegradable: moccasins, bone tools and hide containers. Camping for long periods of time was unheard of here: it was a region where they kept on the move, with only short stopovers.

With Jimmy leading, we went down to the shoreline, where there were the remnants of birch-bark canoes and tipi stone circles. He explained how and why they came to this hunting ground in the past. He told of his ancestors travelling these great distances and their struggle to survive, while occasionally being hunted down by the Chipewyan from the south. He was not only a hunting guide but also a storehouse of cultural information and of his people's history. Fortunately for me, there was always someone willing to serve as translator, either nineteen-year-old Jingo, George Tailbone, or his brother Charlie.

The next day we broke up into scouting parties and went in different directions, in the hope of locating the herd we had spotted. There was talk that we may have missed the migration and that the caribou might very well be out of reach. Two days of scouting passed with no sign of caribou, so it was decided to expand our search. Boats were sent out with hunting parties who were dropped off on all sides of the lake. There were six of us in our party, and we in turn broke into two teams of three. Jimmy Lacorde, Jingo and I formed one, and Pierre Caroseen, George Tailbone and Charlie Tailbone formed the other.

We travelled over an expanse of land made up of rolling hills, all of which, to my eye, were indistinguishable one from the other. Hours passed. I had a hard time keeping up to Jimmy's pace in the cold, wet conditions. Snow squalls came over the hills and dropped wet snow on us. We met up with the others, consulted, and then split up once more; this time it was George Tailbone, Jimmy Lacorde and me as a team.

We continued to scout for tracks without success and skipped a tea break because the scrub brush normally used to start a fire was so coated with wet snow. We just kept on moving. The wind gained such strength that we concluded it would be impossible for the boat to navigate the lake to pick us up. Realizing that, we decided to work our way back toward the main campsite.

The footing was treacherous as we contended with terrain littered with boulders. At one point, we heard some shots being fired. We searched the horizon in the direction from which the sound came, but there was no sign of anyone. I felt frozen to the bone and was anxious to get back to the heat and comfort of the camp site. We lost the warmth of intermittent sunshine as the clouds began to close in. My binoculars were useless as they fogged up quickly, but with Jimmy constantly scanning the horizon there was little need for them.

Then, below us, in one of the valleys, we spotted movement. A small herd appeared as if out of nowhere, but we were still too far away to take a shot. Jimmy stood silently watching the herd, and I watched him.

"Even if we shoot a caribou, I'm not sure if I've got what it would take to carry one to the camp," I muttered to George. I had always prided myself on being a sturdy young woodsman, but this pace was on a whole different level.

"Follow me," Jimmy said to us as he pointed to the darkening sky. "A big storm is coming." No sooner had he said those words than a violent gust of wind struck us. In the direction where the caribou were, I saw a low-hanging, fast-moving weather front of turbulent black cloud. The caribou were quickly engulfed in this shroud of snow pellets and rain, a driving wave of sleet. The wind swirled violently as the cloud engulfed us. Our rifles were disabled, their mechanisms coated with ice. Jimmy signed for me to empty out the cartridges. I scraped at the ice furiously with my knife as I sheltered the rifle with my body. Groping with numbed fingers, I managed to empty and reload and put the rest of the shells in my pants pocket. Huddled down for shelter behind a large rock, we could only see a distance of about ten feet.

Suddenly, Jimmy stood up and walked headlong into the blizzard. He did so with the clear authority of a man who knew what he was doing. In the midst of this chaos, he sensed it was time. We followed. It didn't seem to me to make sense to move out from shelter into that swirling craziness. But we trudged down the valley, moving deeper into the darkness of the storm. Half blinded by the sleet, I struggled to keep my two companions in sight. Everything around, rocks and shrubs, was getting coated. My impression was of being on the inside of a cloud.

Moving ahead of me were the ghostly shadows of George and Jimmy. They were my focus. They both stopped. I caught up. We stood there, side by side, as time seemed to stand still. I looked around and could not credit what I was seeing. We were encircled by ice-encrusted caribou. They were everywhere around us, standing like ice-coated statues not more than ten feet apart. I looked at Jimmy. He smiled, and in the middle of this eerie scene he motioned for me to pick my caribou.

He spread out his arms and signed as if to say, "Pick a fat one; help yourself. Pick the best that nature has provided." All this in a single look and gesture. In this remarkable moment, although numbed to the core, I was totally focused and the natural instinct of the hunter surfaced, all else forgotten. I understood everything Jimmy had implied. The three of us raised our guns, carefully picked out our caribou and shot. Three caribou fell.

Almost in keeping with that moment, the storm cloud began to dissipate. The herd just wandered away, showing no sign of panic; it was as if we hadn't discharged our guns in their very midst. We watched them almost casually ascend the hill ahead, and as the cloud lifted, they disappeared from sight.

We were encrusted from head to toe with ice. I was told to empty the shells from my gun for safety's sake. I struggled to get my frozen hands to unload the shells—such an elementary thing to do. I turned to George in frustration.

"I can't do anything, George; look at me. I'm shaking from head to toe." My words slurred through frozen lips.

"Don't worry; you'll soon be warm." Jimmy said, with George translating. "So far you've been like a Dogrib and have wanted to learn everything we do, so do as I do." He told me to get my cup, walked up to one of the downed caribou and lifted its head as he said a prayer. He cut the jugular vein and filled the cup with blood. He drank it. As vapour rose up from the cup, I watched intently. I reached for the cupful of blood and drank. As it passed my frozen lips I felt revitalized.

Jimmy gave the customary thanks over each animal. He then peeled back the skin from the belly of one and directed me to stick my frigid hands between the hide and the body. Within moments I had recovered enough energy to carry on skinning and preparing the carcass for transport. We wrapped the meat of each caribou in its own hide and left nothing but a gut pile behind. We each carried our caribou on our backs, wrapped in our tumplines, and headed back to the camp.

This was a life-affirming moment, one that pushed me beyond my limitations. It holds a special place in my memory, one I will want to revisit until the day I die.

CAMPING ON THE HUNT

We headed back toward our tents, cold and exhausted. Along the way, we met up with the other three men from our hunting party. They had also shot some caribou and were returning to camp because of the storm. They had left the carcasses behind, planning to go back to get them the following morning and hoping that a Barrenlands grizzly would not beat them to it. We also met up with another hunting party that hadn't had any luck, and we descended into the valley, to the welcome sight of smoke rising from the camp stoves.

I was ready to fall asleep as soon as I had eaten. If I had done so, I would have been the only one. The day was far from over. We all huddled in our respective tents and were having difficulty drying out our wet clothes. It was decided to arrange three tents end to end, making a large elongated one, where we all huddled together, creating a great sense of camaraderie that chased away fatigue. The warmth generated there helped dry out our clothing as the night wore on.

Caribou hide bedding was spread out on the floor. A number of the men knelt on the bedding, facing one another in two rows, as others tuned their hand drums by warming them on the small stove. Then the drumming began. Everyone joined in a chorus of loud, rhythmic chanting. I sat there, listening in quiet awe, as the sound and mood of celebration spread throughout the tent. I could feel the beat of the drums deep in my chest. The chanting was an expression of thanks for the day's good fortune, a wish for success on tomorrow's hunt, and hope for a safe return to home and families.

The drummers took a break as they set things up for the hand game. The game sticks were placed in the center, between the two kneeling groups. This is a form of gambling where the men on one side pick up a bullet, stone or stick and hide it in one of their hands. Having picked up the item, they now place their two hands behind their back, decide in which hand they will hide the item, then return their hands to the front, sometimes crossed over one another and sometimes outstretched. It is the task of the opposing team to guess in which hand the item is being held. Bets are placed, won and lost. The drummers stand behind the players, chant and beat their drums, contributing to a rising tension as the game proceeds. The ritual, in all of its aspects, was mesmerizing to see, to hear and to feel.

The young and old, who just hours before had faced the extraordinary challenges of the hunt, put all behind them as they laughed, chanted and drummed in the intimate confines of the tent. For me, that tent housed a larger than life presence. I stood behind Charlie Tailbone at the beginning of the game, pestering him with questions about it. He explained things to me as he played. The next day, he came up to me and asked why I had not come to the hand game. He had been so caught up in it that he had no recollection of our exchange during the game.

After a while, I was asked to join in. They gave me a quick lesson on the strategies and some complicated hand signals. We played late into the night. I watched as Louis Flunkie lost his gun, shells and blanket. I had trouble understanding why he would do such a thing and found out later that he would not be expected to give up his possessions until we returned to the village.

The next morning, I heard that one of the other men, Pierre Caroseen, had hurt his back and had to leave his pack of meat behind and was worried about it. I volunteered to retrieve it and made two trips for him and another one for Bruno Mantla. I was young, full of energy and willing to push myself in the circumstance. I was at school in the Barrenlands, eager and learning so much.

It was the practical nature of this kind of schooling that made me eager to learn. It was in stark contrast to the school classroom model I had experienced in Winnipeg, one that failed to inspire me in any way. Not to mention how the Church and Government had failed these people in every imaginable way with abusive residential schools that mandated assimilation and completely ignored the importance of this type of traditional cultural way of teaching.

LEGENDS OF EDZO

We had a day of rest with no hunting while camped beside the famous treaty site on the Barrenlands. Everyone who went out to hunt after that returned empty-handed, so it was decided that we needed to change our location. I was told we would face a tough portage that ran roughly five miles over a barely visible trail and along a dry, boulder-strewn old river bed. So, with this facing us, we were urged to get as much rest as possible. Early that morning, just as the sun was rising over the hills to the east and we finished our morning prayer and fed the fire, I was told that Jimmy wanted to take me to a historic site nearby that was of great importance to his people.

I met up with him and one of the other guys, who acted as an interpreter. We walked a short distance from the camp, and he told me to look at a spot where the sun was rising from behind a hill in the distance. He pointed at a huge bolder at the top of the hill.

"That's Red Cap's rock," he said.

"Who's Red Cap?" I asked.

"He was the young son of chief Edzo. He got his name after he got a red cap as a gift from his father. They sold them at the Hudson Bay Company store at that time." Jimmy then gave some further background to the story he was about to tell, saying, "We heard many legends about Edzo when we were growing up. Most of them took place around the time our people made first contact with white people. Some tribes gained advantage over other tribes as they learned new things or got new tools or weapons. This led to fighting between tribes. This troubled Edzo, who was admired not only for his feats of bravery and strength, but also because he wanted his people to live in peace with other tribes."

With that introduction, Jimmy proceeded to tell me one of the stories about Edzo. It entailed the conflict between Akaitcho's and Edzo's people and how they put an end to the long-standing antagonism between their tribes and celebrated the event with a tea dance. "That tea dance happened right over there," Jimmy said and led us to a sandy area he was referencing. Neither Charlie nor I could detect anything by way of markings, so Jimmy had us follow him up the hillside. He pointed down to where we had stood and asked if we could see the area he was talking about. We still could not see any markings. He took two sticks, stuck them in the sand, one in front of the other, and, using the tops of the sticks like a gun sight, he said, "Look along the tops of these sticks, line them up and look beyond." We did what he asked. A well-defined circle came into focus, a circle worn into the surface of the Barrenlands by dancing feet many years ago.

The next day, the weather worsened and once again delivered driving sleet. The portage was downright treacherous. How no one broke an ankle or leg was a matter of luck and the excellent physical condition of the men, what with all the slipping and sliding we did over rocks and boulders as we carried the boats. We finally stopped and set up camp.

One particular question that intrigued me was: what happened to the fabled Edzo? My curiosity was piqued because the topic had never come up in my presence, and I thought, surely such a legendary figure's gravesite would be hallowed ground, to be visited and revisited after he met his end.

However, it appeared to be the custom not to ask any questions, but to wait, knowing the story would eventually be told. The location where this was most likely to happen was in this legendary setting where we were camped. Later that night, after all the chores were done, everyone gathered in the large tent to share stories. One of the stories to be shared was the story of Edzo's final days. My question as to how he met his end was answered. However, no one knows where he was laid to rest. I found out later that the manner in which he met his end can vary depending on who is telling the legend.

THE CHANGELING

We continued on our journey the next day and arrived at Parent Lake, the last big lake before the Coppermine River system. We launched the canoes and a short time later ran into high winds. Jimmy directed us to head ashore. We disembarked and Jimmy told everyone to stay by the boats while he scouted around. He appeared to be concerned about something but a short time later signaled us to unload the gear. Later that night, he told us why he had to check out the site before we unloaded, and through one of the translators, here is what he had to say.

"Twenty years ago we came to this place and saw a white wolf. The wolf was a changeling. We watched it go behind a hill, and a short time later a person came out from behind that same hill. We watched as he went behind another hill and didn't come out, but a white wolf did. There was no man to be seen anywhere. We were worried, but the wind was so strong that we could not go back onto the lake to get away from there, so we set up camp. While we were setting up camp, we heard the sound of a baby crying and we went in search of it, but the crying stopped. A while later, we heard it again. One of the men walked to where we had first seen the wolf, and at that hill he found a male baby. He took the baby back to camp but was told to get rid of it. One of the elders said no and that we must keep the child. The elder took care of the child and brought him back to Fort Rae. We hunted the next day and were successful. The weather got better and so we headed home."

I later met this found child when he was a young man. The name they gave him was Eskimo. He was obviously Inuk, judging by his appearance. He made no effort to investigate his roots in Inuit country; he had grown up a Dogrib and continued to consider himself one. The Dogrib and Inuit feared each other and yet shared the same hunting grounds, because they followed the same migrations of caribou. The changeling stories feed that fear and suspicion they have of one another and, consequently, the two groups work to avoid contact.

Early the next morning, we were about to launch the canoes and head for the Coppermine River when caribou were spotted not far from our camp. We hunted them successfully, and continued for a few more days till everyone had enough meat to take home to their families. Then we started out on the arduous journey back to Gamèti.

As Rae Lakes came into view, guns were loaded and the hunters announced themselves with gunfire. The community rushed to the shore and responded with volleys of their own. Quite suddenly, the shooting on the lake stopped. The boats arrived on shore in silence because one of the hunters had accidently discharged his gun while pulling it out of its sheath and was killed instantly. Grief displaced celebration. The hunter's name was Jimmy Wedawin. The normal celebrations that followed a successful hunt were cancelled, out of respect for Jimmy's family.

The meat from the hunt was distributed throughout the community from the chief's house. I repaid my debts to everyone who provided me with gear and moccasins for the hunt with bundles of dried meat I put together. The work boots I had left behind on the first portage had been picked up by one of the hunters and returned to me. The families of the men whose meat I had helped carry back to the camp supplied me with pounded meat and bone marrow by way of thanks.

This was a coming of age experience for me personally. It was a privilege to have been given this unique opportunity to participate in the Dene tradition of hunting in the Barrenlands.

HUNTING IN THE BARRENLANDS

The following description of hunting practices in the 1970s on the Barrenlands reflects what I saw as I hunted alongside my Dene friends.

At daybreak, while out on the hunt, the hunters roll up their bedrolls, pass a washbasin, bar of soap and towel, and everyone washes. That's followed by a quick meal of boiled meat, usually mixed with oatmeal, or grilled fish along with hot tea with sugar. One or two people scout for firewood, which is usually meagre brush pickings, and place them by the stove to dry. Then they decide in which directions the hunting parties are to go. Curiously, no one person makes the decision as to who teams up with whom. It just falls into place smoothly in an unspoken way. It is the practice to travel in groups of at least two members in case of injury or having to deal with the barren ground grizzly.

The terrain is hilly and rocky, scattered with small shrubbery, with the odd exception of shrubs as high as six feet in some valleys. In the valleys the brush can be difficult to see through. A bear could be ten feet away and not be seen. Consequently, a hunter who shoots a caribou in these areas needs to be aware of danger while skinning the animal.

Eddie Camille and the end of a successful hunt

When the hunters return to camp after a successful hunt, they hang the meat up on poles far back from the campsite and create a smudge fire to keep flies off the meat and to deter bears. On some hunts it may happen that grizzlies approach a camp and go straight to the meat stages to enjoy a feast. This usually happens around the start of the caribou migration. Shooting the grizzly is out of the question. You move camp.

The bears have acclimated to the sounds associated with modern-day hunting, the roar of the plane and the sound of gunshots. To them, these sounds are no longer to be feared; they are the sounds of the dinner bell. They will scavenge gut piles or meat that has been left behind for one reason or another.

Hunters take very little baggage. Each man carries his gun and one box of shells, usually a lever action Winchester 30-30. A tumpline for carrying the meat, a small packsack with one teapot per group, tea and a teacup, sugar, protected matches, a set of skinning knives in a canvas wrap, a small coil of rope, and a file. Clothing is whatever the weather requires, plus a pair of moccasins with below-ankle rubber overshoes.

Removing the head

After an animal has been shot, a form of thanks is given, the head cut off and the animal skinned. The head is removed right away in the belief that this prevents a parasite from migrating into the body meat.

The hide is placed flesh side up on the ground and readied to create a carrying device. A length of rope is laid down around the perimeter of the hide, leaving a margin of about three inches. Then the three inches of hide outside of the rope is folded over the rope and fixed in place. The carcass is butchered and stacked on the prepared hide. The ribs are placed in the center to serve as a reinforced base onto which the meat and glands are loaded. The head of the caribou is sometimes tied on the top of the pile. The only thing left behind are the lungs, intestines and esophagus.

This bundle is pulled together by the rope, making two loops, one on each end. The load is placed on a rock to make for ease of lifting onto your back, and the tumpline is attached to make the load more portable. The headpiece of the tumpline is placed on the brow, which makes for greater ease of transportation. Upon returning to camp, the meat is deboned and hung up to dry; the fat and gristle on the hide are scraped off.

Readying camp on the edge of The Barrenlands

On many of these hunting trips, they brought next to nothing by way of food and lived on fish until they got game. An all-fish diet over weeks for breakfast, lunch and supper can get to you, and I had occasion to experience this regimen a few times. (I never did adjust fully to the fish diet and was known to smuggle onions and my trusty HP sauce with me to spice up my meals.)

When firewood is plentiful, food is cooked differently. The first thing cooked is the animal's head, be it moose or caribou. The head is split and the brain baked in the skull. The jaw and nose are cut away, the tongue and nose being a sought-after delicacy. The brisket is suspended on a stick over the open fire. The meat is sliced in strips the thickness of cardboard and dried. The bones, with whatever meat is left on them, are boiled and the soup produced is left to cool until the hardened fat congeals on top. That layer is usually about a half-inch thick and eaten with dry meat or stored to be eaten later with pounded meat. The boiled bones are broken open, the marrow extracted, and that, along with the fat, is eaten with the pounded meat.

Pounded meat is processed by taking the toughest pieces of dry meat and pounding them with a stone or the back of an axe. It is then stored in a bag made from the caribou hide from the lower part of the legs. This section of hide is the only part of the hide that does not shed its hair. Another word used by southern tribes for the pounded meat is pemmican. Once pounded, the meat has the consistency of tobacco and needs bone grease or marrow to help make it edible.

They had descriptive ways of naming some parts, curiously some with Christian liturgical references. For instance, the intestine of the caribou is encased in a transparent veil of thin, stretched membrane. This they call the chasuble. Then there is a multilayered piece of fat resembling a book; they call it the bible. On the caribou's back there is a layer of fat about two inches thick with the texture of coconut. This is occasionally eaten off the freshly killed animal. At times, the leg ligaments are eaten after a successful hunt and are believed to give strength to the hunter.

The hunt may not be successful, and when that happens they feed on blueberries, raspberries and cranberries, but the most desired berry is the muskeg berry, called the gots oka. The yellow berries are found only in bogs and muskeg and are as sweet as jam.

Only the undamaged hides of the fall caribou are kept. Damage to the hide is caused by the warble fly, which lays its eggs in the hide. When they hatch, the larvae burrow out and leave holes in the hide. Hides obtained in winter don't have these imperfections and are used to make coats, pants, duffel bags or socks. Two of each item are made, one with the hair on the inside and the other with the hair on the outside. You can sleep outside at fifty below in this clothing.

In the event that they ever encounter Inuit, the practice is to camp on the opposite shoreline. This follows a tradition of sharing the hunting grounds but not one another's company. When hunting close to the region of the Coppermine River, it was not uncommon for Dene hunters to come in contact with Inuit hunters and families.

A GIFTED STORY

A few years after that first Barrenlands hunt, when I learned a great deal about the legendary chief Edzo, I chanced to be in Snare Lake, (Wekweeti) and mentioned my interest in stories regarding Edzo. Word got around and I was asked to come to the house of Joseph Pea-a, an elder. An old woman met me at the door and directed me to sit and have some tea, bannock and dry meat. As I ate, the house started to fill with people, who squatted down under lantern light. The woman sat in a corner with a young girl by her side, who acted as translator. After people settled down, she began to speak. "I am the last direct descendent of Edzo. I have no children. My grandmother was one of his thirteen wives," she announced as she began her story. "I know most of you believe you have heard all the legends there are to hear about Edzo. I have a story about him that has never been told before. I'm getting old and feel it is time for me to pass the story on." Then she directed the following comment to me. "This story is for you to pass it on to others. This will now be your story to tell." With that said, she began.

"Each of Edzo's wives had different jobs, preparing dry meat, gathering wood, keeping the fire going, setting up and moving camp, checking nets or making dry fish. My grandmother had one very special job, over and above her other work. She had to take care of Edzo's medicine bags and prepare things for ceremonies as directed by him. Edzo was well known as a great shaman and that is how and why he was so powerful. In one of these bags there was something that the Dogrib had never seen before. They were creatures that were not of the area and were a source of medicine for Edzo. These creatures possessed strong powers, and Edzo knew how to use them, and this was one of the reasons his people feared and respected him.

"It was my grandmother's job to take care of this special medicine. They were kept frozen in winter, but in summertime had to be kept safely in a bag and fed. It was her job to make sure they didn't escape as she fed them. It was also her job to pack and carry them with her every time they pulled up camp, which in those days could be quite often.

"One day, when they were about to make a move to another winter campsite, Edzo's wife decided she had had enough of having to carry this bag of frozen creatures to the spring hunting grounds, where they would come to life and she would have to feed them once again.

"She decided to put an end to all this in her own way. Without consulting Edzo, she took the stone she used for making pounded meat, placed the bag of frozen creatures on a large rock, and pounded them to a pulp in the bag. She then went to Edzo and told him that if he wanted his medicine bag, he could carry it himself from now on."

Everyone there had a great laugh, particularly the women. "Good for her!" was likely what they were thinking. As it turns out, what she had been carrying all those years was a bag of snakes. The only location in the Northwest Territories where snakes are common is around Fort Smith, close to the Alberta border. Edzo must have traveled there at some time, possibly to get salt, which was available in that region, and learned of the snakes, collected some and brought them back home, where they served as a source of medicine for him.

I often chuckle when I think of this legend about the famous warrior who could perform great feats. He is shown to be a man no different than the rest of us, facing some of the same problems that we face from day to day. The Edzo legends, more often than not, laud the feats of this particular chief, eternalizing him as a teacher and great leader. This one legend depicts him as a family man having to come to grips with a decision taken by his dissatisfied wife.

I gave thanks to the old woman for gifting this story to me, and in keeping with Dene tradition, I am honoured to pass it on here.

THE JOKER: DZÈHKW'II

One spring day, shortly after most of the snow had melted, a story spread around town about a dream one of the elders had. This elder, Pierre Washee, had recently arrived in Rae Lakes from Fort Rae. He dreamt that his ancestors came to warn him that things were changing and the old ways and traditions were at risk of disappearing forever. He was instructed by them to pass on one of those ancient traditions by staging a particular ritual, which took the form of a game. Old Pierre was a sick man of bent posture who was convinced he was going to die soon and believed that if he did as instructed in his dream he would live a longer life.

The story of the old man's dream spread quickly throughout Rae Lakes, and at a community meeting the two medicine men discussed the implications of conducting the game. The people had been warned by the clergy that the old rituals and traditions were evil and they were urged to set them aside. Governments suppressed the traditional practices of many tribes in North America. This game was one such tradition. After much discussion, it was decided to allow this elder to play the shaman's game. I was fortunate to be at the meeting at the time when this issue was being discussed and decided upon. The word dzèhkw'ii was being used throughout the discussion to describe or name the ritual the old man wanted to conduct, and I wondered what the word meant.

"What exactly is dzèhkw'ii?" I casually asked at the meeting. All became quiet. Nobody spoke up to give me a translation of the word. A young man around my age picked up a deck of cards, searched through the deck, pulled out one card and held it up.

"What do you call that?" he asked me.

"The joker," I replied.

"That's what dzèhkw'ıi is. He is the Joker, a mysterious character with magical powers," he said. This became the English word commonly used to refer to the ritual from then on. Very few people in the community had experienced the game, so for many this was to be a new experience and one that would be long remembered.

The rest of that day and the next, stories circulated about how the game was played and how it had evolved over time. There was one aspect of the game that all of the stories had in common, and that was that the game was very dangerous. People could be hurt, but if you played and got hurt, the shaman could heal you on the spot. I became intrigued and felt comfortable enough with the people in the community to ask if I might join them in the game.

"No," I was told. "This is a spiritual event from the past and part of the tradition is that it be held away from the community and away from the white man's influence."

Because I identified so strongly with being part of the community by now, I persisted and approached a respected elder with my request to attend the event. He did not answer yes or no to my question, but went on to tell me that there was a dress code that applied to anyone who attended: no shoes or boots or belt-buckles; only traditional leather wear or cloth was to be worn. He said that in the past it was played with spears, but that nowadays they used an axe. The event, he said, would take place about a half-mile out of town. I listened intently, became even more intrigued and left that meeting knowing more about the game, but without a response to my request to attend. I took this as a polite no.

That night, I watched as crowds of moccasin-clad men, women and children headed out of town. Then a young boy ran up to me with a verbal message from one of the elders at the event. He told me I was to come and meet them at the first fire.

I rushed home, took off my belt, and, since I was already wearing moccasins, just slipped off the rubber overshoes and ran to catch up with the young lad. As I passed through the community I noticed that it was unusually quiet.

I caught up with the tail end of the crowd as they gathered in the failing light at the designated spot in the bush. It was a relatively small, open area of sandy ground with some snow patches still showing between the surrounding jack pine, spruce and birch trees. It was a park-like setting with very little undergrowth and three bonfires in the making. I went up to the first fire, as I had been instructed. As I did, some young people approached me to say that I should not be there. Before I could respond, two of the elders, along with the old shaman, approached us. They thanked me for coming and assured me in the presence of the young people that I was welcome to participate, where they left to prepare.

Then, out of the darkness, the Joker slowly appeared. There, in the flickering light of the fires, he stood straight and tall, not bent and stooped as we knew him. He had on a mask of birch bark, the whiteness of which reflected back the firelight. Two slits were cut in the mask, and a tuft of straw was attached to the top of the mask. The slits for his eyes left him with limited peripheral vision. He held an axe above his head and approached the gathering slowly at first, and then, with a burst of energy, ran directly at the first fire.

The people scattered in panic in every direction. He hurled himself headlong at the fire, swinging the axe, plunging it into the fire and scattering flaming embers about. He backed up suddenly, stood upright and plunged the axe into the ground.

He began to tremble. Every joint in his body—his ankles, knees, waist, elbows and wrists—began to waver and wobble. It looked like he might collapse. The two medicine men approached him, looking confused and obviously concerned. No words appeared to be exchanged, but something was communicated. The Joker relinquished the axe to one of the elders, who went to a nearby tree of the appropriate size, cut it with two strokes of the axe, and began to trim and shape the wood. Meanwhile, the other elder asked the owner of the axe to come forward.

"Did your daughter use this axe today?" he asked.

"Yes," he replied.

"Dzèhkw'ii says your daughter has had her first period today. Is this true?" he asked the man. The father quickly conferred with his wife and daughter and found this to be true. The elder went on to say, "This is a special occasion and powerful time in her life, but this has altered the shaman's medicine. She must leave and we will correct the situation by changing the axe handle and burning the old one." Meanwhile, the other elder had shaped a new handle in a matter of minutes. He thrust the axe head in the fire until it turned red, removed it, drove the old handle out and, with a rock, hammered in the new handle. He then dipped the axe head in a nearby patch of snow and checked to ensure that the head was secure. He returned it to The Joker. While this went on, I saw the young girl and her mother quietly leave the area.

The Joker took the axe and the trembling subsided. He raised it over his head, waved it from side to side and started to dance and chant. At times he stepped forward and stirred the fire, his masked face looking stiffly to the left and then to the right. Slowly he turned his head as he continued to sway with the axe at shoulder height. He leapt forward and struck the fire, glared into the crowd, his eyes visible through the slits in the mask if he looked around.

Suddenly, he leapt over the fire and ran straight at one individual. People scattered in all directions. In a matter of seconds he stood directly in front of the man, axe raised. The man stood for a moment, frozen in a state of shock. Then, like a rabbit suddenly realizing it is cornered, the man tried to make a run for it but to stumble only a few steps before being overtaken by the axe-wielding shaman, ready to strike. You could hear a collective breath go out of the crowd.

"Get down. Play dead," someone yelled close by. He dropped to the ground in terror. The Joker stopped, turned and looked for another target.

The pattern of the game continued like this for quite some time. The sequence was as follows: he targets you and when he catches up to you, you drop flat on the ground, look away and never make eye contact with him. The Joker then dances on one side of you and over to the other. He chants and speaks in Dogrib. He then rubs the head of the axe from the back of your neck to your tailbone, all the while chanting this phrase: "The caribou are lean; they have no fat. They are too skinny."

Then he raises his axe with his back to you, and as he swivels to bring the axe down, the signal is given for the individual to get up and run. That is when the axe strikes the ground, exactly where the person lay.

It was unnerving to watch. There was a kind of frenzy to it. This frail old man never seemed to tire. After each attack he turned slowly, fixed his gaze on a new quarry and then stalked them. I was so caught up in the strangeness of things as I watched the crowd and the menacing figure that I lost sight of the fact that I was part of the scene. Then, suddenly, I found myself face to face with The Joker.

I froze, bewildered and confused. I did not anticipate for one moment that I would be targeted. This was their game, and I had come as a spectator, or so I thought. I was frozen in the moment and panicked.

Is this the moment of revenge for the ancestors? Will I be sacrificed as the outsider? There he was, glaring at me through the slits in the white, featureless mask. The axe was raised.

"Run," someone yelled. There was no lying down on the ground for me. I turned and ran for the darkness of the forest, literally believing my life to be in danger. I ran in panic, with him following. A fallen tree lay straight ahead; someone stood to the side of it. I leapt over the tree trunk and plunged into blackness and safety beyond the firelight.

I stopped, breathless and relieved to see that The Joker was no longer after me. He approached the person I had passed who stood beside the fallen tree trunk. As The Joker approached him, someone gave out a loud yell telling him to drop, and he did. I circled back to the safety of the fire, breathless and trembling.

The fellow on the ground beside that fallen tree trunk was my translator's father. He was blind in one eye. Although he was not supposed to move, he did in order to use his good eye to see what was happening. At which point, he heard the death chant of The Joker. He saw the axe being raised, leapt up and ran for his life as the axe was driven into the ground directly where he had been.

The game continued. I made a point of avoiding eye contact with The Joker. Finally, he and the two medicine men and everyone else gathered around and said a prayer to the ancestors. The three men faded back into the darkness of the forest and the game was over.

It was a night that I will never forget. The next morning, the old man wandered around town, bent as he had been before, but, as some people noted, he appeared to have a spring in his step. As for me, I felt a new kind of acceptance, whether in the community at large or in people's homes.

This shaman, possessed with the spirit and vigor of a young man, had captured the hearts and minds of all who were there. The fear and laughter that night was filled with ritual and tradition and emotion.

Wrapped in a cloth bundle was a collection of bone knives and scrapers, along with a traditional game made from the foot bones of a caribou.

In 2019, I had a conversation with the shaman's son Alexie about the event and commented on what a remarkable experience it must have been for him to see his father become such a powerful and mythic figure for that one night. He then related what his father had said to him at the time leading up to the ritual. "In four days' time people will come to ask me to perform an ancient game. If they do come, it is then I will know the dream I had was truly from the ancestors." His son described how two medicine men actually did come to their home and asked his father to perform the game.

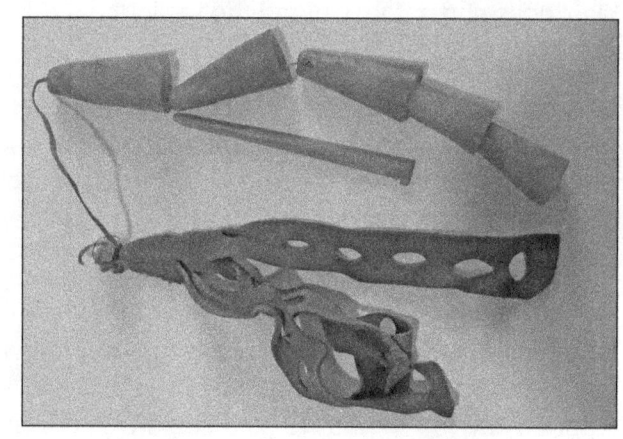

Cup & Pin Game

I also had his Eldest son visit me in Ft. Rae about 1986. His father heard my eldest brother was in town and he told his son to gift my brother a very special item, a game. His instructions were for my brother Gerry to keep it and that he was to tell people on the outside that the Dene still have medicine power and that I (his younger brother) was a witness to that. This bundle was then gifted back to me a few years ago and helped inspire the writing of this story in memory of that man, Pierre Washee. The game was intriguingly near impossible to play, but his son could perform it effortlessly. A game of hand eye coordination that required the utmost skill imaginable. Little did I know the importance of his request at that time.

NÀHGA: THE BUSHMAN

While working on the church in Rae Lakes, I met Alphonse Apples. I checked nets with him in the evening and on days off and often went duck hunting with him. During these trips, I made attempts to learn more about Dene culture. On one occasion we passed an area known as the Valley of the Hills, not far from the community. I asked him if there was a lake in the valley and he said there was, but, when I suggested we go hunting there, he said we couldn't because the Bushman, Nàhga, lived there. This led to conversation about the Bushman. Although the Dene description of Nàhga varies from story to story—sometimes it is a physical, living thing, and sometimes an invisible presence or even an area of inexplicable danger—the name remains the same: Nàhga.

Some stories describe Nàhga as a hairy creature that kidnaps children or women. If you see him, you must leave where you are and go elsewhere. I heard these stories over many years and in many places in Dene territory. Some people are reported as having killed one. The trouble is, if you kill one, all kinds of things are thought to be likely to happen to you, because the Nàhga has strong medicine and will always get even with you. It is without doubt a threatening concept or presence.

An old man in Fort Franklin was supposed to have killed one. I met him in later years. He was dark skinned, but had large white blotching all over his body, which he claimed had occurred after killing a Bushman. It was said that after he turned all white he would die.

Folklore in Dene communities holds that upon killing a Bushman you must dispose of the body in a flawless manner. The Nàhga must be dismembered, every joint in the body disconnected and thrown away in a different direction. The old man claimed that he was in the process of doing this when he heard other Bushmen talking nearby. In fear, he threw away the last hand without dismembering it, and ran. He was plagued with worry that the Bushmen knew who he was and would come for him one day.

I asked Alphonse to drop me off at the head of the valley that he had refused to enter and to pick me up that night. He refused. I was told by others that no one ever hunted or trapped in this area. When I spoke to Father Amourous about this, he gave me some background.

"It's understood that Nàhga lives in that valley and, should you go near it, the mountain will rumble." One day Father Amourous, who had also had been warned not to go to this valley, was flying to Rae Lakes with an elder. He asked the pilot to fly over the lake in the valley of Nàhga. The elder cautioned him not to do that, but the pilot flew into the valley anyway. As they entered it, the plane wobbled violently and the pilot had a struggle with the aircraft to climb back out.

"I told you not to go there," the elder remarked. Father said that this was the kind of incident that only reaffirmed the legend in the community. Father Amourous and the pilot were convinced it was just a thermal wind effect.

Here I'm hunting near the Nàhga region where a forest fire is burning

There was another spot farther to the southeast of the community with a different Bushman. This one was invisible and left no tracks. A trapper, ten years before, had gone into an area where no one had trapped before. The trapper did not return the next day. His family went in search of him. They came across his trail and found his dogs but no trapper. There were no tracks leading away from or around his sled. He had disappeared from the back of the sled. There was no explanation. This confirmed the area as taboo, and no one trapped there again. Remarkably, many years later, I found another possible answer to the question of how the trapper disappeared.

A friend and I had a hobby trap line in similar terrain. We were travelling on a well-defined trail that passed over a small lake and into the woods. We had just come off the lake onto the shore when my friend suddenly veered his sled to the side. There was a circle of water three feet in diameter in the middle of our trail. I went over to have a look, cut a ten-foot branch, trimmed it and pushed it down into the water. It met no resistance. The branch penetrated to its full length and did not touch bottom. Where did this pool of water come from, and why did it not freeze over? We didn't have the answers, but we gave the pool a wide berth.

Many years later, I posed a question on an Internet site regarding the anomaly I had observed that day. I got a response from someone in Russia. He explained it as a salt spring and not an unusual feature to be found in the kind of terrain I described.

Getting back to the missing trapper, my speculation is that his team walked over the thin ice on one of these saltwater holes, and the trapper likely stepped off the sled and went through the ice.

I have heard many other cautionary tales about Nàhga, the Bushman, and never grew tired of listening to them, because the Bushman reshapes itself in form and function in the different communities. He is a spirit, yet killable, a presence with power in air, on water and on land. In some ways, hearing these stories was like watching a sci-fi movie series, where the storyline and shape of the central character may change episode by episode, but Nàhga is the common theme.

HANDBALL GAME: GOHZÌI

John Bekale came to me after work one day to inform me that people were gathering outside between Chief Andrew Gon's house and Harry Simpson's place. They were going to play handball, or gohzìi as it is known in Dogrib. John was quite excited as he explained to me how much fun it was.

We rushed over to find a group of people already gathered. I was surprised to see some of the shyest ladies in town were standing there giggling, anxiously waiting for the game to begin. The women formed a large circle, and about five or six men were coaxed to stand in the centre. One of the women arrived with a small caribou-hide ball that just fit in the palm of her hand. It was soft, not unlike a beanbag. There was a great deal of chatter and teasing going on. Once the men were settled in the center of the circle, the woman holding the ball threw it high into the air towards the women on the other side of the circle, who were expected to catch it. The circle's edge was three or four bodies deep in places. Once the ball was in the air, it was the men's task to try to intercept it.

If one of the men did catch it, the women descended on him to pry the ball out of his hands. The women's hands were as strong as or stronger than those of many of the men because of their daily chores of scraping, pulling and stretching hides. The women were allowed to tickle the man at the same time as they pried his hands open. Each time they retrieved the ball, the circle formed once more and the game started all over again.

The amount of body contact involved brought everyone out of their shells. Normally shy people were in the thick of it. How often do you have an opportunity to tickle your neighbor without being worried about the consequences? Everyone pulled, pushed, pried and tickled; women, men, children, and even the wide-eyed infants perched on their mothers' backs were caught up watching it. A mentally challenged lad joined in the game as he jumped, laughed and moved with the shifting crowd chasing the ball.

The game had gone on for quite a while when I was invited to participate. I became totally involved and ended going home with a sore stomach from all my laughter.

I was getting ready to leave Rae Lakes at the time, and this simple game was just one more thing that enhanced my sense of belonging to and my regrets at having to leave this community. I suspect that the resurrection of the game at this time was a result of The Joker shaman, whose recent intervention had stirred the community's interest in revisiting the old ways.

I had supper at Harry Simpson's house and on the way home came across a little girl, Frances Quitte's daughter, playing with a doll. I chatted with her and her friends and went home intent on making a doll house for her as a parting gesture. I gathered leftover pieces of lumber from the building site and used them to assemble a small dollhouse. The next morning, I dropped it off at the young girl's place. I met her again many years later, when she was a woman of about thirty. She remembered the dollhouse as the most special present she had ever received and expressed her thanks once again for my thinking to make it for her.

I flew out of Rae Lakes rich in spirit but poor in pocket, and arrived at the Yellowknife airport where I was picked up and brought out to Fort Rae. There, the priest who hired me to build the church, Father Pochat, surprised me with a paycheque. I reminded him that I had undertaken to do the work without pay. However, he insisted.

"The money is not for the work you did, Kieran, it's to pay you to buy some new clothes," he said, as he noted that the clothing I was wearing was in tatters.

CAMBRIDGE BAY

I had finished my work in Rae Lakes in the fall and remained short on money, with no work options. Then I got a call from Father Pochat asking me if I would be willing to go to Cambridge Bay, also known as Iqaluktuuttiaq in what is now Nunavut, to build a church. It was a timely offer; I accepted and boarded a plane heading into the Canadian Arctic to undertake another construction project, not for the Dene this time, but for the Inuit of Cambridge Bay.

Once I was settled in my accommodation, I took a walk around town and came to an area where huge plywood crates were scattered around on the still-frozen ground. As I passed one of these crates, I suddenly realized that they were being used as homes. They had holes cut in them, with plastic stapled over the openings that served as windows.

I was invited into one of these dwellings and told that these crates had been used to ship snowmobiles to the Northern Store. Dozens of people were living in these salvaged crates and raising their children in uninsulated wooden boxes in one of the coldest climates on the planet. These makeshift homes were called matchbox houses throughout the Arctic. As I talked with the residents, I was told there was a long waiting list of people asking for housing. Many of the new people on that list were living in conditions worse than those of the home I was visiting. This family saw no prospect of getting a house. To think that government officials were aware of these horrific living conditions and were doing little to address them! To add insult to injury the Government had a liquor store so large that had it been converted into an apartment complex it could have housed half the town.

Added to the desperate living conditions was the even more serious matter: that those living there had suffered broken spirits. Their traditional beliefs and practices had been undermined to the point where many people had lost their pride in and connection with their culture.

The Inuit had thrived for millennia in one of the coldest climates on Earth, while many outsiders, like Captain John Franklin and his crew, had perished because of it. But here, at this time, the Inuit were rudderless, uprooted from their traditional territory and way of life. It's no wonder that the actions of both church and state here have come to be regarded as a form of cultural genocide. It was all there, happening right in front of me. They were reduced to wearing cast-off western clothing and living in discarded shipping crates. They had abandoned many of their traditional ways and were drinking themselves into oblivion. At that time, and in that place, there appeared to me to be an overwhelming sense of hopelessness.

Living conditions for the Inuit in Cambridge Bay have improved dramatically over those of the 1970s. The community has made a remarkable recovery from that despairing time to become a modern town that now serves as the government's administrative centre for Nunavut.

Towards the end of my stay, I took a stroll out onto the tundra, along with my dog. I came to a hill ahead with a pile of unusual stones on top. I climbed it and found bones scattered in a wide circle. I knelt down by the cairn, identified a human skull, and realized that this was a burial site. This burial practice was similar to that followed by some traditional Dene, where the body was disposed of in such a manner that it becomes one with the nature that surrounds it. I stayed there for some time, contemplating and trying to visualize the life lived by this Inuk and his fellow hunters.

I left there feeling very much at peace. I returned to town and told the priest what I had seen. "The remains you saw out there on the Barrenlands would have been that of an elder who asked for that kind of burial. The people here believe that after they die, whatever insect, bird, plant or animal feeds from their body carries their spirit. In short, the dead go on living in the world. That's their traditional idea of the afterlife." He was an understanding cleric, one who didn't put down the traditional ways. I was to hear a similar concept of the afterlife described some years later while talking with a Dene elder, Joseph Rabesca, in Fort Rae.

The Cambridge Bay experience gave me a new awareness of the destructive impact colonization has had on Indigenous communities, be they Inuit or Dene. I carried that troubling awareness with me as I headed back south to Yellowknife and to the community of Rae Lakes once again.

RAE LAKES COMMUNITY HALL

Shortly after I returned to Yellowknife from Cambridge Bay, I was asked if I would be interested in going back to Rae Lakes to build a log community hall there. I went to the government office to look at the plans for the building. It was to be an octagonal-shaped structure. I looked over the plan and asked the man who had offered me the job: "You do understand that I've never built a log building before?"

"I was given to understand that you're building a log cabin," he replied.

"Yes I am, but it's a work in progress and it's only three logs high."

"Well?" he said with a smile and added, "That makes you more qualified than anyone else we know. Besides, you're familiar with the community and they've requested that you be given the job." I felt good about the acknowledgement and agreed to take it on. He continued, "There won't be any sub trades involved, so you're in charge of the entire job from start to finish. Okay?" I nodded agreement. This was to be my first experience in running a job without being able to draw upon the expertise of skilled tradesmen.

I landed in Rae Lakes to a welcoming reception from a large gathering of familiar faces. A young boy, Leon, Harry Simpson's son, came along to help me unload some of my gear onto a homemade wheelbarrow made completely from logs, wheel and all. My living quarters were at the back of the church, a small room with a wood stove for heat and cooking.

Here I was, in a settlement with next to no contact with the outside world, in charge of a work force of thirty-five people, few of whom spoke English. This was to be a challenge and also a crash course in project management. I was twenty-two years old at the time and surprised myself at having the confidence to take on a job like this. Maybe I would yet become that log building contractor I had hoped to become when I first came north.

My first task after settling in was to come to grips with the octagonal form of the building. I drew the shape and played around with it, over and over, without reference to the blueprints. Late into the night I came to what I felt was an understanding of it. I figured I could start the next day at least with a handle on the form the building was to take. The matter of how to put it together would hopefully follow.

The building supplies had come in on the winter road. One thing I did note that had not been considered was that we needed extra piles, because this building would be used for functions such as drum dances. I had seen drum dances held in people's homes and remembered the floors shaking from the pounding, so much so that nails popped and the plywood flooring came loose.

I calculated that we had to harvest and haul about 150 logs to the site. That task was left to the men and their dog teams. They were soon to be seen moving up and down the lake at all times of the day and night. Those doing the hauling were paid by the log, a motivator that led to feverish activity. One of the many issues that made this job a big challenge was the shape of the logs. They were conical, twelve to sixteen inches in diameter on one end and only six inches on the other. I learned many lessons about log building on this job, skills that earned me a reputation in the north as a competent craftsman.

Each evening I worked on solutions to the technical problems we faced. I needed to know what I was talking about when I gave the men instructions. But I wasn't left alone to do this. I had John Bekale working beside me. He was always there, any time I needed him. Sometimes, long after everyone had gone home, he watched me struggle with the blueprints as I laid things out for the next day and bounced ideas off him to get his valuable input. Even though he had all kinds of responsibilities at home, he was eager and willing to spend time helping.

It wasn't a matter of all work and no play. There were the usual drum dances and hand games every once in a while. People like John Bekale and Francis Quitte and others around my age encouraged me to attend these events. I went and was rather shy about dancing at first. But before I knew it, I would be pushed or shuffled into the line by someone, to share in the joy of the occasion.

This was the first time many people in the community were earning a paycheque. The newfound prosperity was shared by every home in the community. They had arranged it so that at least one person from each household had a job on the project. They could now afford the small extravagances: fabric for curtains and new colourful scarves for the women, or they might even save enough for someone to fly out to go shopping or to visit relatives.

What are young people like John and Francis going to do with themselves when the job is finished? I often wondered to myself. I'm sure they had concerns about that also, but they were not given to expressing them. They were, however, filled with curiosity about what was happening outside their community and asked me endless questions in that regard, as I did about their world. We fed off each other's inquisitiveness.

The octagonal community hall in Rae Lakes

The people in the community never stood still. They were always hooking up dogs to go somewhere or pushing off in a canoe to hunt ducks, some making dry meat or tanning hides, others hauling or splitting fire wood, gathering fish from their nets or feeding the large number of dogs staked out near their homes. Everywhere I turned, I saw activity. Children were well looked after and in constant physical contact with someone, being carried, wrapped up on someone's back, or being swung on a baby swing in the corner of the home.

My time spent engaged with the community was to shape my future in ways I would never have imagined. It was in Rae Lakes that I felt I had found the sense of purpose and connectedness that I lacked while living in the south.

RAE LAKES AIRPORT

While working on another log building in Rae Lakes, I was told that the government had decided to fund the building of an airstrip for the community. The airstrip was to be located just behind the village, in a flat, sandy area that was heavily treed. It was badly needed to address emergencies during spring break-up, and it would provide further employment opportunities for the community.

Once the officials had finished inspecting the site, they said that they would send in a dynamite expert to blast the rocks and clear the strip in about three weeks' time. These rocks were large, as much as ten feet tall and around eight feet across. Two more flights would be needed because the blasting caps had to be transported on one flight and the dynamite on another. After the inspectors left, the elders called a meeting, because they were having a hard time understanding why they had to wait for a blaster to deal with the large boulders. They knew they could do the job themselves without a blaster and just needed to get organized.

The next morning, I watched from the community hall job site as a large group of men headed to the airstrip. They had a huge bonfire going in no time. I asked someone how the job was going and was told that the old-timers didn't want to wait for the blaster and had set to work on removing the boulders themselves.

"What do they plan to do?" I asked one of my work crew.

"They're in the process of burying them," he replied. I headed to the airstrip to see what was going on. They had already disposed of one car-sized rock and dug under the second rock, undermining it on one side while the rock was secured from moving with strategically placed heavy poles. When the hole was considered deep enough to bury the rock, they removed the support poles and pried the rock forward until it pitched into the excavation.

They buried another the next day and had decided on a different plan for dealing with the third rock, which was the size of a Brinks truck. They gathered some of the trees that had been cut down, piled them around the enormous rock, and built a fire. They fed the fire for a long time. Containers of water were then brought up from the lake, and they proceeded to throw water on the heated rock. The quick cooling caused it to crack and shatter into pieces, bit by bit. This process of heating and dousing went on for two days, and in the end the rock had been reduced to a pile of rubble. All of this material was then carted away and buried nearby, leaving not a trace of a rock or boulder on the proposed airstrip.

In background, smoke from a fire used to break up the giant boulder

A government representative returned by plane, bringing the blasting caps for the dynamite. He said that the blaster would be arriving on the next plane and he would need help to move his large rock drill to the airstrip site. I was the person selected to break the news to him as to what had happened. Without saying much, I invited him to come with me to check the site, and I added that I thought he would agree that there would be no need to fly the blaster in after all. He looked puzzled as we headed to the airstrip.

When we got there, he walked up and down the airstrip, trying to figure out what had happened to all of the rocks. At first the community played him along and told him that they used medicine power of ik'ǫǫ to do the job. They let him think on that for a while, and then he was finally told the whole story of how it had been accomplished, all to his great amazement.

HOTTAH LAKE YQHTSIK'E

During that summer when I worked in Rae Lakes building the community hall, the town began to run short of food. There was no freezer in the community to store food, and the supply of dry meat from the winter hunt was running low. Fish was mostly what was available. An enormous quantity of fish was needed, not only to feed the people, but to feed all of the dog teams in town. There were a few ducks now and then to supplement the diet, but even rabbits were in short supply and moose had not been spotted for months.

The chief requested that people go on a moose hunt to supplement the food supply. Groups of hunters were sent out in different directions. I was asked if I wanted to join one of the hunting parties, which was to head north on the Camsel River system. I asked what to me seemed like a reasonable question of David Quitte junior, nicknamed Anwa because of a duck's call that he was great at imitating.

"How long will we be gone?" He looked at me somewhat puzzled.

"Till we get a moose," he said, implying: what does time have to do with it? I got the message.

I thought to myself, How do you plan for a trip not knowing how long it is going to take? I crammed as much stuff as I could into my packsack.

"Pack lighter, Kieran," Jimmy Mantla cautioned me. I unpacked some items and then scrounged around town for some dried fish.

The weather the next morning was miserable, but nonetheless we set out. I remember a few of the names of those in my party. There was Alphonse Apples, whose boat we were using, Andrew Quitte, Jimmy Mantla and Anwa, one of the Quitte family. We skirted all the bays on Gameti Lake and portaged along the Camsel River system, looking for ducks as we travelled, but without any luck.

Our canvas canoe was powered by a twenty-five-horse kicker, and not long into our journey the motor started to falter and then quit altogether. Anwa told one of the younger fellows to pull the spark plug so that it could be checked. Using a crescent wrench, he unthreaded the plug and, as the threads reached the top, the plug fell to the side, rolled off the motor and plopped into the water. We watched helplessly as it sank into the depths. It was too deep and cold to consider diving to retrieve it. Now what do we do? I thought. No motor, and miles away from home without food, and no moose to take home to the families.

Anwa directed us to paddle to an island close by where we could set up camp, warm up and decide what to do next. Anwa and Andrew got into a deep discussion, pointing in different directions as we paddled. Andrew finally told us that we would begin to look for an abandoned motor that was somewhere nearby.

"Years ago, my father and I left a motor on one of the islands along this stretch of the lake," Andrew said. "If we can find it we might be able to salvage the spark plug. It could be this island, but I'm not sure."

BURNT SNOW

We landed on the island, split up and went in different directions. The chances of finding the old motor were slim, as were the chances that the plug could be salvageable, and then there was the difficulty that plugs vary greatly from one motor to another. We had no luck. We regrouped and went from island to island until Andrew recognized the one where the abandoned motor was located for sure. So searched once again, with more enthusiasm this time.

Then we heard Andrew calling out that he had found it. It was in the middle of this granite island, standing upright on a makeshift stand. I had never seen such an old motor; it was a museum piece. It had a flat top made of solid steel that was rusted badly, nothing like the aluminum block on our motor. On the top of this motor there was a huge sparkplug. Oil was applied and left to soak in for a while. Then we took an axe and lightly taped it over and over, eventually managing to work it loose. The base of the plug was much larger than the spark plug hole in our motor, but that didn't seem to discourage anyone.

They made a fire, brewed some tea, and Anwa sent me to the boat to gather up all the files we brought for sharpening our axes and knives. I had a handsaw file in my kit. They then went to work to file the huge plug down to size. We worked in shifts through the night.

It helped that we had almost twenty-four hours of daylight at the time. Our fingers got raw and in some cases to the point of bleeding by the time we had the plug down to the size required. Anwa then took my handsaw file and proceeded to file threads into the solid steel plug. When he took a sleep break, Jimmy and I took over, and slowly but surely we got what resembled threads. We woke Anwa. He fitted the plug onto the motor slowly, turning it with the wrench, tapping it lightly with the axe as he went. He then removed it and, using the deeper imprint of the thread on it, finished filing it a little deeper. He then turned it into the block to a depth he thought would work.

We got the gas hooked up to the motor and proceeded to pull-start it. Over and over, we pulled as we made adjustments to the plug and tried again until our arms and shoulders ached. Just when we were beginning to think that all our work had been a waste of time, the motor bucked and, BARUMMMMMMM; it started. We turned it off, hooked it on to the boat, loaded our gear, and got ready to push off. Anwa pulled the cord; the motor kicked in and ran perfectly. As we pulled away from shore, Anwa turned to me and posed a question.

"So, which way? Head home or head north for moose?"

It was an unexpected question, and I wasn't sure if I was expected to answer it or not. He waited and I reflected quickly.

"Go home empty-handed, or, go north and break down again and have twice as far to paddle home. Tough choice!" I said. Anwa didn't take that as an answer. He insisted I make the decision.

"Ne koawo, you're the boss," he said.

"Nope! I am not the boss." I quickly responded, and, remembering a favorite Dogrib phrase, I reached into my pocket and added, "Soomba kaowo," meaning money is the boss. With that, I took out a coin, flipped it and said, "Heads north and tails south." Heads came up. "Okay. Soomba kaowo," I said. "We head north to hunt moose." That got a chuckle out of them. I'll never know for sure if they were playing me along or not, but I suspect they planned to continue to hunt whether it came up heads or tails. A short while later, we saw a duck fly past ,acting like it had a broken wing.

I knew of other birds who would do that to draw people away from the nest but was surprised to see a duck trying to do the same. We combed the shoreline and found the nest. It had eggs and ducklings. Anwa gathered the eggs up in his head kerchief. He broke one open, emptied it into his mouth, and I could hear him crunching the bones of an embryo. He asked if I wanted one. I closed my eyes, broke the egg into my mouth, crunched and swallowed. We kept the ducklings for making soup later on.

Anwa with ducklings for our soup

On and on we travelled, with no sign of moose. Then someone made the unwelcome announcement that we were now past the halfway point for our gas supply. "Now what?" I thought for the second time. But I was learning not to predict doom when travelling with this creative crew. Andrew said he was trapping on Hottah Lake last year and left some gas at his camp about halfway up that lake.

"We have enough gas to make it there," he said. I felt a question coming.

"What do you want to do? You're the boss. Do we go back or go ahead Ne kaowo?" Andrew asked once again. However, this time he encouraged me by saying that he knew the Hottah Lake area well and that it was a good spot to find moose. He was a Slavey married to a Dogrib woman and this was Slavey country. I was not going to be pressed into another decision.

"Soomba-kaowo," I said and flipped the coin. "I guess we're going north again." No one argued.

We now tackled the last portage into Hottah Lake, through clouds of sand flies that swarmed us. We were about to embark on a journey across a huge lake where, if we ran out of gas in the middle of the lake and bad weather struck, there were no islands to serve as shelter. But nobody appeared to be concerned. The lake had only recently been freed of ice, giving rise to a light fog as the air warmed. This was understandable, since we were only about 130 miles from the Arctic Circle. We moved slowly into the fog, with Andrew navigating on his home turf.

Mornings started very early with these guy,s and at times we travelled all night and slept on the go. As we glided along, at one point, the motor suddenly cut out. The spark plug popped up out of the block, but fortunately stayed attached to the plug wire. We threaded it back in and carried on, and then it popped out once again. This cycle went on for a while, slowing down our progress. We had no compass, yet Andrew pointed us onward through the fog that came and went. During one of the breaks in the fog, we came across three beautiful swans. They didn't fly off as we slowed to a stop and sat quietly admiring them. I asked if they were going to shoot them; after all, we were hungry. The answer was no, because it was against the law, but I suspect it was more because the sound of the shot would scare any shoreline moose back into the bush. Then they went on to tease me, telling me how delicious swan meat was.

The fog lifted clear of the water, and we could see out onto the great expanse of Hottah Lake. After a short while, we came to three small, flat, rock islands almost completely devoid of trees. Andrew signalled for Anwa to slow the boat down. Almost simultaneously, we heard the boat run aground on a rock, making an ominous scraping sound, bad news for a canvas canoe. Ice-cold water gushed in through three large gashes in the canvas.

"At least we know it's not deep here," Anwa called out calmly. He maneuvered the boat toward a flat outcrop of rock close by and drove the boat right onto it. This island was about sixty feet by twenty feet wide. We unloaded and flipped the boat to assess the damage.

"What are the chances of someone finding us here?" I speculated. The obvious answer was, no chance. It was an ongoing concern for me, but the others did not appear to share that concern. We looked around. There were scraps of driftwood in some rock crevices, dry grass and shrubs here and there, and two trees about eight feet tall and two inches thick, if that. We gathered wood and made a fire. Anwa walked around the island, came back and asked for a frypan.

With the fire going and fry pan warming, Anwa started scraping one of the trees. The trees had been damaged, likely by ice in breakup, and the sap had run and hardened in the small wounds on both trees. He took this sap resin, melted it in the frypan and quickly poured it over two of the smaller rips in the canvas. He spread the sap into the tears with a hot knife and sealed the damage.

There was still one more rip to fix. He asked everyone to empty their packsacks to see if we had anything that might be used for the purpose. I had an empty bread bag to keep my matches dry. He took it, wrapped it on a stick and set fire to it. Then he took it to the boat and let the melting plastic drip onto the rip, and he again used a hot knife to spread it. It was not quite as good as the sap for the purpose, but it worked. We let the craft sit for a while to give time for the patch to adhere fully. This trip was a course in survival attitudes and techniques for me, yet all this appeared to be taken for granted by the rest of the crew.

We had a cup of tea before we left. The urgency to get the hell out of there was hanging over our success. We headed towards the west shore located halfway up the lake. By way of paying our respects, I was instructed to "pay" the lake, and did so with some .22 shells. It was hinted that our bad luck so far could have been due to the fact I had overlooked paying the lake when we first entered it.

Anwa heating sap to fix the canoe

After a short time, we came upon some ducks. We were approaching the bay where there was a possibility of moose, but our hunger won out over our better judgment of not wanting to scare them off, so we shot four ducks. We eased our way slowly into the nearby bay, to find a streak of muddy water not a hundred feet away where a moose must have rushed up onto the shore and away in response to the gunshots.

We parked the boat and Andrew directed us up to the top of a hill, where we built a fire and the smoke gave us some relief from the bugs. We cooked the eggs we had gathered from the rock island, plucked and cooked our ducks. We were discouraged at the lost chance of bagging the moose, but the men talked about the fact that the bugs were so bad it would not be too surprising if the moose came back to seek refuge in the water. I stood up to put another log on the fire and, just as I did, far below I noticed the moose moving back to the spot in the bay. I pointed as I ducked down, groping for my shells and gun.

"Dedii, moose, moose," I muttered. Everyone grabbed their guns. Anwa signaled us to hold fire. He had noticed something. We waited with our gun sights trained on the moose as it entered the water. Then, to our astonishment, another moose came from our side of the water and started to swim across. Once it arrived on the shore, we were given the go-ahead to shoot. Two of us were to shoot and two others acted as backup, in case we missed. Then followed the sharp crack of two guns firing almost simultaneously. Both moose dropped. We had done what we came to do.

We finished our meal and then headed downhill to the work at hand. This was my first time to shoot a moose; they had given me the honour of the first shot; had I missed, they had backup shooters ready.

After we had given the traditional thanks to the creator, I took careful note of the butchering process that followed. When we had finished working on the carcasses, we filled the bottom of the boat with more boughs and loaded the canoe to the brim. The only parts left behind were the gut pile and the lungs. When everyone got into the boat, there was only a few inches of freeboard.

We went a little farther north to get Andrew's fuel cache. It was there and intact. We were on top of the world with newfound enthusiasm and heading home to the families with plenty of meat. As we crossed the lake, we knew we had to get a move on, knowing that if a wind came up while loaded like this, we would be in serious trouble. When I think about it, this trip, with all of its ups and downs, was an example of living on the edge. We made it to the portage at the bottom of the lake and unloaded, and now the work of portaging began.

Back and forth we went over the portage, carrying this mound of meat. The bull flies were out now, teaming up with the no-see-ums. I have never been more bitten in all of my travels. I suspect the smell of that meat brought them out in clouds. By the next two portages, my wrists began to swell from the bites, like a bracelet as thick as a half-inch rope. Some of us had head nets, which helped a little. There was Anwa, no head net, no gloves and all exposed skin. His only defense against the bugs was his kerchief sweatband; he had pulled it down and covered his nose and mouth like a bandit. He showed no signs of any significant swelling from the bites.

We had layered the meat in the boat with spruce boughs between the layers so that they would not build up heat. This mass of moose flesh had to be turned and shifted throughout the journey. When we stopped to camp, I looked forward to the break and to a hearty meal of pan-fried moose steak, a historical meal fit for a voyageur. An hour must have passed from the time we landed till we were set up. We made a stage to hang the meat and then got a smudge going to keep the flies away. We set up our mosquito nets, got a fire going and were finally ready to eat.

I was sizing up the hind leg to cut off a large steak and pulled out the frying pan. Jimmy came over and interrupted me in a quiet, respectful way as I prepared to cut my steak.

"Kieran, we came all this way to hunt for our families. We're here to bring home as much meat as we can," he said. I nodded, feeling embarrassed because I now realized that the others were eating the leftovers from our egg and duck dinner. The whole crew sat looking at me, standing there with my knife poised. Then they started to laugh.

"We know it's your first moose hunt. Let him go ahead," someone called out. Jimmy cut off a piece from the right lower front leg, a really tough piece of meat, and gave it to me to me to cook.

This was an eye-opening experience for me, but for the crew it was all in a day's work. That night we ate moose head, considered a great delicacy. I was given a lesson on how to skin and prepare it. The head was placed in the fire, turned over and over, and after about twenty minutes it was removed and skinned. The tongue, which had been removed earlier and was the most desired piece, was cooked. Following that, the jaws were split and every scrap of meat on them eaten, by scraping it off the bone with a knife. The skull was then split in half, using a large knife struck with the heel of an axe. The brain inside was cooked and ready to be eaten.

This was total immersion in the way of life on the hunt and how things were done. There were unwritten rules on process and protocol. Each night on the way back, we went through the same ritual, making smudges and hanging the meat so that it wouldn't spoil. The thicker portions were sliced thinly to keep them cool and help in the drying process. The more we did this, the lighter the load became. We now were into mostly river travel with its many rapids and portages, and few breaks were taken. Speed was of the essence.

We came to a set of long, treacherous rapids. The portage would have required more than one trip, so it was decided to navigate the canoe that had the meat on board through the rapids by lining them. It was my first experience of lining a rapid of that size, and I began to realize the extent of expertise required. Two people worked on one side of the river and one on the other. Long ropes were tied to the front and back of the canoe. Andrew took the responsibility of guiding the boat with the help of a long pole and shouted orders to those on shore. One of his jobs was to secure the boat at various intervals using the pole, then signal for the rope to be passed on to the next man, who then placed himself in an appropriate location to allow the canoe to be advanced slowly. We got through the torrent and out into the calm eddy without damage or injury.

We were now on the last leg of the journey. As we approached the settlement, a boat came out in answer to our warning shots, and we unloaded half of the meat into that boat so that we could manage the rising waves. We made it back with a plentiful food supply for the community.

That evening, they held a feast at Andrews's house. At the feast, the story of the trip was told, the entire community feasted, and families left with their supply of uncooked meat to be taken home and processed in traditional fashion. It was fortunate that we managed to get our moose, because none of the other hunting parties had success.

The next day, all of the smoke tents in town were going full tilt. Outside, the women scraped and prepared the moose hides, carved dry meat, kept smudges going and crushed bones to extract the bone grease. It was a busy and happy time. I received the gift of a pair of moccasins from one of the women for my contribution to the hunt. A drum dance was held late into the night and, tired or not, we all participated.

The following day, we went back to work on the octagonal community hall. I now had an even greater appreciation of having a rewarding job and of being able to live a way of life the likes of which I could never have imagined. I could also add to that list the satisfaction of having played a role as part of a team in adding to the community's depleted food supply.

WHAT HAPPENED TO BEAR LAKE ALEXIE?

Alexie Tauye

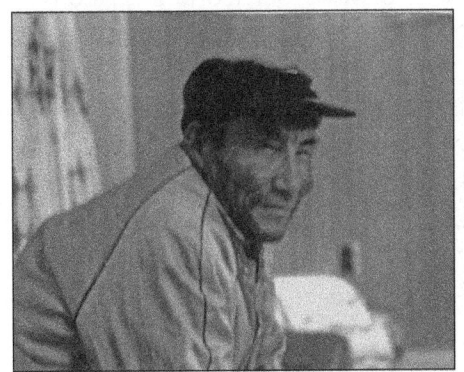

It was springtime in Rae Lakes, and most of the snow on land was gone. The ice had melted a good forty feet out from the shoreline. All of the dogs were tied up on the outskirts of the community, people were painting their canoes, and those who had kicker motors were tuning them up. The ice was now starting to candle, and it was getting too treacherous for travel. Large masses of this ice can shift with the winds from one end of the lake to the other in very short order, eventually breaking up on the rocks and islands along the shoreline.

Early one morning, after a few hours of shingling on the community hall roof, we lay back to bask in the warm sunshine. Our bodies luxuriated in it, having suffered through the long, cold winter. One of the men beside me commented that he thought he could see something moving in the distance, out on the ice. I looked in the direction he pointed and could make out a small, moving speck.

"Maybe a wolf?" someone speculated, and a few minutes later, "It could be a lone caribou." We all sat up and gazed intently into the distance. One of the work crew then exclaimed, "It's a dog team!" Sure enough, we could now see it twist and turn. Since everyone had their dogs tied up at this time, no one could understand who this might be out there or where he could have come from, knowing that everywhere south of us, the ice conditions would be worse than we were experiencing here in Rae Lakes.

Word of the sighting spread quickly. A small crowd gathered by the shore and watched as the team drew closer. Charlie Gon launched his canoe and paddled towards the ice floe as everyone watched. The team pulled up at the ice edge and Charlie talked for a while with whoever was there. They then transferred the man's gear to the canoe and, holding a line tied to the lead dog, they got into the canoe. Charlie paddled back towards the shore as the man pulled his leader into the water and the rest of his dog team followed, pulling the empty sled along with them.

They got to the shore and the new arrival shook hands with everybody as he wandered through the crowd. After a while, someone showed him where to tie up his dogs. He went to my friend, blind Johnny Arrowmaker's house. Word went around the town that he had come all the way from Yellowknife via Lac la Marte and that he was on his way to Fort Franklin on Great Bear Lake. I was astonished at what I had just seen and decided that I would visit the man after work, and Johnny could help with translation. With all I was hearing, as the day passed, it was obvious this man was a very special visitor. He was a medicine man by the name of Alexie Tauye, who went by the name of Bear Lake Alexie.

From what I heard, my curiosity about him was aroused. I went to Johnny's house that day and got introduced. I asked why he had come to Rae Lakes, and he replied, "I'm here to rest my dogs and myself and then I'll carry on to Franklin."

"Why are you going to Fort Franklin?" I asked. He laughed shyly and replied.

Ice conditions at the time of Bear Lake Alexie's arrival in Rae Lakes

"To find me a wife." He was between fifty-five and sixty at the time, and he never did find that wife he was looking for. After that first visit, I felt drawn in a powerful way to the mystique that was very much a part of the man.

He was a true nomad, travelled alone with no apparent restrictions, no deadlines, no one to worry about, and no one to worry about him. He was heading for Fort Franklin with no apparent concern about the fast-melting ice.

Given the ice conditions he had just left behind him, I was thinking that maybe old Alexie was being overly optimistic. I was planning to go duck hunting by canoe shortly, and here he was targeting Fort Franklin by ice. One morning a short time later, I noticed Alexie's dogs were gone, so I went to Johnny's place.

"Where's Alexie?" I asked. "I notice his dogs gone."

"We heard him moving his dogs last night, and when we got up his blanket was gone as well," Johnny replied. I went back to work and told the work crew. They said it was more likely that he set up a tent somewhere close by. Talk spread through the community, and word came back that no one had given him a boat ride out to the ice, which was now fifty feet from shore. No one had seen him. So where was Alexie?

Part of the search team taking a break

A decision was made to paddle around the island, a day's journey, to see if we could spot him anywhere along the shoreline. We took three freighter canoes, traveled all night and encountered no ice issues, nor did we find any signs left behind by Alexie or his dog team. There was no place where he could have forded to solid ice out on the lake. There was the curious fact that we became more puzzled than concerned.

The search party

We returned home perplexed. The elders showed no sign of worry. In their minds, it was Alexie's way to make his journey, however and whenever he wanted to. We returned to our normal activities, but I continued to wonder. The path this medicine man traveled was to cross with mine time and time again over the years.

Heading home after futile search for Alexie

I asked for information around the community about the man and what he did, but all I found out was that he was a medicine man and a wanderer. This was rare in the Dene culture. Few people wandered alone for months on end, other than when working a trap line. People tended to travel in groups when undertaking long journeys or to go hunting in places like the Barrenlands. One of the few stories that did emerge about Alexie was a legend of sorts, regarding two people who claimed to have run into him in a bar in Yellowknife.

He had just returned from the bush and had traded his furs from a winter of trapping. Alexie had a relative in Yellowknife, Muriel Betsina, at whose place he stayed. He was drinking in the bar there with other trappers when a large Chipewyan walked in and approached their table and demanded that Alexie buy him a drink. Alexie ignored him. The man repeated his demand. Alexie said nothing. The Chipewyan leaned forward threateningly and everyone backed away, expecting trouble. Alexie put down his drink, collected the change the waitress had left on the table and closed his fist over the change. He looked the man in the eye and, with his arm outstretched, opened his hand again. The change he held was now melted into a solid glob of metal. The Chipewyan backed away and exited the bar.

I heard this story of Alexie while siting with a group of people, some of whom nodded or made comments like, "Yes. I've heard that story before, or yep, that would be Alexie." It was just a part of the legend that this man had become.

As time passed and I thought about Alexie, I considered it curious that his disappearance was met with such an apparent lack of concern. People were no longer talking about searching for him, and no one was expecting him to turn up. I was left thinking that if anything happened to him, no one would know and years might pass before any one realized he was missing.

This man is traveling on his own schedule with no commitments and with no expectations of anyone, I thought to myself. He's not concerned about what people think or don't think about him, and he lives his life as he wants to live it. At that time, there was no way to contact anyone to help track him down. I slowly came to understand that the seeming lack of concern about Alexie's disappearance was a sign of respect for the man's space and his choice of a way of life. He had come unexpected, and now he had left unexpectedly. That was Bear Lake Alexie.

Almost a year after I was finished building the log community hall and was again in search of work, I was contacted by a government project officer and asked if I would be interested in going to Fort Franklin to build a log fire hall. I gladly accepted, and it occurred to me that, at the same time, I might find the answer to the question that haunted me: What happened to Bear Lake Alexie?

I told two friends in Yellowknife that I was heading to Fort Franklin, Alexie's destination. Both of their wives were from there, and they gave me the names of two people to check in with, Charlie Neyelle and Elisa Blondin, their mother. I made the connection with Charlie, and he took me to the site where I was to build the log fire hall. As we talked, Charlie told me that his dad was given a contract to use a portable sawmill to square the logs we were to use for the building.

"Do you by any chance know a man who goes by the name of Bear Lake Alexie?" I asked him.

"How do you know Alexie?" he asked. I told him part of the story. Charlie blurted out, "Say no more. This is an amazing coincidence. I'm the one who found Alexie after he left Rae Lakes. Do you see that house right there?" he said, pointing. "That's where Alexie stays. Meet me there tonight at eight o'clock. You'll meet Alexie and get a chance to tell your story, and you'll get to hear Alexie's story as well." It was common practice to get together at people's houses to hear a good story about trapping or hunting, or survival stories like Alexie's. This time I had the privilege of being part of the story that was to be told.

Needless to say, I went to Alexie's place that night full of curiosity. The place was packed with people, young and old. Here I was, on my first day there and about to experience a significant community event, the telling of Alexie's story.

I scanned the crowded room and, off in a corner, sat Alexie, enveloped in a cloud of smoke as he puffed away on a cigarette. We smiled and acknowledged each other. I found a place on the floor but very quickly was ushered to a chair at a small table. After tea was served, Charlie introduced me to everyone and explained that I was there to head up the job to build the fire hall and was looking for people to work on it. He then told them that I also had an interesting story to tell.

I explained that my story was very short. I went on to tell them of Alexie's dramatic arrival in Rae Lakes in very bad ice conditions, and followed that by describing the equally bad ice conditions that existed at the time he went missing from Rae Lakes. I then told them about the search that was conducted to locate him.

"How did you manage to get off the island of Rae Lakes and make your way to Fort Franklin in such bad ice conditions?" My question was translated for all to hear. The old traveller took his time to respond, and with a little coaxing and a few more puffs on his cigarette, he began. He told it in his own language, Slavey, and Charlie Neyelle translated for me. In my words, and to the best of my recall, here is what Alexie said.

While he was in Rae Lakes he watched the weather carefully, until one night when he saw a change in the wind direction that was favourable to him. He brought his sled and dogs along the shoreline on the north end of the island. Late that night, the change in the wind direction caused the ice floe to come ashore. He moved his dogs onto it. A short time later, the wind direction changed once again and moved the main ice floe away from shore and back out into Rae Lake. This answered the question about his sudden disappearance; he simply knew how to read the weather and the movement of the ice floe.

Once on the main ice, he traveled the rest of that night to the far end of the lake. In a bay there, he axed a chunk off the ice floe large enough to raft himself and his dogs to the shore. But spring was following right on his heels as he travelled, using the ice floes at night to cross various lakes along the way. He slept by day and shot jackfish along the shallows, and muskrat and beaver to feed his dogs and himself. Eventually, he made it over Grizzly Bear Mountain on Great Bear Lake, where he managed to shoot a moose when he was close to running out of food.

The weather began to change, and a huge sheet of ice that had broken loose from the main ice floe on the north end of the lake blew ashore close where Alexie was camped. He upped camp, hauled his dogs, gear and a pile of spruce boughs, firewood and his moose meat onto the ice floe. He set up his tent and waited patiently for the wind to change.

After a while, the sheet of ice broke free of the shore and floated back out into the middle of Great Bear Lake, and for a while all went well. He slept out of the winds in his tent. He woke up to the sound of his dogs howling and stepped out, only to see that they had been separated from him by a gap in the ice. His ice raft had split into several pieces. He tore down his tent and threw everything onto the larger sheet where the dogs were staked. He used his sled to span the gap and walked across it to join his dogs.

The ice floe continued to fragment. He spent sleepless hours making many moves on the slowly melting sections of ice. Finally, he came within sight of Fort Franklin and figured that his ice raft was unlikely to last another day. He gathered his tent poles, firewood and spruce boughs, and made a fire after dark in the hope that someone in Fort Franklin would notice it.

Back in Fort Franklin, it was a miserable evening and nobody was out and about, with the exception of one man, Charlie Neyelle. He was on his way home from his janitorial job at the school. He looked out onto the lake, wondering if he would be able to get his boat into the water any time soon to go hunting. It didn't look promising; there was still too much ice jammed in the bay. Then he noticed a strange glow in the middle of the lake, miles away, and wondered about it. He continued on home, woke his wife and had her come out to confirm what he had seen. They concluded that it was probably firelight on the ice.

Charlie immediately launched his boat into the mush ice. He poled and pushed his way through ice floe after ice floe to get to stretches of open water. He eventually spotted a man and his dog team by a fire on an ice floe and made his way to them. They loaded Alexie's gear, sled and the dogs into the boat and struggled back to shore in driving sleet.

During the telling of this story, there was not a sound in the room. When Charlie finished, many comments were exchanged and there was much laughter. The rounding-out of Bear Lake Alexie's story by Charlie reinforced my respect for Alexie, a self-assured man with such a depth of traditional knowledge. He was truly an independent spirit. When in his element, he pushed himself beyond normal limitations and dared to do what few others would ever consider attempting, a humble man with an indomitable spirit.

Many people in both in Rae Lakes and Fort Franklin believe that it was at Alexie's command that the wind blew the ice to his assistance. His arrivals and departures were all according to his personal clock and cloaked in mystery. He was undoubtedly the stuff of legends, lived life on the edge and all in his own way. I saw him as a role model, one whose self-sufficiency I would strive to achieve.

FORT FRANKLIN: DELINE

The Rae Lakes community hall completion led to my getting hired to build log fire hall in Fort Franklin. This was another unique challenge for me. I boarded a Twin Otter loaded with the building materials, my tools and gear, along with my ever present companion, Akaitcho, who I acquired as a puppy at Akaitcho Hall in Yellowknife.

My ever present companion

Fort Franklin, at the time, was a small town on the shores of Great Bear Lake. There were a few old log buildings mostly on or near the shoreline. It was a treeless town with gravel roads. The most prominent landmark was a beautiful, octagonal-shaped church that had been constructed by a well-known priest, storyteller and artist, Father Bern Will Brown.

I was given a room at a hostel built for transient government employees and anyone else coming in to serve the community. As soon as I was unpacked I took a walk with Akaitcho in search of Charlie Neyelle, this man who had been described to me as one of the nicest persons you could ever meet. I found him and was invited to his house, where I met his wife. He was about ten years older than me, and we hit it off right away. I told him how Bertha and Alice (the two people in Yellowknife who put me in touch with him) were doing, and he immediately suggested we pay a visit to their parents.

We arrived at a sparsely furnished, modern home. After meeting Elisa, a joyful woman, I heard a shuffling noise behind me in the bedroom. Her husband, Edward Blondin, was maneuvering his way towards me, pulling himself along the floor with his one usable arm. The absence of furniture facilitated his maneuvering about. He had suffered a massive stroke from which he lost all his speech and much of his mobility, with the exception of that one arm.

We were introduced and shook hands. After chatting for a while, I learned that Elisa had been a camp cook at a mine. So we struck a bargain, and there and then and I hired her to cook for me for the duration of my stay. She had one specialty I could not get enough of, her cinnamon and raisin bannock. They had two sons; one worked the barges on the Mackenzie, and the eighteen-year-old son lived at home. The daughters and their husbands, whom I knew, lived in Yellowknife.

Elisa & Edward Blondin

I was told many stories about old Edward Blondin. It was very unfortunate that Edward had lost his speech, for I would have enjoyed hearing more from him about his unusual life experience. He was in his eighties at that time, and his wife in her fifties. I visited him almost daily and kept him informed on what I had done that day. It was a bright spot in his day to know that someone understood that he would be interested in hearing about what was going on outside his home.

One of the first tasks related to my contract was to establish if there were enough logs available to do the job. I had to make sure that they were harvested and delivered before freeze-up. We were nowhere close to having enough logs, so I talked to Charlie Neyelle, who introduced me to Isadore Yukon, a Dene and retired riverboat navigator on the Mackenzie and Bear rivers, who towed our log booms. He told me they had had very bad weather and unfortunately lost some of the booms when they broke, and the loose logs were floating toward the Bear River.

Isadore Yukon on the Nanook

I made arrangements to join him the next day to go in search of our lost logs. It was a cold, calm day as we headed out in the Nanook, an old RCMP Arctic coast patrol boat. We spent the next two days collecting most of the missing logs. When we arrived back, Charlie's dad showed up with a wagon, loaded the logs, and took them to where he had his sawmill.

The next morning I went to where the logs were to be cut and saw Charlie's dad jacking up the tractor by himself. He blocked it up at a distance of about fifty feet from the mill, then mounted an eight-inch-wide belt to the mill and tractor. He lined everything up by eye, started the mill running, adjusted the belt, and in no time had the cage for the logs rolling and the sawblade whirring. The capacity of many people in the community to take on complex jobs like this no longer amazed me, but rather I became attentive to their skills and learned much from them. Charlie's dad was doing his job, and now I must do mine.

They were as good as their word. I had that entire crew work with me right up to the end. When the job was over, Jim Burke took me aside one day, inspired enough by what he saw that he asked, "How would you like to be a game officer?"

"What makes you ask that?" I queried.

"I've never come across anyone who worked so well with the locals as you do. We need people like you in the Game Department," he said. It was a passing comment that contributed to building my confidence at the time. With hindsight, I realize that if I had taken him up on the offer, I would have a decent pension right now. But then again, look at what I would have missed.

Fort Franklin log fire hall

CHARLIE NEYELLE

While in Fort Franklin, I asked Charlie Neyelle if he would introduce me to Joseph Naedzo, a prophet to the Dogrib and Bear Lake Dene, about whom I had heard so much from people in Rae Lakes, where his picture hung in every home. Charlie had great respect for him, and he agreed to take me. Naedzo, in his mid-eighties, was unable to speak English, and he was now blind. I don't recall anything of our exchange, but during my visit I noticed he had a hand drum nearby. I asked if I could look at it. The caribou hide drum was two feet in diameter. What intrigued me about it was that I couldn't detect a joint in the wood hoop.

I asked Charlie about it as we headed home. He smiled, surprised that I had noticed such a small detail, and told me that his father had made the drum for the blind prophet, Naedzo. He had watched his dad feather the ends of the piece of wood to match the grain so perfectly that no joint was visible.

Charlie and I also went hunting together. On one occasion we traveled by boat along the shoreline of Great Bear Lake and went ashore and then walked inland along an ancient trail, through bush and muskeg, hoping to find game. At one point, he stopped and inspected an area beside the trail and, like a stereotypical woodsman, observed, "Woodland caribou—be real quiet; they're not like Barrenland caribou. You get just one chance with them."

We continued in silence until we arrived at a small lake. On the other side, we could see five caribou already fleeing to the west of us. A missed chance. Charlie threw some dirt into the air to check wind direction. "Follow me," he said. "They'll go downwind of us; they move fast." He turned and led the way back in the opposite direction. I had thought of myself as being fit, but I had a hard time keeping up with him. Just as Charlie had predicted, the caribou had come full circle and were almost within shooting range. I approached

Charlie from behind as he was setting up to shoot. Unfortunately, I was not treading as lightly as I should have and ended up spooking the caribou before he could get a shot off. Charlie took it all in stride, and we returned to the boat knowing we came close, but no caribou.

When we got back to town, the barge I was waiting for had not arrived. Charlie told me he was going to make a trip down the Bear River to Fort Norman to visit relatives and asked if I wanted to go. Seeing as I couldn't get started on the job, I jumped at the opportunity to travel with him again. Just as we came close to the Bear River docking station, I was surprised to see a barge loaded with lumber, with a four-foot-high sign spray-painted on it that read, KIERAN MOORE, FORT FRANKLIN. I went to the office and was told they would deliver the lumber in about two days. So it was still okay for me to carry on to Fort Norman with Charlie.

Charlie Neyelle from Fort Franklin

Once we arrived in Fort Norman, we visited Charlie's relatives and sat down with them to relax over a meal of tea, bannock and moose stew. As already noted, Charlie was not a man who sat still for long, so, in short order, we finished our meal and headed back upriver at a much slower pace as we fought against the current.

This was not the comfortable, Sunday picnic boat ride that I had imagined. The craft dipped and kicked as Charlie navigated the current. It was draining for me just to hang on. For every creek and river we passed, Charlie had a story to tell, because of his many years trapping and hunting in the area with his father. These were the kinds of landscape stories that help the Dene navigate the land and its rivers without maps as confidently as Charlie was doing.

We made it home in the dark, by which time the barge had arrived.

DON'T BURN THE SNOW

I learned many lessons as I lived, worked and hunted with the Dene. Even the act of making tea over a campfire had a lesson in it. When we stopped to make camp in winter, one of the first things we did was to make tea. I noticed that, when other people made the tea, it was ready sooner than mine and always tasted better than anything I brewed.

I never gave much thought to this until one bitterly cold day, when I was traveling a trail with my friend Charlie Niellie. We stopped at one point along the way and set up camp, then built a blazing fire to warm up and to make tea. We began filling our individual six-by-six-inch, open-topped Hudson Bay teapots with snow scooped from a nearby snowdrift, to be melted down to make water for our tea. I wasn't aware that Charlie was observing me packing the snow into my teapot until he spoke.

"Don't burn the snow, Kieran," he cautioned me.

"Burn the snow?" I said quizzically and laughed.

"Yes, you can," he replied. "You need to take the snow from the bottom of the drift, not the top."

He suggested that we both continue to scoop snow as we had been doing. While doing that, he carefully described the differences between the many layers and how the snow crystalizes differently in each of them. The layer at the bottom that he was using looked like a tightly compressed, ice-like layer of miniature marbles, while the snow I was adding was light, flaky and felt dry to the touch in the extreme cold we were experiencing, of close to minus-forty degrees. Once the open-topped teapots were filled and I was getting ready to hang mine above the blazing fire, Charlie passed his to me and asked me to observe the difference in the weight of the two tea containers. I could tell that my pot weighed much less than his.

I hung the pots above the blazing fire. While observing the pots, Charlie showed me a technique he used to speed the process up of melting. He picked up a small stick and used it to give his pot a few light taps on the sides every once in a while. This, he said, caused the snow to settle and melt quicker. In a short time, Charlie had a generous quantity of water in his pot. He had me tap mine in the same manner, without success. The snow in it didn't settle, and more than that, it became stained by the smoke. He took my pot off the fire and pushed the snow aside, revealing that there was very little water below the large pocket of air that had formed between the snow and the bottom of the pot, and what was there was evaporating as quickly as it pooled. He also pointed out that I was pushing scorched smoke-stained snow to the bottom, where it melted, a slow process at best and one with bad results for my tea.

"You'll be packing that smoke-stained snow in there for a long time to make enough water for your cup of tea and, when you finally get your tea, it will have a burnt taste," he said. When the water in my pot finally boiled, we tasted the water from both pots. His tasted clean and fresh, and mine had a distinct burnt taste.

"So now you know," he said as he smiled. "Don't burn the snow!"

My Irish mother would have been suitably impressed, and she knew how to make good tea; now maybe I would be able to do the same.

FORT FRANKLIN TO RAE LAKES

The fire hall job dragged on. Early one bitterly cold morning, with ice crystals hanging in the air and the willows along the shore glistening with hoarfrost, I sat on top of the wall of the almost-finished fire hall and took a break. As I sat there, I remembered a promise I had made to myself when I had left Winnipeg. It was that, either on New Year's Day or my birthday, I would assess my life's direction. If I was contented, I'd stay put; if unhappy, I'd make a change. Christmas was coming, and at this moment I felt that something was missing in my life. I thought about Bear Lake Alexie and made my decision.

I resolved that I would make the same journey that Alexie had undertaken, but in the reverse. I would journey back to Rae-Lakes from Fort Franklin by dog team, not during breakup as Alexie had, but in winter; the same journey, but with a different set of challenges. I mentioned my intention to my boss in Yellowknife and, surprisingly, he replied with an offer of another job.

"It just so happens that we need you to build a large Co-op store in Rae Lakes. The sooner you get here, the sooner you can get started on the job," he said. I'd had my share of these unsolicited job offers before now, and this one was particularly timely.

"Okay, as soon as I'm finished here, I'll arrange to fly my tools out and follow them to Rae Lakes by dog team. I'll get there when I get there," I told him. He had no problem with that.

I proceeded to make plans and bought a team of dogs from an elder in town named Moise Bayha. I took two overnight trial runs up the Willow River. It was bitterly cold and, although these dogs had not been used in years, they were happy to be in harness, by God, and so was I. The leader was very responsive, even though his command language would have been Slavey and mine was English with a sprinkle of Slavey.

I had loaned my five-star sleeping bag to a man in the game warden's office who damaged it, and I ended up with a three-star to replace it. The topographical maps I ordered didn't arrive. It was two days till I was scheduled to leave. Things were stacking up against the trip going ahead. Regardless, I was determined to leave, come hell or high water, on my birthday, February 19, and set my mind to make that happen.

I went to see my friend Charlie Neyelli with the thought that he might have a topographical map of the area, but no such luck. Charlie, in his usual laid-back manner, took out a package of cigarettes, emptied it, tore it along one of the seams, unfolded it and asked his daughter for a pencil. He then drew a map on the back of the package. As he penciled in directions, he identified certain landmarks for me to look out for along the route.

Ready for my trek to Rae Lakes

He pointed at one of the lakes and said, "When you get to this lake, you will see that there had been a forest fire to the left of a big hill that marks an opening to a valley. You head towards the valley, and just before you get there, in a small bay, there should be a large pile of snow about a hundred yards from shore. They just finished a hunt there and left caribou meat in a cache. That's where the entry to the portage you need to take is located." No coordinates were given or considered necessary, just geographic reference points in the Dene tradition of traveling by landmarks or by descriptors such as: "This portage is named sih nek'e, or wind between the hills. Very strong winds blow through there. We seldom stop on this portage."

Charlie and the author with cigarette package Map (45 years later)

Charlie continued to describe other landmarks along the way and concluded by wishing me luck. I thanked him and his wife and went home feeling better informed and more confident, with his rapidly sketched trail map in hand. Alexie would not have had to use a map of any kind. The geography of the region was all in his head.

I went to old man Blondin's place to say goodbye to him, Elisa and their son. I sat with him for quite a while and told him what I was intending to do. Elisa made tea and cinnamon bannock and translated as I talked. I had the sense that Edward understood that this journey was profoundly important to me. Although paralyzed and unable to communicate, he projected as being intensely interested in everything I had to say. We sat on the floor, eyes fixed, as I talked, and he appeared to be seeing the trail he knew well. I packed Elisa's bannock into the caribou hide packsack I had received from an elderly Rae Lakes woman, and he took time to admire the stitching. We hugged, shed a few tears of respect and said our goodbyes.

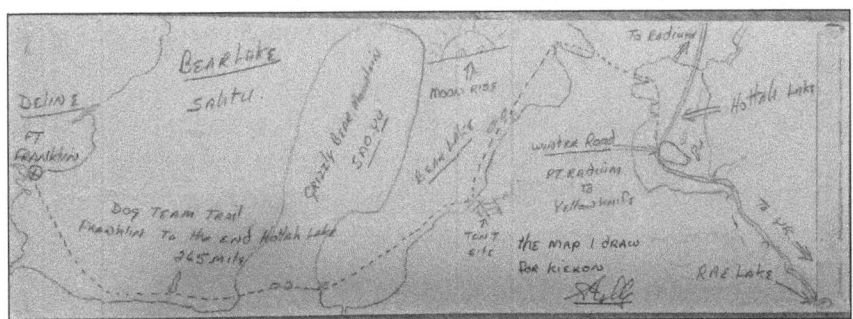

Cigarette Package Map

The following morning was very cold. I hooked up the dogs. The water truck was out delivering, every chimney in town had smoke rising from it, and there wasn't a soul to be seen or to say goodbye to. I headed onto the lake into a light morning breeze, which within an hour had turned into blinding windstorm. The prominent landmark of Grizzly Bear Mountain, which I had counted on using to set my direction, was obscured behind a wall of blowing snow. I had to rely solely on my compass. It was a tough way to start out. To my knowledge, there was no one else out on the land that week but me. Even Christmas Tree (a man Charlie and I had visited by snowmobile earlier that month) would be tucked in his tent, and the trappers from Johnny Hoe would have already returned to Fort Franklin.

My first target, but not a stopping point, was Christmas Tree's camp and the landmark trees he staked stretching out into the lake. The trail I was following eventually disappeared under the snow, and the dogs continued to plod headlong into the blizzard, straining at the harness. I eventually saw the line of trees at the camp and followed them to the shoreline. From there, I continued heading straight into the wind, the cold biting at my face. I ran alongside the dogs to help them and to get my blood flowing, and from time to time I sat on the wood stove in the sled with my back to the wind, relatively well-protected with my wolverine-lined hood up and a scarf across my face. Then, on one occasion, as I went to take my seat on top of the stove, my heart sank. The stove door was missing. I had disconnected it as I hopped on and off, somewhere back on the trail.

It was still daylight, but the dogs were slowing down, so I headed for shore. I had a tough time making it through the deep drifts and hacked at the protruding willows that snagged in the snowshoes. It turned out to be a bad decision, because I ended up having to carry the dogs to the camp one by one to avoid the hazard of the sharp pointed willow stumps I had just hacked.

I hauled the sled to the campsite, cut down tent poles, set up the eight-by-twelve prospector tent, assembled the stove, made a spruce bough floor for the tent and the same for the dogs, and cut enough firewood to last the night, the normal ritual of setting up camp.

First campsite on dogsled run to Rae Lakes

Once the tent was set up, I emptied out everything I had in the sled to see if I could find something to replace the missing stove door. A frying pan lid I had was perfect for the job. I poked holes in it and made hinges with snare wire, and a handle, and got the stove going. However, the tent filled with smoke caused by downdraft, and I ended up refashioning a lard can I found close by to form an elbow extension to the stovepipe. I settled in as it began to snow, feeling satisfied with my progress on this, my first day on the trail. I slept well that night. The wind had diminished overnight, and it had stopped snowing by the time I got up.

I fed the dogs, broke camp, dragged the sled onto the lake and loaded it up. I continued to make good time that day and got to the base of Grizzly Bear Mountain as darkness fell. I was now close to the portage marked on Charlie's map. I spotted a large tree with plenty of dead branches and so headed to shore and set up camp once again. I had plenty of firewood but not enough trees of a size that could serve for tent poles, so I decided to go without the tent. I gathered boughs for beds for myself and the dogs and laid them out close to a huge fire. The heat from the fire created a cavern-like spot. I lined the cavity with the pine boughs, creating a comfortable spot to spend the night.

I looked to the east and saw a bright light through the trees. I thought that Charlie must have been wrong; the trappers from Johnny Hoe must be out there and heading this way. I was excited at the thought of having some company and made a fresh pot of tea. A short time passed, and the light coming through the trees grew brighter than any Ski-Doo lights. I thought maybe it was Jim Burke in his Bombardier, but I couldn't hear any sound. Strange, I thought. The bright light had now turned from stark white to brilliant orange and rose up from the forest floor at an alarming rate. It left me without any explanation, other than the silly notion of a UFO. I looked at the dogs. They lay there, unperturbed.

"Calm down! The dogs know better than you," I told myself. Eventually it showed itself for what it was. Not hunters, a Bombardier, a Ski-Doo or a UFO. I was staring at a full moon rising. The appearance of forward motion as it rose had confused my senses. The mind plays tricks when you're a rookie on the trail at the end of a hard day's travel. I drank the tea I had prepared for my visitor and toasted the beauty of that extraordinary full moon. I tightened the circle of the dogs closer to the fire and crawled into my bag in the cozy lean-to as it began to snow once more.

Come morning, I fed the fire, dusted off the snow and dried everything I was to wear, had a quick breakfast, packed up camp and took off in search of the portage. But as soon as I hit the lake, the dogs took me by surprise and immediately headed in the wrong direction, back towards Fort Franklin. I yelled at Akaitcho, who was second to the lead dog. He stopped, but the dogs taking up the rear stumbled over him, turning the harness into a tangled mess. I flipped the sled to anchor them and managed to get reorganized and moving under better control this time. I was beginning to realize that I was definitely an apprentice without a master and very much alone in this white wilderness.

After an hour of worrying about finding the portage, I identified it, and it was still morning when I arrived at the other side. There was no sled riding from there; it was a hard trek just breaking trail in front of the dogs through the fresh snow. I came to the realization that I had packed too many items in the sled. I was carrying everything I needed to live comfortably for the rest of the winter in my tent in Rae Lakes. This made for a long, slow haul on the McVicar arm of Great Bear Lake. Alexie would have asked the question.

"What's this guy doing loaded down with all this stuff?"

When I arrived at the portage heading east to Hottah Lake, I remembered that Charlie had told me about this place called Tote-si-tweigh, and to be wary of the winds in this area. I arrived early in the afternoon, and as I approached I saw the two outcrops of rock on each side, almost cliff-like, about 200 yards apart. All of the trees between the cliffs were dead. Straight ahead, the land rose gradually but was of an unusual color. It looked like a lava flow of yellow ice, about eighty feet across and stretching back for about 300 feet, which looked easy enough to cross. I trudged into the valley with the dogs at my heels and soon noticed that my snowshoes were getting clogged with a yellow slush the consistency of pastry flour. I tried to move as fast as I could, hoping to make it through, but in ten or fifteen steps I could no longer lift my feet. I reached for one of the dead trees and leaned on it, exhausted. I pushed the snow aside and saw that my snowshoes were in about six inches of overflow.

I backtracked, kicking my snowshoes against the trees to break the ice off. There appeared to be higher ground to the east of this buried swamp. I trudged on slowly, trying to skirt the area, but it got worse the nearer I got to the cliffs. As I floundered around, the dogs became locked in this ice-cold sludge and howled in their misery. I worked my way back to the sled, which was frozen in place, and used my axe to break it free, then tied a long length of rope to the front of the sled and pulled with all my might as I yelled to Akaitcho. He leaped into the air and the rest followed suit. The sled broke free. Eventually, after several repeats of this exercise, I made it through to solid ice.

I still had to get the dogs and sled up and over the rise ahead. I removed my snowshoes, picked up the rope and took a run for the top, all the while urging the dogs to pull. Once the last dog had made it up the icy slope, I went behind the team and yanked the sled over the edge onto level ground. I lay down, along with the dogs, utterly exhausted.

I stayed put at this location, set up the tent and got the stove going to get rest and to address a problem I was having with frozen feet. Having fed the dogs, I thawed out the lacing on my moccasins, got them off and removed my socks. The big toenails on both feet were torn loose and blood-clotted, but were still lightly attached. I must not have felt the damage occurring because of numbness as I kicked against trees to break the ice off the snowshoes. But the same numbness made it possible for me to remove the nails and do a cleanup without too much discomfort. That done, I put on warm socks and moccasins and stumbled out to the dogs.

They were unusually restless. I thought this might have something to do with the unusual number of wolf tracks I had seen in the area that day. Later that night, I was drawn out of the tent by the sound of the dogs as they answered howling wolves. It was an incredible night, a clear sky, a beautiful display of northern lights, and all accompanied by the eerie sound of distant howling. One at a time, I brought the dogs in and spent time tending to their paws. I felt badly for the ordeal I had put them through, but I was much more the worse for wear.

The next morning, I packed the sled, headed down the portage in sunshine and arrived at the large lake with many bays. I consulted the cigarette package map and went in search of the bay where the cache of caribou meat was supposedly left by the hunting party Charlie had mentioned. I came across a wolf trail leading into one of the bays and followed it. We arrived at a circle of packed snow about fifty feet in diameter. This was obviously where the cache had been located, but it was no more. The wolves had found it and left nothing behind. This meant no food supplies for either the dogs or myself.

On the upside, I could make out the hill referred to on my map, and I felt that sense of relief that comes with knowing I'm where I'm supposed to be. This was still an alien environment for me, and I drew comfort from these landmarks that indicated I was still on course. I headed along the wolf trail once again and found the portage, a well-defined trail all the way to my next point of reference, Hottah Lake.

As I approached the lake, I could make out the two islands in the distance that I had been advised to use as reference points. According to my map, I would find the winter road to the Echo Bay mine on the opposite shore that would take me to Rae Lakes. My supplies were dangerously low, and I worried because I was only halfway through my planned journey. I built a fire, made tea, and dried things out before heading out between the two islands.

I finished my tea, loaded firewood and birch bark, and took off. Once I arrived at the two islands, I noticed the dogs' ears were up and their noses sniffing the air. I got my gun ready, for what, I didn't know. When we moved clear of the gap, I rode on the back of the sled for a while, looking back down our trail, and spotted what was bothering the dogs all along. There were three wolves standing on the cliff edge on one of the islands. I was learning to read the dogs, even if the terrain was giving me more than my share of difficulties. I reached the snow banks thrown up on the plowed winter road, crested the top of them and came down onto the level, ice-covered surface. The sense of having reached something more familiar to me than the winter wilderness gave me comfort.

The sled skimmed over the ice like it had no weight on board. I was elated to see the dogs in such good form, and what a relief it was to travel without snowshoes. Hours later, after covering the length of the lake and around a bend at the end of a portage, I came to a campsite of three tents with chimneys billowing smoke. Two young girls were splitting wood outside one of them. When they heard the harness bells, they looked up, saw me, and ran for the largest tent, yelling, "Na Gon! Na Gon!" They believed that they had seen a Bushman with a dog team. Now, that would have been a first!

Then silence. As I pulled up to one of the tents, an old woman came out, took one look in my direction and quickly withdrew. I had startled them. Then two women peeked out. I tried to reassure them in a mixture of Slavey and Dogrib. Suddenly, I recognized the oldest lady. She was Jimmy Lacorde's sister, close to about seventy years of age. She had traveled in my sled from Hislop Lake on the occasion of my first dog team trip a year ago and had given me a dry meat bag made of caribou hide as a gift for the help I had given, moving her family to Rae Lakes that day.

She obviously didn't recognize me, and I was puzzled as to why not. Then I remembered the small hide bag she had made, located it and handed to her. She studied it for a moment, looked up, beamed a smile of recognition and dragged me by the arm into the tent, all the while talking a mile a minute and explaining to the other woman who I was.

The tent interior was like a huge spruce bough raft, all cozy and welcoming. One of the women, whose last name was Football, spoke some English and explained why they didn't recognize me, and at the same time held up a mirror. I took one look at myself and immediately understood the problem; my eyebrows and ears were covered in ice. The hair on my face was caked with ice and my cheeks were badly frostbitten, black in places and blistered. It was no wonder the kids thought I was the Bushman. I was handed a washbasin with warm water and soap, and one of the women went outside to tend my dogs. As I washed, I noticed my hair was caked in a hardened pus that covered my frozen earlobes. With that and my damaged toes, I was a bit of a mess.

A meal of fresh bannock and jam, along with caribou and boiled oatmeal soup, was followed by the traditional pounded meat and bone grease. It was a regular feast, and such a traditional welcome and totally unexpected break in my journey. I was in my glory with a full stomach and could hardly wait to curl up in a cozy corner and catch some sleep. The tent was so warm that the two-year-old child was shirtless.

When I got up to bring in my gear, one of the women said that it would be better if I left right away, so that I could join the two dog teams that had left a bit earlier. The suggestion caught me off-guard. I tried to explain that my dogs would be too tired, not to mention myself. However, these people of the land, who have used dogs all their lives, assured me that if I left right away my dogs would pick up the scent of the two other dog teams heading for Rae Lakes and would travel well with no problem. They told me that the two men were from Fort Rae and would be traveling slowly because they were loaded down with fresh meat.

Somewhat reluctantly, I readied the dogs and headed away from what I had hoped would be an overdue good night's sleep. Just as the women had said, the dogs kept up a good pace with no need for direction. At dusk, as I rounded a bend in one of the portages, I spotted dog teams in the distance. The two hunters had seen me and stopped, likely wondering who I was and where I had come from. I pulled up, introduced myself, and gave them a short version of my journey. The older man studied me intently and gave an approving smile. When I connected with him again some years later, I found out that while this trek was a first for me, running into a white man with a dog team on that trail was a first for him.

They were surprisingly happy to have me join them. The women were correct; it was a fitting way to end up traveling to Rae Lakes, with two experienced Dene hunters for company. It was a fortunate meeting and one that had implications for me and my future when we would meet again under totally different circumstances.

Campsite set up on our way to Rae Lakes

On we traveled, eventually setting up tent in a clearing halfway down one of the portages. I'm sure it was to their surprise that I knew what needed to be done as part of the team setting up camp.

When we settled in by the stove and cooked some caribou meat, we began to exchange stories. They spoke little English, but we managed to communicate. The older man was in his sixties and the other, his son, around my age. He behaved in an unusual manner at times, talking to himself a lot, but always in great humor. He talked with the dogs till late that night and made sure they were comfortable before he turned in.

The young man and I teased each other from time to time. He enjoyed making fun of my blend of Slavey and Dogrib. His father was a quiet man, strong and limber, and had an air of dignity about him. As we set up camp, I noted that he got everything he needed to do done with a minimum of exertion.

After two days traveling together and just hours away from Rae Lakes, we camped. The next morning the old man was in no rush; he told his son to melt snow and warm the water. The young man filled a basin, got his father a bar of soap and a towel, and the old man washed up. When he had finished, he asked his son to get water for me and I followed suit, washing myself as he did. He opened a leather carrying case, took out nail clippers, comb, scissors, a mirror and a shaving brush, and proceeded to shave the faint trace of stubble he had on his face. He changed into a clean shirt and put on a beautiful pair of beaded moccasins. After all this preparation, he explained that it is the proper thing to do when you visit another village. He was from Fort Rae and was going to stop in Rae Lakes for a while to rest the dogs and do some gambling.

We set out for Rae Lakes, and as we traveled, hoarfrost coated the dog blankets and harness. Not a noise was to be heard in the stillness, save for the swishing of the sleds and the ringing of harness bells. We arrived at our destination well rested.

I went straight to Harry Simpson's home, where I was welcomed as if I were family. They insisted I stay there. Their young daughter seemed to be intrigued with this strange man in the shaggy red beard. He was no longer quite the same man as the one who left Fort Franklin a number of days ago, following in the footsteps of Great Bear Alexie.

A COMMUNITY HUNT AND A DOG CALLED JESUS

While I was working on log buildings in Rae Lakes, the community began to run out of meat, because most of the men were now salaried employees and less dependent on the hunt for food supplies. Yet they still had kept most of their dogs. In the recent past, the clans knew the whereabouts of the caribou herds, and this information was passed on between the clans. Such was not the case at this time, which complicated the task of locating the caribou if anyone decided to go on a hunt. Regardless, the community leaders decided that they would undertake a community caribou hunt.

The men working for me said they needed to take time off from work to go on the communal hunt. I was asked if I would like to accompany them. I immediately agreed. We were to leave on Friday and hopefully, after a successful hunt, return in time for work by Monday.

That Friday, the town came alive with the buzz of preparations for the hunt. It was an altered atmosphere, filled with excitement and anticipation. Guns were cleaned, hunting gear assembled, sleds loaded and harnesses prepared. Then the howling began. It was something so foreign to my unpracticed ear. The howling began with a single dog team, at the house of the first person to take the harnesses to their team. Very soon, every dog in town began to howl, leaping to the ends of their chains and restlessly pacing. The sound created a sense of urgency. Every household in the community had at least two dog teams and their offspring, all of which made for an impressive chorus. Unfortunately, it is unlikely that anyone will experience this in the future on this scale in any northern community.

All was ready. One by one, the sleds sped through town and headed out onto the lake, where they strung out in single file, forming a narrow trail heading in a northeasterly direction. There were thirteen teams in all. Some of the hunters were Harry Simpson, Philip and Louis Zoe, John Bekale, Sam Mantla, George Tailbone, Alphonse Apples, and Romie Wetrade's brother. Most of the teams consisted of seven dogs, for a total of almost ninety in all.

We formed a snake-like procession, winding our way across lakes, around islands, along creek beds and over portages, all in single file. I was about eighth in the line for quite a while, working hard with my ragtag dog team. It had snowed steadily for several days before we left, and as a result our trail took on the form of a trough cut in the fresh-fallen snow. As usual on such a hunt, we traveled with very few provisions; just the sled, gun, knives and sleeping bag. We traveled along the same lake route and portages as the canoes take to get to the Barrenlands. We were now well into a long day of mushing, and as we hit deeper snow, nobody was riding the sleds, out of consideration for the dogs.

John Bekale on the community hunt

Later that day, after I had fallen a bit behind, I saw that Harry Simpson and Philip Zoe were taking turns breaking trail on snowshoes ahead of the dogs. The two of them did that into the late evening, demonstrating remarkable stamina. I thought I was fit, but these men were in a league of their own. I was the last of the thirteen teams, and by the time I caught up they were already setting up camp. They had the tent set up and had a large bonfire going. I came to a stop, left my dog team in the snow trench, and made my way to the fire, needing to pass several teams lined up in single file. Partway along the lineup, I attempted to cross to the other side by stepping over a set of harness. I was immediately told, in no uncertain terms, never to step over another man's harnessed dogs. The point was made that these are working dogs and it is important not to risk injury in interacting with them.

I made it to the tent, which was already full of people sharing the warmth and having a cup of tea. The tent was too small to house everyone for the night, and some of us had to set up our beds on the sleds. So I crawled into my sleeping bag in the sled and quickly fell asleep.

I woke up to the sound of axes biting into frozen tree trunks, and the smell of wood smoke billowed from the tent stove. The thirteen of us worked as a team to get things done around the camp and then attended to our dogs and gear. We gathered around the fire to cook, boil tea, warm up and to undertake the ritual of a snow wash. The process involved a bar of soap being passed around, taking a handful of abrasive snow crystals and rubbing them vigorously between the hands, along with the soap, to make the lather. It was a wash that certainly reee-freshed.

An early morning snow wash

While we traveled, a loose dog was spotted, trailing along behind us. I mentioned this to Harry and asked him if he thought it would be okay if I harnessed it to my team. My dogs were slow at the best of times, and this dog looked young and fit. Harry agreed and, shortly before bedtime, one of the men caught the dog and brought it to me. I chained it up while one of the men set to work to make a lamp wick harness, made from the wick used for coal oil lamps. They had it sewn together very quickly. In the morning, I had the new dog harnessed up with the team and ready to go.

I could sense the excitement of the younger men as we had our morning tea. It was a unique experience not only for me but also for most of them, now that they were busy working instead of hunting and trapping for a living. The older hunters were more stoic about things as they sat around the fire smoking. When the time came to leave, no one person gave the order. We all moved more or less simultaneously to take our place in line. Just before we left, Harry cautioned me about the dog I had added to my team.

"The reason the dog wasn't picked up by any of the other hunters was because he bites harness. So watch him closely," he advised. I thanked him and told him I would hook him up as my wheel dog, the position closest to the sled, so that I could keep a close eye on him. I hooked him up just as the sleds ahead of me began to disappear around a sharp left turn in the trail leading down to the lake. That bend in the trail was about to save the day for me.

After hooking up the dogs, I went to the back of the sled and yelled the command to go. Snap! Snap! In a split-second following my command, the stray had severed both of the harness straps, and off sped the rest of my dog team at full speed, leaving me standing there with the sled and the culprit.

There was no way I could catch them by chasing down the trail. Instead, I flipped the sled and leapt off the trail at an angle, hoping to cut the team off just beyond the bend in the trail. I plowed through the snow frantically, intersected with the trail and lunged headlong onto it just as the dogs were set to speed by. I grabbed the last dog's harness and brought the team to a halt. I led them back down the trail to the sled, rehooked the team, knotted the harness together where it had been cut, and set off once more. Fortunately, there was no further trouble and I caught up with the others. We traveled all that day, with Philip and Harry continuing to break trail, but there was still no sign of fresh caribou tracks.

When we camped that night, I told the story of the severed harness and they all had a good laugh. One of the crew dug into his pack and brought out heat liniment, which he gave to me saying, "Put this on the harness ahead of the dog and he won't be tempted to bite it again." I did just that as further insurance and with good results, because there was no repeat of the incident. By the end of the following day, we were at the edge of the treeline. Still no sign of tracks. We had all of the dogs, thirteen trappers and a community of 150 waiting to be fed, and we seemed no closer to doing that than when we started.

Harry Simpson or Philip Zoe breaking trail

We reached a large, windswept lake and fanned out. When we regrouped in the middle of the lake, no one had any sightings to report. We were discouraged, and as we stood there trying to decide on our next move, we heard gunfire in the distance, about six shots in all. The dogs went wild with excitement. We puzzled as to who it could be. There were no sled tracks anywhere around.

One of the hunters said that it must be Romy Wetrade, who, he said, had decided to go out hunting on his own. It had taken us three days to get to where we were on the accepted trail to the Barrenlands, so how could Romy have made the same journey cross-country and somehow arrived here at the same time we did? It was a bewildering question for me. Three teams headed in the direction from which the shots had come. As they disappeared in the distance, Harry turned to me and pointed.

Regrouping to decide on our next move

"See the ravens in the direction those guys are headed? There're swooping around and making a fuss. That could mean there's something dead out there. Go check it out." I took off, and in a short while I pulled up at the site of the ravens' feast. It was a picturesque hunting scene. At the base of a rock overhang, the three teams were there and had already butchered a large bull caribou. A wound it had received in the rear leg had become gangrenous. It must have died recently, or the ravens would have made short work of it. As Jingo was packing up what was left, I sliced a piece off the gangrenous leg to see if the dogs would eat it; they would have nothing to do with it. Jingo told me to store the putrid meat in a separate plastic bag. He obviously had plans for it.

I continued on with them, and a short time later we met up with Romy. There he was, on the back of his fully loaded sled, coming downhill toward us looking all so casual, with his pipe sticking out of the side of his mouth. He pulled up beside us, shook hands, and said he had left three caribou out on a lake on the other side of the hill. His dogs were long-legged, powerful creatures, the canine equivalent of a Clydesdale horse and reputed to be quarter-bred wolf.

I marveled at how the slightly overweight, five-foot-two man tackled this challenging environment alone with such apparent ease, breaking his own trail miles away from the route we had followed. He didn't let aloneness scratch at his spirit. We made our way to the lake where Romy had left the caribou, butchered and loaded them, and headed back to join the other men.

Hunting party on the trail

When I arrived back at the campsite with the plastic bag containing the gangrenous meat, I was directed to make a separate fire and throw the contents of the bag directly into it until they were charred. I did this, chopped the charred chunks into pieces, and divided it among the teams for feeding the dogs. They ate all of it without hesitation. We cooked one of the caribou heads and shared what little meat was on it.

The other teams were already heading away while I was feeding my dogs; there would obviously be no sleep tonight. It got so bitterly cold that everyone curled up in blankets, and we continued to travel that way at a crawl, only stopping once in a while to rest the dogs.

A bitterly cold day on the trail

I grew concerned as I fell behind once again. I heard some yelling and looked to find that Jingo's dogs had tangled their harness. He didn't appear to need any help, so I passed by with my head buried in my blanket. A while later, the bells on the harness indicated that my dogs were faltering, so I hopped off and noticed I was at the junction of two trails. One of them would have been the trail on which we had headed north originally; the other, the trail the teams ahead of me were on. But I couldn't tell the difference. Fortunately, Jingo arrived behind me, got off his sled, took one glance at both trails and pointed to the trail to the right without hesitation. By the time we caught up, the other teams were already seated around a blazing campfire, having tea.

I mentioned to Jingo that my dogs were worn out and unlikely to be able to continue for much longer. He didn't seem concerned and assured me that the dogs would pick up the pace as soon as the moon rose high enough for them to see their own shadows. I was still at the point of not questioning statements like this aloud, because they were usually delivered with quiet conviction. A full, bright moon hung low on the horizon as I got into the sled and bundled up, and off we went at the same pitifully slow pace. An hour later, I heard a distinct difference in the sound of the harness bells. I looked out from under my blanket to see a full moon throwing distinct shadows and the dogs moving at a brisk pace.

It was an otherworldly sight to see twelve dog teams strung out ahead of me in bright moonlight and the of breath from men and dogs crystalizing in the air above them, leaving a trail in the air. The assuredness with which everyone took on the challenges presented left me aware that I still had a lot to learn.

We were now well into an almost nonstop, twenty-four-hour journey. Morning came, and we were still on the move. Quite a few of the hunters were on their feet and running behind their teams to warm up and give the dogs some help. But then, something strange happened.

My third dog dropped in his tracks, as if dead. A few of the other mushers came to see what was wrong. The dog appeared to have stopped breathing. We all assumed he was dead. Then I remembered an incident when I was a young lad, out walking in farm country with a friend and his dog. The dog chased a passing car, collapsed quite suddenly and, like my sled dog, appeared to be dead. My friend got down on his knees, gave the dog mouth-to-nose resuscitation, and revived it. His dog was prone to doing this. I applied the technique to my third dog; he got up, shook himself and was ready to go. Nobody there had seen anything like this happen before.

On we traveled, and the same thing happened twice again in quick succession. With me following the same procedure, the dog revived. Then he collapsed a fourth time, and Jingo and I took turns trying to resuscitate him, without success.

"What should I do with the dog?" I asked.

"Just don't bring it back to town," I was told. So I unharnessed him, lifted him up, put him into a four-foot drift of powdery snow and gently covered him up. A few hours later, with John Bekale's team of beautiful huskies taking the lead, we arrived in Rae Lakes, but without the traditional gunshots, since most of our sleds were empty of game.

The following day we went back to work, and after a few hours into the job, one of the men spotted what they thought was a wolf in the distance, out on the ice and approaching the settlement. Then someone made an excited observation.

"It's not a wolf; its tail's up. It's your dog, Kieran; he's come back to life."

We ran to the shore, and others joined us as the dog came off the lake, oblivious to the fuss we were making. I greeted him like a long-lost soul and tussled his frost-covered fur. For days after, people came up to me offering to buy the miracle dog, but I told them that he was not for sale and that he had a weak heart.

"Why would anyone want to buy him?" I asked on one occasion.

"Because of his spirit, his will to survive. He came back from the dead, didn't he?" came the answer.

In the centre, the celebrated dog that came back from the dead

I eventually gave him to John Bekale's father. I told people I was considering renaming the dog Jesus, because he had come back from the dead. Given the looks I got and what they implied, I backed off doing that. However, I will always remember him as a dog called Jesus.

MAKING CONNECTIONS

I left Rae Lakes after finishing all the log projects then moved back to Y.K. for a short time. I found no work prospects so I packed everything I owned into the trailer and truck box, and headed down the Mackenzie Highway. I got to Fort Providence (Zhahti Koe) and crossed the river on the Merv Hardy ferry, disembarked and, as I continued on my way, spotted a sign for Kakisa Lake village. I had seen it before and paid no attention to it, but this time I decided to check it out. It was a peaceful location, sitting in the middle of a stand of good-sized trees. I noticed smoke billowing from the chimney of one of the cabins, but I also noted a significant absence. There wasn't a dog team to be seen anywhere, and no sign of a snowmobile.

I approached the cabin and knocked. A young girl of about seventeen opened the door with a surprised look on her face and stepped to the side. A middle-aged man sat in a corner of the cabin smoking his pipe. I introduced myself in English and Dogrib and, by way of breaking the ice, I explained that I had recently come from Rae Lakes. The man put his pipe down and waved me in, paying particular attention to my moccasins. He instructed his daughter to make tea, and I mentioned that I had some dry meat and asked if he would care for some. He was delighted with the offer and said that he hadn't had pounded meat in a long time. I took out my bag of pounded meat and marrow and gave him some. I was invited to join them for a breakfast of stewed oatmeal and rabbit.

We sat there chatting for a while, he with his broken English and me with the mix of Dogrib and Slavey I had picked up in Fort Franklin and Rae Lakes. He told me about his small and fast-dying community and the fact that so many people had moved to the town of Hay River. He then said something that I was hearing more and more of late. He said that no one was interested in trapping anymore. Most of the houses in the village were now empty and there was nothing by way of construction happening in Kakisa Lake. However, he did suggest that I might find work near the old village across the river from the town of Hay River. He directed me to take a small dirt road that wound through the woods that would lead to the home of Chief Dan Sonfrere.

"He might have work for you," he said. "Tell him I sent you." I thanked him, took my leave and made my way to the chief's home.

I was greeted there by Dan Sonfrere's wife, who ushered me in to meet her husband. My first impression of Dan was that he was the same height and stocky build as my father and even had a facial resemblance to him. He spoke English well. Once again I shared my dry meat and brought him greetings from his friend in Kakisa Lake. We chatted for quite a while on a whole range of topics related to the Dene community. However, when I asked if there was any work in the area, he said he there was none but suggested that I keep in touch with him. I left his place a little discouraged, yet feeling that I had made a solid connection. Over time, Dan and I developed a strong friendship and mutual respect. As I grew to know him, I came to appreciate his acute intellect and strong sensibility when it came to the changes happening around him. He was politely astute when it came to taking action on matters of concern to his people.

Many months later, on an early fall morning, I went to pay him a visit. The air was cool and a fog had rolled in, making for poor visibility as I drove down the gravel road that wound along the shore of Hay River and past the new village. Although this was called the "new" village, the houses were already old-looking shacks made of well-weathered plywood. Peering through the fog, I saw some movement on the road ahead. It looked like a large vehicle, but there were no lights showing. I slowed down and found myself following something I never suspected existed north of the 60th parallel, a horse-drawn wagon. It was being driven by an elderly man. He halted the wagon, stepped off, lifted a forty-five-gallon drum off a platform in front of one of the houses, and heaved it onto the wagon. Each house along the road had a similar drum sitting on a similar small platform, built at the same height as the bed of the wagon. I was in no hurry, so I followed, watching him at his work.

It was such a peaceful image. This elderly man moved at such a leisurely pace, the breath from the horses became one with the fog that surrounded them. I'm prone to romanticizing things from time to time and fell into doing that with ease on this occasion.

What a great job, I thought. He's plodding along without hustle or bustle, no noisy vehicles speeding by, just the sound of the horses' hooves splashing through puddles or crunching on scattered patches of snow. Here's a man and his two working companions; each knows what to expect of the other. An otherwise humble job of collecting waste was transformed in front of me into a calming morning ritual. I inched carefully by, trying not to disturb the horses or the man, and went on my way.

The elderly man on the wagon was Jim Lamalise. He was what he appeared to be that foggy morning, a person of calm disposition. He was a prominent elder in the community, and I was to have some cloak-and-dagger dealings with him and Chief Daniel Sonfrere a couple of years later, in their negotiations with the federal government regarding the Hay River First Nation. It was an occasion that had huge implications for the future of Chief Dan's and Jim Lamalise's Hay River community.

STEEL SPACE INDUSTRIES

I eventually found a roofing job in Hay River, a town close to Chief Dan Sonfriere's Slavey community. I was wrapping up the job when I got wind of another job possibility. I was told that a guy in one of the local hotel bars was looking to hire carpenters. I went there with a fellow worker, and the scene that greeted us was right out of the Wild West. It was standing room only, and we watched as tray after tray of alcohol was unloaded onto tables already half-filled with beer glasses. My fellow worker pointed out a crew of guys sitting at one of the tables along with their boss, the man who was looking to hire someone.

I approached him and noted that he was already good and drunk. I told him I was looking for work and had heard he might have need for someone. He had one of his employees give up his chair so that we could talk and, after a brief exchange, promised me a job that included accommodation in a wing of the hotel reserved exclusively for his workers. I stayed for a short time and ended up being pressured by his crew to buy a round of drinks. Shortly after, I left the bar a little poorer but satisfied that I had secured a job and a place to live.

Early the next morning, I packed my tools, hooked up to my trailer and headed for the old town on Vale Island, to the Pioneer Hotel, where the accommodation for the work crew was located. I approached the front door, where the boss was briefing three or four of his employees on their duties for the day. I waited until he was finished. As he was putting his coat on, he turned and asked what I wanted. Somewhat puzzled, I told him he had hired me the previous night and that I was here to start work and move into my accommodation. He gave a dismissive laugh.

"I never hired you, and even if I did, there's no room available here," he said.

"What do you mean? I've just wrapped up my other job and I'm ready to take the position you offered me," I said with an edge to my voice. That was of no interest to him. I bristled, thinking that last night's promise must have been a barroom scam to get a round of free drinks out of me. This guy didn't give a shit whether I was jobless or homeless. Seething, I went back to my truck and thought the situation over. I wasn't going to put up with this kind of treatment. I went to the hotel, barged into his room and confronted him.

"You hired me in front of witnesses," I told him bluntly. "You've no choice but to give me the job. If you don't stand by your word, I'll be in touch with your company's head office," I threatened.

"I can't hire you," he continued to insist. "And besides, the hotel has no extra rooms and every hotel in town is booked up."

"Really?" I said. "You made a commitment with no intention of keeping it? That's your problem, not mine. I'm going to the building site to start work right now, and I better have a room when I get back here tonight." Still fuming as I was leaving, I turned and said, "I'll have your job for this, you lying bastard!"

I was no longer that naïve youth from Winnipeg, lacking in self-esteem. It took an unfair situation like this to trigger the person I could be, aggressive and ready to stand up for my rights. This was undoubtedly the product of both my recent experiences in the North and the example set by my parents, who believed in fairness, honesty and standing your ground when it came to matters of principle. In this particular situation, I knew what was wrong and what would make it right.

I went straight to the job site with my tools, ready to work. There was a large polyethylene hoarding set up on the building to shelter the bricklayers as they worked, but they hadn't yet started work because it was badly ripped and blowing in the wind. The regular work crew showed up, and, when I suggested we fix the hoarding, they told me to wait till the boss arrived. I ignored the suggestion, grabbed my tools and told them they could wait if they wanted but that the hoarding needed to be fixed. They were slow to move, but we began to work on the hoarding.

The boss showed up about two hours later and had everyone get ready for a scheduled concrete pour. I had poured a lot of concrete before and knew what needed to be done. During that day, I learned the name of the company for which I was now working. It was Steel Space Industries.

I was called to the boss's office at the end of the day. When I walked in, he gave me a room key and I gave him my social insurance number. Not a word was exchanged. I went to my room, had a welcome bath, lay on the bed and reflected on what had happened that day. I went from being jobless and homeless in the morning to being employed, with accommodation and a guarantee of three meals a day. I didn't know it at the time, but this was to be the beginning of a stable and rewarding career path for me.

I worked under this boss for about a month. He began to show up on the job site later and later and came half snapped when he did. I slowly gained the respect of the workers, who had at first resented this young guy making decisions. They began to feel better on the job and saw that the boss's neglect was making their jobs more complicated than they needed to be. To top this off, the boss failed to put in an appearance for two days prior to a big concrete pour. On the third morning, a cement finisher showed up and could see that the plastic hoardings we had worked on had ripped overnight and needed fixing. He became agitated.

"You guys are in deep shit; you're not ready. A whole fleet of trucks is loading up right now and heading this way. On top of that, I'm told that they're using a new technology for the cement pour called foam create." I listened to him, and my heart sank. We weren't told anything about this. The crew wasn't sure what to do to prepare for this new process and wanted to wait for the boss's instructions.

"He was drunk this morning and wouldn't get out of bed," someone offered. This was the last straw for me.

"Enough already!" I exclaimed. "I'm not going to sit around and wait for that idiot. Who's with me?" Three people out of about eight got up and joined me. I decided to press the others once more.

"Look guys, the trucks are on their way and the boss is not, so let's pull together on this." They had a quick discussion and came to an agreement to join us, and within minutes the whole place was a whirlwind of activity. We caught on quickly to what was required to work with the new quick-setting product. The cement finisher was working himself half to death, all the while cursing and claiming that our boss had promised a crew of finishers, but they never materialized. In the midst of all of this, I ran back and forth to the office to consult the drawings, make decisions and coordinate the crew.

We finished the nonstop pour at about ten at night. We were an exhausted group, yet proud of what we had managed to do. Not only was there no resentment among the crew at my having taken charge, but they took the time to thank me as they left the job site.

Two more days passed, and there was still no sign of the boss. The building owners came to inspect the job and told me that they had talked to the subtrades and had been informed of the circumstances on the site prior to and during the concrete pour. They informed me that the Steel Space representatives were recommending that I take over as supervisor and asked if I was interested. I accepted, on condition that the work crew agreed with my appointment, and told them I would let them know my final decision the next day. I approached the crew, got their support and agreed to take on the job.

Our boss was let go the following day, and I took over his position. I had inadvertently done what I said I would do the day he refused to honour his promise. I told him, "I'll have your job for this."

One of the things I noted when I arrived on the job was the absence of Indigenous workers in the work crews at Steel Space Industries. One of the primary objectives I set for myself when I took my new position was to focus on finding Indigenous workers and craftsmen whenever possible. It was a decision made on principle that paid off over and over again for those I hired, and for me as a responsible foreman and recruiter. It also reflected my values.

IF RAVENS COULD TALK

I arrived at the Hay River hardware store one day and noticed a congress of ravens circling above.

Old Slim, the owner of the fish truck, must be parked somewhere near there, I thought. As I got out of my truck and headed for the door of the hardware store, I heard a voice.

"Hello." I looked around, but there was no one to be seen. I heard it once again and looked up to where the voice appeared to be coming from, only to make eye contact with a raven perched above the door and looking straight back at me.

"Hello," I said hesitatingly.

"Hello." the raven responded.

I continued on into the store, incredulous and shaking my head. I told the salesperson what had just happened.

"Oh yeah, I know," she replied. "He comes here occasionally, but you'll usually find him wherever crowds gather. He likes people."

"How did he learn?" I asked.

"No one knows for sure. Some people think that he may've split his tongue eating out of a tin can at the dump and found that he was able to mimic people," she continued, adding a bit more detail. "He hangs out around the church. As you know, when people arrive on Sunday there's lots of handshaking, and the people and priest greet one another with a friendly hello. They say that's how it probably started," she added. "But he also hangs out around the schoolyard a lot. He could've picked it up from the kids there. They get a big kick out of him."

The raven became a popular fixture in the community, welcoming one and all wherever he landed. I noticed one day that it had been a while since I had seen him, so I stopped at the store and asked the girl at the till if she had seen him around.

"No, unfortunately," she replied, "And we're not going to see him, either." Then she broke the bad news about the not-too-surprising disappearance of my welcoming friend. It seems that his capacity to expand his vocabulary with such ease unfortunately ended up being to his detriment.

One Sunday, he was at the church as usual and got the welcoming wave from the priest as the congregation began to arrive. But instead of being welcomed by the familiar "Hello," they were treated to a totally new greeting from the church steeple where the raven was perched.

"Fuck off!" exclaimed the raven. Apparently he repeated it over and over again, and the traditional handshake on a Sunday was put aside as dismayed parishioners scurried into the church. But there was no refuge there because, as mass proceeded, they could hear this new greeting echoing down into the nave through the rafters above. "Fuck off! Fuck off!" over and over again. As much as people may have been shocked, I'm told it also brought a smile to more than a face or two.

The next day, the raven disappeared, never to be heard from again. It turned out that the kids in the school playground had taught the friendly raven how to swear. He was quick to learn and paid dearly for his ability. I suspect the local priest had something to do with the disappearance of the Hay River raven, whose vocabulary unfortunately grew to include more than a simple "Hello."

BEAR LAKE ALEXIE COMES TO HAY RIVER

I hadn't realized it, but I had grown accustomed to and missed the taste of wild game in all its forms, such as pounded meat mixed with bone marrow grease. I hoped to pick some up in Rae Lakes, when I took a few days off work to visit friends before the winter roads closed. I asked Chief Dan if he would like me to bring some back for him. He was delighted at the offer.

I set out on the Mackenzie Highway with half a dozen jerry cans of gas in the back of the truck. I got to Edzo, where the winter road begins, but the sign on the turnoff read: ROAD CLOSED. I had officially missed my chance; the winter road season was over. Rashly assuming the sign had been posted recently, I ignored it and fortunately made it safely to Rae Lakes that evening, in what was the beginning of a whiteout.

I went straight to Harry Simpson's house, where I was given the usual warm welcome and invited to spend the night. As we talked, I told him about Chief Dan's request for dry meat. Harry directed me to a home nearby that had an ample supply. I purchased as much as I could and returned to Harry's place to share a meal with the family.

Harry had a bush radio switched on at his place and heard that the storm had increased in strength and had already hit Fort Franklin. Then, we heard a distress call coming from Fort Franklin. A group of young people had left there just before the storm hit, were poorly dressed and not equipped for this kind of weather, and had not yet returned. It was thought that they might be headed to Rae Lakes for shelter. They requested that someone with a truck in Rae Lakes head to Hottah Lake to possibly intercept them and take them to Rae Lakes until the storm blew over. The town was abuzz with concern for these young people. My jeep was probably the best vehicle available for the job, so I volunteered to head to Hottah Lake, along with John Bekale, to see if we could find the lost crew.

Out into the whiteout we went, with only the winter road snow banks as our guide. We were aware that there would be no snowplow coming to our rescue if we did get stuck, and, if we did, I was more worried for the truck than ourselves. We could find our way back, but chances were that the truck would go out with the ice in the next few weeks. Foolhardy? We went anyway. The only relief from the whiteout was on the portages.

We made it to Hottah Lake and were getting close to the spot where the young men would likely have entered the winter road. I was about to give up and turn around when something caught my eye ahead and off to the left of us, but there were no snowmobile lights showing, so it wasn't the lost kids. As we came together, I stopped the truck and rolled down the window. It was a man and a dog team. He pulled alongside and approached the truck. He was wearing totally traditional caribou hide clothing, which was encrusted in frost and snow, and his face was buried deep within a ring of wolverine fur. He greeted us with, "Dàąt'e?" This was none other than my mysterious friend, Bear Lake Alexie. I jumped out of the truck and shook his hand vigorously.

"Where are you going?" I asked, somewhat bewildered.

The answer he gave was almost comical. "To K'atl'odeeche [Hay River]," he responded. Here we were, passing one another on a blizzard-blown lake, going in opposite directions, but now with the same destination in mind.

He was clad from head to toe in caribou-hide clothing, one layer with the fur facing inward and an outer layer with the fur facing out. His brown, furrowed face was barely visible, buried within his hood. The dog team was impatient, unlike Alexie, who tied his mitts behind his back and accessed a cigarette and somehow lit it in the stormy conditions.

"Where are you going?" He asked in return.

I answered with the first thing that came into my mind. "I'm here to pick you up; we're going to K'atl'odeeche." We both smiled and shook our heads in disbelief at this extraordinary chance meeting. We loaded his sled on the roof of the truck box and we packed seven reluctant sled dogs into the truck.

We told Alexie the reason we were out in this storm. He told us that he hadn't come across any snowmobile tracks while traveling on the lake. Consequently, there wasn't much sense in our continuing on from there. We surmised that the group was likely camped in the protection of the woods, out of the blizzard. We turned around and headed back to Rae Lakes. Once in the truck, drained and weary, Alexie fell asleep. The return journey was the most challenging four-wheel-drive journey I have ever undertaken.

On numerous occasions we became stuck in the deepening snow. We didn't disturb Alexie as we drove through the storm or worked to dig the vehicle out of the drifts along the way, as the wind filled in the trenches almost as quickly as we dug them out. We finally made it to Rae Lakes, staked out Alexie's dogs and found him a place to sleep. As it turned out, a radio message had come saying that the young people had managed to make it back safely to Fort Franklin.

I was now concerned as to how Alexie and I were going to make it out of Rae Lakes and over the 150 miles to get back to Hay River in these weather conditions. I mentioned my worries to John Bekale's father. He had great news. Because the store was short on groceries, the Chief had arranged for one more delivery of groceries and fuel, which meant the ice road would be plowed and be back in service and open for our use.

Sure enough, that morning the huge trucks started arriving. A convoy had come through the blizzard, with the African Queen plowing ahead of them with her massive V-shaped plow blade blasting a clear path through the snowpack and drifts. Truck drivers with bigger trucks, with all the modern amenities such as radios, cassette players and good heaters, would talk of giving up a trip for the thrill of getting one crack at driving the African Queen on the winter road. On one of the occasions when I met up with the African Queen, I shared coffee in the cab with the driver of that notorious snowplow and got the story attached to it.

African Queen on the ice road, hauling uranium

In short, the African Queen was the pride of the snow-clearing fleet, and every northern trucker knew her history. After spending her princess days in the desert sands of North Africa during the fight against Rommel's forces, she was dispatched to the High Arctic to be a plow truck for the winter roads. She was so effective at her new job that she replaced the Caterpillar trains that pioneered the opening of the winter roads at that time. She had sunk through the ice three times, only to be retrieved and lovingly restored by a corps of mechanics who venerated her. They anointed her The African Queen. Eventually, she was barged south to Yellowknife, where she spent her last days hauling along the winter roads to Great Bear Lake, where I often crossed paths with her.

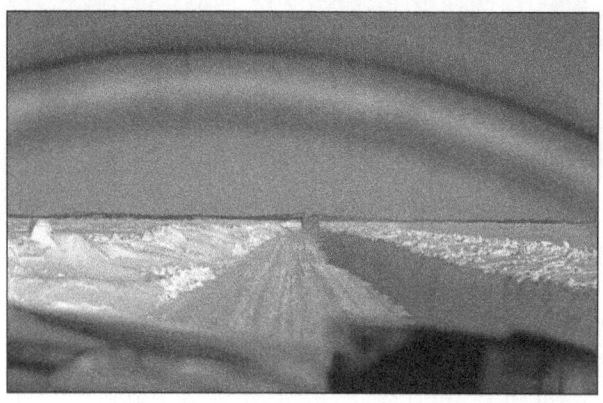

The ice road as viewed from behind the steering wheel.

The morning we were scheduled to leave Rae Lakes, Alexie made arrangements for someone to care for his dogs, and he and I took off in the truck, maneuvering along the winter road south to Hay River. I asked him why he was heading there. He said he had heard via the bush radio that there was an independent fur buyer, George Piper, there who would give a better price for furs than anyone else. To pass the time on that long journey, we exchanged stories, and he also gave me a history lesson in his limited English.

He talked of the old days before the white man came and of how his people lived before the introduction of steel and metal. He mentioned that a team of seven dogs like his was unheard of. People only had one or two dogs, and maybe three if they were doing well. If they had means to feed three dogs and a family, they would be considered well-to-do.

Dogs were an important part of a nomadic lifestyle. However, there was no such thing as restraining dogs with chains. Anything made of hide would be eaten through, so the dogs were not tied up. They were free to roam. The animals and people learned to live together. People lived in small clans, because the larger the group of people, the greater the number of loose dogs. That would be a safety threat. To feed these dogs, it was necessary to catch most of the fish required in the fall and to make stick fish to last the whole winter. This was necessary because they did not have steel chisels capable of chipping through five feet of ice. Their nets also had limited capacity because they were made of willow bark and were no longer than twenty feet. Caribou were plentiful, and the migration came much farther south. When that didn't happen, it meant hardship for families and long journeys to get to the caribou, much like the hunts of today into the Barrenlands. These nuggets of traditional information opened my eyes and gave me a view of the past that I had not heard before.

When we arrived in Hay River, I took him to a restaurant for a meal. He was still wearing his trapper's clothing, which had that strong, smoked hide smell, and he looked the worse for wear. I didn't particularly care if we brought a little discomfort to the patrons. What was important was to ensure that Alexie had a decent meal before he did what he was here to do: sell his furs, visit old friends and spend some of his money.

We went to the Hay River First Nation settlement nearby, where Alexie knew he had a place to stay. He knew the community well, so we drove around until he identified the place. It was a dilapidated structure without running water. I was aware the place had a questionable reputation, but the choice was Alexie's. I held on to his furs at his request, and as I dropped him off I arranged to pick him up the next day to meet with the buyer. He had no money on him and so borrowed forty dollars from me to get him through the start of his few weeks' visit. He was received warmly and was delighted to connect with his friend.

The next day, I picked him up as arranged and we headed out with his two large packsacks, or ohchi, which were made of hide and stuffed with the furs of wolverine, white fox, marten, lynx and wolf. We went to the Game Office, where the proposed prices were not to his liking. So we located Mr. Piper, who offered good prices for most of the furs. Alexie felt the prices for wolf in Yellowknife would be much better, and so he held on to those particular pelts. He certainly knew his business when it came to trading furs.

I took him back to the house, and before he went in he pulled a huge wad of bills out of his pocket, extracted about a hundred dollars, handed me the rest and asked me to hold onto it for him. He specifically instructed me not to give him back any of his money, even if he asked for it, until the day he was to fly out to Yellowknife. I agreed. He showed up drunk at my job site a couple of times over the next few weeks, asking for his money. I refused and repeated his own words back to him. He accepted my decision without argument. I assured him that he would have the money in his hands the day he left for Yellowknife to finish his trading.

He eventually came and asked me to take him to the airport. He was not well versed in airport protocol, so I purchased his ticket for him. We stepped up to the check-in desk behind a woman dressed in a beautiful white fur coat. She had just checked her suitcase through and was about to walk away as we plunked down Alexie's two ohchi. They were soiled with years of use and smelled of campfire smoke. The ticket agent was about to pull the ohchi through when the high-heeled lady in the fox fur coat pushed forward.

"Remove those filthy bags," she demanded of the agent. He was in the process of complying, so I stepped forward, put my foot on the scale and blocked the bags from being removed. She may have had a somewhat legitimate concern, but I was ticked off at her arrogant attitude.

"Listen, mister," I said to the agent. "This man has traveled 150 miles by dog team and 300 by road and has traded most of his furs in your community. He's now on his way to Yellowknife to trade the remainder of his furs. He's paid his fare; I assure you that his baggage is going with him."

"What's in the baggage?" the agent asked.

"The furs of white fox and wolf, along with some smoked dry meat." I told him. With that, I pulled a piece of dried meat from one of the packsacks and showed it to him.

"Oh! You mean like beef jerky?" he exclaimed. The woman, meanwhile, railed on in protest. She demanded to see the manager. I turned and spoke directly to the woman.

"This man is a well-known and respected elder and trapper, and you, madam, may very well be wearing furs he has trapped. Where do you think that white fox on your back came from?" I turned to the attendant and added, "I too would like to see the manager, because if these packs are not on board this flight, I assure you that a welcoming committee from the Indian Brotherhood waiting for this man's arrival."

The agent provided us with some plastic bags for the packsacks and weighed them, and we watched them go through. Alexie gave me a look that needed no words. As I said goodbye, I handed him his money. He took it with a smile and we parted company, two good friends who understood and appreciated each other in a deeply meaningful way. I later called the "Indian Brotherhood" office and they confirmed he and his belongings arrived intact.

CHIEF DAN'S DILEMMA

Chief Dan Sonfrere of the Hay River Band
– credit-N.W.T. Archive / Rene Fumoleau

I got to know Chief Dan Sonfrere quite well while making frequent visits to his place. On the occasion of one of my visits, I mentioned the unusual experience of watching the elderly man with his horse and wagon traveling through the early morning fog. He listened as I spoke of the impression that this casual meeting made on me. He asked me to come back later that day, and when I did, he told me we were going to a meeting at the horse and wagon man's home. I was pleased at the thought of meeting him.

Later in the day, we went to the old village to meet an elder and member of the Band council by the name of Jim Lamalise. Another councillor was also at the house, Ted Bugghins. The purpose of the meeting was not only for me to meet Jim but was also to see if I met with the approval of Jim and Ted to act as a participant in an important upcoming meeting, the nature of which was to be confidential. We sat around a table where the politics of their small village was discussed, sometimes in English and the more heated discussions in Slavey. They asked me questions about myself in the manner of a job interview. As the meeting went on, I picked up on the key concern they had met to address.

These men were worried that large corporate businesses wanted access to their traditional lands. This control over their own lands was at the core of their concern. Hay River's business and political community had ignored the Hay River First Nation community over the years. They did little or nothing to assist the community, other than to push through a winter road across the ice to Hay River to give them access to town. In a word, the corporate or political interests in Hay River were not positively disposed to paying attention to the needs and wishes of Chief Dan's community but were highly attuned to the corporate interests, such as those involved with pipeline construction.

The situation that the Hay River Band faced was complicated by intertribal disputes among the Dene from the NWT as to how they should tackle the matter of land claims with the government. The Dene tribes had formed an organization known as the Indian Brotherhood of the NWT, a large alliance of tribes committed to negotiate with one voice with the government on matters related to land claims for the Dene. They believed that a united front gave them more clout at the negotiating table. Their worry was that if bands pursued small, individual land claims settlements, it could mean the establishment of small reserves, and the organization wanted nothing to do with the reserve system. At the root of it, they wanted to achieve the loftier goal of self-government with their having jurisdiction over their lands and resources. This collaboration was something Chief Dan and his Band councillors initially supported and were excited about at the beginning of the negotiations process in the early 1970s.

Dan saw evidence in his area that the pipeline project was ramping up, with or without the approval or participation of the Dene. All around him, there was evidence of development activity, in particular where the islands in the river were being transformed into platforms for loading facilities. Dan alerted the other Dene tribes early on as to what he saw happening, and they used this information to help weld together their alliance of the tribes that would be affected. But Dan's enthusiasm for the alliance waned.

After a while, it became evident to Chief Dan that the alliance's approach was not going to address his concerns. He realized that it would take years for the Dene alliance organization to reach a land claims settlement. It was a complex process, with many levels of decision-making involved, not the least of which was that each band would have a final say regarding the application of the terms of any treaty to do with their specific, traditional territory. He realized that this would slow the whole claims settlement process down, and in the meantime the exploitation and development would proceed regardless. Some form of drastic action needed to be taken by the Hay River Band. Then some key information came to his attention.

One day in 1972, a young woman from the village came to speak with Dan. She was employed by a company contracted to do work related to the building of staging facilities for the pipeline. Knowing of Chief Dan's concerns, she informed him that she was aware of the existence of documents that would be of interest to him. They indicated that the staging facilities being planned were to be located on the site of the old village and on the very land on which Dan's house was located. According to her account, everything in the designated area was to be bulldozed.

Chief Dan called his Band Council together and shared this information. They weighed their options. The pressure to stay within the Dene alliance was strong. All could see the importance of it, yet somehow, most of them could also see the futility of the alliance's efforts when it came to protecting their village and their lands around Hay River at this very moment. After much discussion, they concluded that the only way to stop what was happening was to forge on ahead on their own and form the first Indigenous reserve in the Northwest Territories.

They knew this would be a highly unpopular move and would meet with much resistance from the Dene alliance. The organization had succeeded in giving voice to the voiceless Indigenous communities in face-to-face discussions with government. They were a symbol of solidarity for the Dene people; they even rallied around their own flag. Dan wanted to support that alliance in its work, but he also wanted protect his community's lands. This was Chief Dan's dilemma.

Dan had to persuade his people and his councillors that they had no choice but to separate from the Dene alliance, even though he knew that the alliance would condemn him. He knew the town of Hay River would condemn him, and his people would suffer repercussions when they announced their intention as a Band. That intention was to bar the pipeline companies from access to the Band's traditional lands, from the use of the river that flowed through those lands, and from the use of the islands in their territory in that river. In simple terms, they intended to bring the whole pipeline machine to a stop.

To convince government of the validity of their case, Dan needed the documented proof of the company's plans. He managed to get hold of a copy of those plans. With this information in hand, he called Indian Affairs to the community and demanded that they put a stop to the planned encroachment on the Band's territory. After many meetings, along with a petition to the Canadian prime minister of the day, the Honourable Pierre Trudeau, the government representatives entered into discussions with the Band Council to set up a reserve. Eventually, they supported the Band's position, put a halt to the building of the pipeline storage facilities in the identified territory, and set the wheels in motion for the establishment of a reserve.

This process of setting up a reserve necessitated getting the support of the Band Council. In any event, the meeting in Jim Lamalise's cabin was about establishing whether they had that support or not. They ended the meeting on the understanding that they could not get unanimous agreement of the Band. They also agreed that I would be an acceptable candidate to take part in a follow-up meeting, as long as I was willing to hold everything said and decided at that meeting in the strictest confidence. I gave my word, still not knowing or asking what specific part I would be asked to play.

Dan often asked my opinion after explaining to me what he hoped to do, but I believe it was more a matter of him wanting to hear himself putting his thoughts into words than looking for my viewpoint. My twenty-three-year-old outsider's brain struggled to get a handle on all of this, and as I did, my admiration for Dan's leadership skills grew.

In September 1973, when the weather had closed in and the snow was already two feet deep, Chief Dan came to see me.

"Tonight is the night I would like you to do that favour I asked of you. Are you ready?" he asked. I nodded assent.

"What exactly is it you want me to do?" I asked.

"I want you to drive. We have to hurry; we're already late," he said evasively. I got into his white passenger van and drove as directed to the village, where we picked up the two elders, Jim Lamalise and Ted Bugghins.

"Where to, now?"

"The airport," he replied without explanation.

We arrived at the Hay River airport and entered the terminal, where Dan immediately approached two men. The stereotypical image the men presented was almost comical. They wore black trench coats and polished, ankle-high leather shoes, and one of them carried a black briefcase. They were from the Department of Indian Affairs. Introductions were made and everyone piled into the van.

"Where to, Dan?" I asked.

"South to the Alberta border," he replied.

The border? I thought to myself. There's absolutely nothing at that border. So I asked again, just to be sure I got it right.

"Just keep going till I tell you to stop." I drove for about half an hour, then Dan asked me to slow down as he peered out, trying to spot some landmark he had in mind. Eventually, he identified a clearing at the side of the road where we could pull in and park the van. A snowshoe trail led away from there, along which we made our way in single file for about 500 yards before reaching the banks of the Hay River. From there, we scampered down the embankment to a small cabin.

We entered the cabin in typical northern fashion, without knocking. This was a trap line cabin, with few amenities. There was an elderly man there, seated and obviously expecting us. He got up, stoked the fire, and then introductions were made as we took off our coats. The owner of the cabin was the chief from Meander River, Alberta, a village just below the border with the NWT. He was a member of a Slavey band, the same band to which Chief Dan belonged. The Band's territory spanned the 60th parallel, and the Chief had crossed over the border to his cabin on the NWT side. The meeting needed to be held here for legal reasons. There were only two chairs in the cabin, a single bunk bed—and eight of us. The two government agents stood as close to the fire as they could, while a small table was cleared and the candle placed on it.

I understood, from previous discussions with Chief Dan, that he needed the signatures of three members of the Band Council along with his to initiate the process of forming a reserve. He had lost the support of one of the Band councillors for his plan. An additional vote was required to get the correct number of councillors to finalize the process, and that's where the Meander River chief came in. Chief Dan knew that the Meander River chief had the same voting rights as a Band councillor when it came to making decisions related to the affairs of the K'atl'odeeche, or Hay River First Nation, even though he was not a regular attendee at Band meetings. This was Chief Dan's proverbial rabbit in the hat needed to secure the additional vote required to initiate the process.

The agents produced the document that would set the wheels in motion for the formation of the Hay River Reserve. All parties present were required to sign the official papers. Then, the unstated reason as to why I was there finally became clear. They required an impartial witness to validate the signatures. I signed, and the meeting ended without any further ado.

With the official Band Council resolution approved, we trod back up the embankment, down the trail, into the van and back to Hay River, having concluded a historically significant meeting in the story of the establishment of the Hay River Reserve. It was an event in which I was proud to have played a small part.

On May 7, 1974, the following communication was sent to Chief Daniel Sonfrere:

"I am pleased to tell you that by order in Council P.C. 1974-387 of February 26, 1974 these lands were set apart as Hay River Indian Reserve No.1."

Signed: Jean Chrétien, Minister of Northern Affairs.

BUFFALO RIVER

Spring had arrived in Hay River, and I was aching to take a day trip by canoe in the Buffalo River.

"Have you ever paddled the Buffalo River?" I asked my friend Frank Fabian.

"No, I haven't," he said. "But Pat Martel has."

So off to Pat's place I went and announced my intention to paddle the Buffalo River to Great Slave Lake and return to Hay River via the same lake. I asked if he had any pointers and if he was interested in coming with me.

"No one had done that trip in years, and at this time of year it's very dangerous." He indicated he was not interested and advised me against doing it. But my mind was set.

"Thanks for the warning, Pat, but I'm still going to do it," I told him, and after chatting for a while I left to get on with my planning.

Pat must have given it more thought, because he came to visit me the following day to urge me not to go. He elaborated on what he had told me earlier, described the hazards of the river in flood and how it expanded its course, creating new channels through the bush, and carrying logs, debris and large chunks of ice with it.

"Frank Fabian tells me you've paddled it." I said. "You seem to know a lot about the conditions on the river right now. Did you ever do it at this time of year?" I casually asked.

"Yes," he said. "When I was young, my father-in-law took me on the river around this time."

"So it can be done in these conditions," I commented. He shook his head, we both smiled, and I thought the matter had been put to rest.

He came back the following day and told me that his father-in-law, Mr. Bugghins, wanted to talk with me. That night I went to his father-in-law's house, where Pat served tea and bannock as I was being sized up. I was young and fit, and the elderly Mr. Bugghins was an arthritic, five-foot-tall man, a bit worn around the edges. Pat translated as we exchanged lighthearted small talk, but once the subject of traveling down the Buffalo River came up, the old man became serious. Mr. Bugghins believed, like his son-in-law, that the river was too dangerous to travel on at this time of year. I listened respectfully without responding.

"When are you leaving?" Mr. Bugghins asked.

"It will be this coming Saturday," I said. No more was said, and I left thinking that must be the end of these exchanges.

Friday came, and I felt something was afoot when I was once more invited to meet with Pat and his father-in-law. When I arrived, they were engaged in a serious exchange in the Slavey language. I sat quietly as they talked and began to feel some guilt at being so resistant to the advice of this respected elder. I was also feeling guilty for trying to convince Pat to come with me, knowing that he had his family to consider, whereas I was single and without such commitments. Just as I was getting to the point of saying I would take their advice, Pat turned to me and blurted out.

"I don't know what to say, Kieran. But my father-in-law insists that there's no way you can go on a trip like this by yourself." Then he added, "He decided that he'll take you down the river." I was floored. I had envisioned taking the journey with Pat, but with Mr. Bugghins? No.

There was momentary silence in the room. I thought, "This man has a hard time walking; how could he entertain the idea of doing this?" So I turned to Pat and made a blunt observation. "Pat, I just can't do that, he's far too old."

"You've lit a fire in his heart, Kieran. You've made him think a lot about this, and now he wants to go. He also wants me to make this one last trip with him as well," Pat explained. "He said he's always wanted to take another run down the river but thought no one was interested and never asked. Now you're here, someone who wants to do it, and he doesn't want to miss this chance. We'll all go together in my freighter canoe." I hesitated and was about to add something when Pat said, "Kieran, he's like you; he won't change his mind. We'll meet you tomorrow morning by the river at the bridge."

We met the next morning at the bridge. Viewed from above, the river was a raging, yellow-brown torrent. Pat continued to be concerned, and I was filled with a reckless enthusiasm, eager and ready to go. Mr. Bugghins shuffled down to the river with his gear and looked it over while we moved the canoe. I asked Pat who would sit where in the canoe.

"My father-in-law wants to take the stern," he said without hesitation. I expressed my concern, and he again said, "It's no use arguing, Kieran. The old man said he wants to do it, and he won't change his mind. He's stubborn, just like you. He takes the stern."

We got into the large canvas canoe and pushed off. Immediately, the boat shot downriver at a furious pace and headed directly towards the other shore at a bend ahead. Blink and it would be over, and we would miss our own end. The old man got us around that bend with ease and, before we knew it, we were riding the swells in the center of the river without requiring a single paddle stroke on our part, as old Mr. Bugghins took full control. All we had to do was sit with paddles at the ready to deflect debris or chunks of ice that came our way.

It gave me comfort to see the old gentleman relive his youth and be so at ease with what he was doing. He even took his time filling and lighting up his pipe while navigating. I had a new appreciation for the fact that he had also taken this trip to safeguard me from myself.

We came to a stretch where the river spilled over its banks, as Pat had described. It flooded far into the woods, and we began to experience calmer waters as the river's course widened. This gave us an opportunity to shoot a muskrat, some ducks and a beaver. However, it soon became obvious that we were unlikely to find a secure spot on the shoreline for a campsite, so Mr. Bugghins made a decision.

"Bad weather's on the way. If we stop we might be stuck out here. We'll travel through the night and get back to Hay River before it arrives." I continued to press that we look harder for a place to stop, so Pat checked once again with his father-in-law, who replied, "This cloud will lift soon. With the full moon, we can continue safely." That addressed any concerns I might have had. A short time later, under a full moon and with good visibility, we stopped paddling and drifted along at our ease, in stark contrast to the conditions we faced when we started.

Pat drew our attention to something in the water a few feet away. Traveling parallel to us, as we drifted, was a tiny mouse, swimming purposefully along. We came so close that we made eye contact with the little critter. I recall thinking: Here's this mouse swimming purposefully downriver at the beginning of its days, and drifting alongside it is an elderly man purposely paddling down the same river, but at the end of his days. I tipped my hat to the mouse as we lost sight of him and looked towards the stern to see a rejuvenated Mr. Bugghins, smiling contentedly.

We continued our journey through the night and emerged from the mouth of the river onto Great Slave Lake. The whitecaps were up and storm clouds closing in as we turned into the safety of Hay River channel, a contented threesome. Two young men taking a chance for excitement's sake and an old man living out his dream and revisiting memories of bygone days.

HAY RIVER RESERVE'S DREAM BUS

I lived the life of a workaholic while employed by Steel Space Industries and had little or no social life to speak of. Occasionally, I'd wander into town and meet people I knew from the area. One person I met there frequently was Chief Dan. He used to take people from the reserve to town for medical appointments or grocery shopping in his white van. It was about a twenty-mile drive from the reserve to the town of Hay River. Few people on reserve had a vehicle, and taxis were costly. Any time I saw his van, I made a point of stopping to chat with him. He had a no-booze policy. He refused to transport alcohol back to the reserve and also refused to transport people who were drunk.

On one of the occasions when we met, he asked if I would visit him at his home that night to talk about an important matter. Dan got down to business as soon as I arrived. He told me that, after years of trying to get the town to provide a bus service to the Hay River Band, he had come up against a brick wall. He now had a plan to get around that. He heard that the town of Hay River had purchased a new bus, so he approached the town officials about donating the old one for the Band's use. He was informed they couldn't just give it away, saying that it had to go up for auction. He asked for an application form and was told that the application wasn't available yet. This happened several times. He suspected that he was being given the runaround. He asked if I would be willing to pick up the application form, fill it out in my name and submit a bid on the bus. If I won the bid and got the bus, he suggested I sell it to him, as chief of the Hay River Band. I agreed.

"I suspect they won't give the application to me because they're worried that if I win the bid I'll bring a lot more people from the reserve to town, and they don't want that," said he.

"You've got to be kidding," I exclaimed.

"No, not everyone thinks like you, Kieran. We're treated like we have some kind of disease and often refused service in town," Dan replied in his matter-of-fact way of putting things.

I was aware that there were people in town hostile towards the Indigenous community, but this situation involving the bus was a form of institutional racism. I agreed to do what Dan asked of me. I saw this as one small way I could do my part in helping to address the lack of fairness in the town's dealings with the Band. It was a great way to circumvent the system, and I was eager to help.

I went to the town office, located beside a storage area for community equipment, where the bus was parked. I did a brief inspection of the large, Greyhound-style bus and picked up the application form. I was told that the closing date for bids was the next day. I asked for and got a chance to take the bus for a test drive, something Dan had requested but was denied. I went to the office, and as I filled out the application, one of the employees made the comment that I was the only one to have picked up the bid forms and could likely get the bus for a song. I looked forward to taking possession of the bus the next day.

I went back to the offices the following day, just before closing time, and submitted a bid of $150, just five minutes before bids were closed. As I handed it in, the guy in charge suggested, "Why don't you have a coffee; we'll be opening the bids for the bus and other assets in a few minutes." I sat and waited. The time came; my bid was accepted. I was given the bus keys and told to come back tomorrow to finish the ownership transfer papers. I immediately went to see Dan and told him the good news. He was elated.

After work the following day, I went to the town office to take possession of the bus. Instead of giving me the papers, I was asked to come to another room and found myself faced by two people. They started out with a question.

"Does your buying this bus have anything to do with Indian Village?" asked one of the men. The other one added, "We've been told that you spend a lot of time over there." I grew angry at this inquisition and, knowing that I was the only bidder and had the keys to the bus in my hand, I responded as I felt.

"Yes," I blurted out. "As a matter of fact, I'm going to sell the bus to the Band for a dollar." They were visibly angry and demanded that I return the key, since they would not be signing over the ownership. I insisted they had no right to do this, since I had bid fair and square on the bus. A very heated exchange ensued.

"There's no way Indian Village is going to get that bus," the man holding my bid exclaimed as he tore it up. The other man added, "Things are bad enough as it is and we don't want busloads of those people coming on this side." Then one of them added, by way of justification, "The bus isn't safe for transporting large groups of people. That's why we're not going to sell it to you." That kind of lame rationale got me even more riled up.

"So it's not safe for the Band to own, but it is safe enough for me to own and drive?" I responded, growing angrier by the moment.

I knew nothing of my legal rights back then and didn't even think to contact a lawyer. I felt powerless and cheated. I was also upset with myself for how I'd handled the confrontation. It was a difficult thing for me to relay the details of what happened when I returned to Dan's place. He showed no sign of anger. In fact, he calmed me down.

"I've learned to expect as much. They get their way whenever and however they can," he said in a manner that had a lot of history backing it up.

Dan put the episode behind him and continued daily to cram as many of his people as he could into his van who wanted to go into Hay River. He never let discouraging incidents like this beat him down. It was a quality of his that I admired and worked to acquire, but I took this one hard.

RAFT RACE

The annual Hay River Celebration is held in the spring of the year. A raft race on the Hay River was one of the events scheduled. The race started at the bridge to Pine Point and ended at City Park. It was heavily advertised in the newspaper, with pictures of previous years' winners. Many businesses and organizations in town participated by sending raft teams to compete under their name. However, the people from the Hay River Band had never sent anyone and had never been invited to participate in the race. The irony, of course, is that the race was held on the very river their ancestors had navigated from time immemorial. I asked Pat Martel, a Band member I knew from work, if he was interested in our taking part and representing the Hay River Band in the raft race.

"They'd never consider letting us enter a team," he answered.

"But this is your river, and your people have been using it for generations. We've got to do this," I insisted, and Pat just smiled. He didn't say yes or no.

I talked with him later on, and he told me about the raft races of yesteryear, commenting that many of the rafts entered in the race were made of light Styrofoam. I suggested that if he joined me we would do something different; we would make an old-fashioned log raft. He shrugged his shoulders.

"Why bother?" he said. "They'll come up with an excuse to keep us out." Pat was a hardworking, respectable guy with lots of self-confidence, a man who felt comfortable directing workers on the job, but he was reluctant in this case, thinking that we could end up in some kind of confrontation with the community on the other side of the river. So I pressed him further, saying that as far as I was concerned, this was to be a matter of making a statement, not just a race. He bought into that idea and making the point that winning or losing didn't matter to him. I made no secret of the fact that I was hell-bent on winning. So we whipped a log raft together that conformed to the specifications required for the race.

I headed out in my canoe the night before the race to get a reading on the river, its currents and any other factors that would help in navigating it the day of the race. When that day arrived, Pat and I pulled up to the river with a sixteen-foot raft dangling out of my truck. Pat stayed at the truck. I picked up the entry form and filled it out while standing in line with the other applicants. I dropped it in the pile and got our identification numbers. I came back with my copy of the application and showed Pat that I had written Hay River Band where it requested the entrant's name. He smiled and shook his head in disbelief. We set our raft in the river a little apart from the launching area.

There was every shape of raft imaginable on the river, but Pat and I had as streamlined a raft as ever you could get. It was sixteen feet long and four logs wide, and this was to be its maiden voyage and our first time aboard. It was slightly tippy and had just enough room to establish a good foothold. We had cut long, strong poles for pushing our raft, while the others used paddles.

The competitors were directed to line up at the start line. The officials spotted us, and we were called aside. They questioned our legitimacy as race participants. "We have our registrant numbers and we've met all requirements set out on the entry form," I told them. They asked to see our entry form, saw it was stamped appropriately and said they needed to measure the raft, which they did, and found that it met all the specifications. Curiously, we noted that none of the other rafts was measured. They then claimed we should have had paddles instead of poles. I was getting furious and told them what they already knew, that there was no prohibition against the use of poles in the rules.

Pat was growing uncomfortable with all this negative attention and, sensing my exasperation, said, "Forget it, Kieran; let's get out of here." I ended the exchange with the officials saying, "We're registered; we've been measured, and we've met all requirements. We qualify!" I exclaimed. With that, we pushed off and moved toward the chaos of the start line. We took our place on the outer edge in the shallows, to take advantage of a solid base to push against with our poles.

After a short wait, the starting shot was fired and the race was underway. Paddlers thrashed and rafts collided as everyone jockeyed for position. The other competitors were either kneeling or sitting in their rafts, whereas we started off standing, legs braced, as we plunged our poles into the river bed and pushed with all our might. The rafts further out in the river had the starting advantage of the stronger current. We poled our way towards the middle of the pack without incident.

Surprisingly, we were soon in competition with the lead rafts being managed by veteran paddlers as the amateurs fell away. The contestants were now spaced widely apart, which gave us a chance to concentrate on coping with the river itself rather than struggling to avoid collisions.

Halfway into the race, we approached a set of rapids with two obvious safe channels on the left side, which the rafters ahead of us chose. Pat let me call the shots as to how we proceeded, knowing I had run the rapids the night before. I knew there was room for our raft to shoot the rapids on a shorter trajectory, to the right of the safer channels, and decided to take advantage of that. Pat was understably anxious as he knelt at the front, with just a foot or two of raft between him and the surging torrent ahead. Into the rapids we shot, with poles extended to keep us away from the rocky outcrops. Both of us were on our knees at this point as we were swept along, barely in control.

What a payoff! We gained so much time that we were now up with the three frontrunners. I knew from reconnoitering earlier that the next turn in the river was a deep channel where our poles could not touch bottom, and we would likely lose ground to the paddle-driven rafts. We headed to the right of the deep channel, where the spring runoff was surging through a narrow gap, and once there, we poked and poled our way through and entered another shortcut of relatively shallow water. As I poled, Pat hopped on and off the raft like a mountain goat as he pushed and pulled us through the shallower sections. This was time-consuming, but it paid off.

We shot out of that narrow channel and found ourselves in front of the nearest competitor by about ten raft lengths. The finish line, which was marked by a small flag and had a handful of people standing beside it, came into view and, poling with all our might, we zipped by the flag to win the race.

We were in disbelief as we pulled over to the opposite shoreline to get out of the way of the oncoming rafts. Once the way was clear, we poled over to the flag, hauled our raft out, and met the second and third place finishers, who congratulated us on our win. Pat and I were exhilarated and replayed the key moments that helped us pole our craft to victory.

We were informed that the ribbons would be presented at a celebration dinner in the Legion Hall. When we got there, we were told by one of the officials that we had been disqualified. The reason given was that the finish was at a point on the shoreline where the flag was placed and not a line across the width of the river from the flag. I argued our case, and they decided to compromise by giving us a third-place ribbon, a clumsy solution to their problem at best.

Amid all this fuss, Pat pulled me aside and stated how he felt. "We know we've won the race, and that's good enough for me, so just forget it; don't make a scene, Kieran." He summed things up well when he said, "I don't care a damn about the trophy. We know we won, and so do they. We won and it feels great."

Even though we knew games were being played on the matter of the finisher placements, we went to the building for the presentations. But when we got there, we were informed that they would give us our third-place ribbon right away and would only make a formal presentation to the first place winner at the meal.

"There you have it, Kieran; they make the rules to suit themselves," Pat pointed out once again.

The newspaper published the results of the race a short while later, and there was no mentioning of the Hay River Band's win or the third-place finish. By that time, I had come to see things the way Pat saw them. We had won that race and were proud that we had done so in the name of the Hay River Band.

THE INQUISITIVE ONE

One thing I managed to avoid while living and working in the NWT in those early years was any kind of life-threatening confrontation with another person. That was about to change.

I was sitting on the dock early one morning in one of the communities in which I was working, when a young man approached and sat down beside me. For the purpose of the story I will call him The Inquisitive One. He didn't say anything right away.

"Is there something you want to talk about?" I asked, sensing he had something on his mind.

"Yes," he replied. "I want to ask you something in confidence, if that's okay with you?" He said he was feeling shy and asked me to promise not to laugh at a question he wanted to ask. I agreed, and so he began.

"The elders want to know something about where money comes from, and I don't know how to explain it to them," he said. "Where does money come from, Kieran? How is it that these government guys arrive in a plane carrying suitcases filled with money to give to us? The elders don't want to ask the priest, and they're confused about the role the government plays in all of this." With that, he stopped and looked at me expectantly.

I needed to come up with some kind of reasonable answer to the question asked by a man who was a few years older than me and one of the best educated in the community. I was only twenty-two at the time.

I had never asked myself that question and can't remember anyone ever sitting down to explain the origin of money to me or how its value was set. I had heard about the thing called the gold standard, had never considered it in any kind of detail, and had a vague idea of how it worked. So with some thought and stray facts recalled, I set out to answer his question to the best of my ability.

"When I was a kid, I had a hobby trap-line on some farmland adjacent to where I lived on the edge of Winnipeg. Around that time, a huge building known as the Royal Canadian Mint was constructed on part of that farmland. In that building, they store gold and manufacture paper money and coins. When I first came north, I worked at a gold mine in Yellowknife and watched as they formed gold into bricks, which were shipped to that Mint and stored there. An ounce of gold at the time was valued at about $35. For every ounce they had stored, they could print a certain amount of money.

"When a person works, they are paid with paper money printed at that Mint, and a portion of the money they get, they give back to the government as taxes." I went on to explain. "The government then distributes some of that money to different departments; two of those departments that you are familiar with are the Income Support Department and the Indian Affairs Department. These departments use the money they get to pay people to build things like community halls or to pay treaty money or to distribute some of it in form of Social Assistance payments to people who are in need." I stopped there. I was unsure of the information I was giving; however, it seemed to answer his question. With that, he thanked me and we went our separate ways.

This question he had asked was not all that odd, when I considered the relative isolation of this community from mainstream Canadian society at that time. His apparent lack of knowledge of the monetary system was no more absurd than my lack of knowledge of the many traditional practices in Dene culture.

HAY RIVER TO FORT SIMPSON

The encounter I had with Alexie as he made his way through the blizzard to trade his furs in Hay River and my subsequent visits with him sparked my interest in the degree of his personal independence. I saw him as someone who lived life as he wished to, with few apparent constraints. He was not accountable to anyone for the decisions he made. Deep down, I was discontented with myself and my circumstances, even though my employer appreciated my work and I had a girlfriend who respected my perspective on life. I was still unable to commit myself to either.

Alexie's way of life held echoes from my own past, when, as a teenager, I wandered alone through the fields and bush on the outskirts of Winnipeg with my gun, traps and snares. I felt driven to regain some part of that early independence when I thought about Alexie.

I chose to break with my existing world by undertaking another dog-sled journey. This time I would do it as Alexie would have done it. I had that youthful confidence that as I closed the one door, another would open.

The journey through the snow-covered wilderness between Hay River and Fort Franklin was a distance of about 620 kilometres.

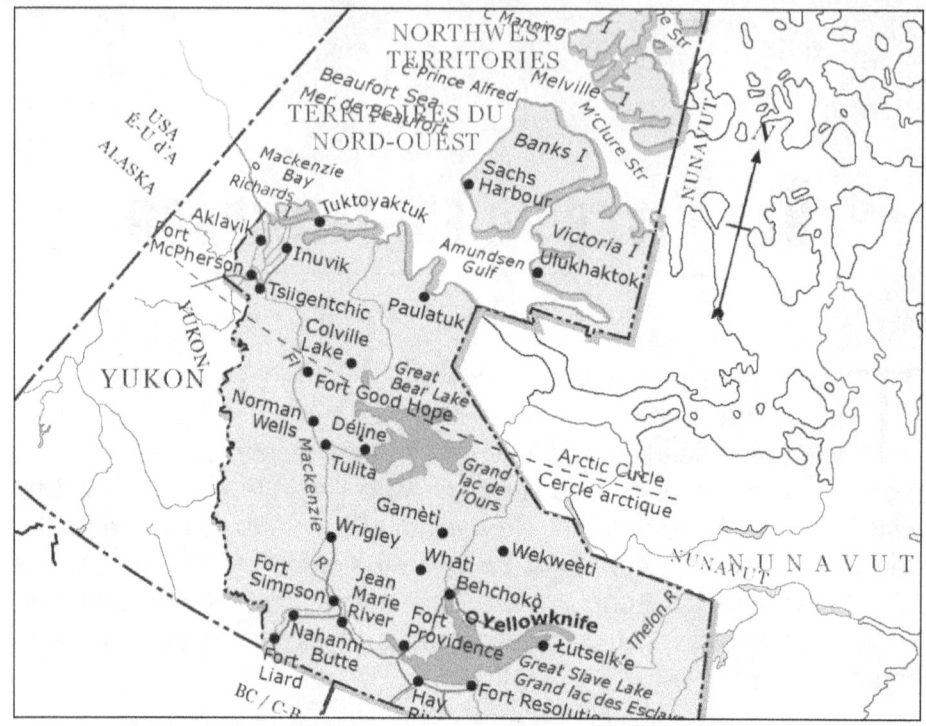

The region I traversed between Hay River and Fort Simpson

I informed my employer of my intentions to move on as soon as I was finished my present job. He obviously wanted to hold on to me, because, as an inducement, he offered me work on any one of the company's projects in Alberta. I thanked him for the generous offer but declined and began my preparations for the trek. The first order of business was to assemble a dog team.

This in itself was a challenge, because very few people were using dog sleds by that time, and they had released their dogs to fend for themselves. A few communities hired people to shoot the loose dogs when they began to pose a safety threat. Others chose to catch the dogs and pen them for seven days. If they were not claimed, they were then destroyed. Hay River had such a pound, and my girlfriend was aware of a good-sized sled dog being held there.

I made my way to the pound after hours, to avoid having to pay what I believed to be exorbitant pound fees, climbed the six-foot fence and nervously let myself down among the growling dogs. I readily identified the dog in question. It was the biggest, most broad-chested husky I had ever seen. I got a collar and chain on him, put one arm under his belly, and gripped his collar with the other. In one quick motion, I heaved him over the fence and into a snow pile on the other side, where my girlfriend had to deal with a bewildered, snarling canine. I scaled the fence, and we got him into the back of the truck.

We collected three more dogs from that compound and now had four dogs, counting my companion Akaitcho. I needed a good lead dog, along with two more dogs, to form a full team of seven. I asked Alex Lafferty, a member of my work crew at the time, if he knew of any experienced dogs that might be available. He said his brother in Fort Resolution had given up trapping the previous year but still had his dogs and that I should contact him.

I headed to Fort Resolution and met with Alex's brother. He said he wasn't interested in selling his dogs. As it turned out, this was just a bargaining ploy that drew me into making larger and larger offers. As I got up to leave in frustration, he ended his bargaining and sold me three of his dogs, the lead dog being one of them. If only I had known more about this particular lead dog's habits, I could have named my price. More about that later.

The last thing on my list of things to get was a pair of snowshoes. My girlfriend knew of traditionally made snowshoes for sale at the nearby village of Indian Cabins. We drove there and looked over their locally made snowshoes. They were the elongated Athabaskan type that stood as tall as me and were commonly used by the Slavey people and recommended for the kind of travel I was planning to do, so I purchased a pair.

I took short practice runs up and down the Hay River, and all went well. The deadline I'd set to leave arrived. I had my sled packed with just enough dried fish to get me to Fort Providence, where I could restock. Morning came and my girlfriend helped me load. Even though we were parting company permanently, there were no hard feelings. I visited her many years later in Edmonton and expressed my regret at the manner of my taking leave that day. It had bothered me, like a nagging toothache, over the years. She was married with two children and was employed in an unusual occupation for a woman at the time: she trained bush pilots.

I hopped aboard the sled and sped northwards, noting the lights of Old Town fading away. I looked ahead into the white wilderness that was Great Slave Lake, with neither an island nor distant landfall in sight. The lead dog was doing his job. He was an older, healthy-looking dog and had the company of his brother trotting along behind him. I was enjoying the comfort of seeing how well the newly assembled dog team was performing. They moved effortlessly for the first two hours as they hauled the heavily loaded sled, with me standing at the back.

Suddenly, without showing any earlier signs of faltering, the leader just stopped and sat down. The rest of the dogs tumbled over each other, tangling the harnesses. I hurried to the front, untangled the dogs and inspected the leader head to toe but found nothing wrong with him. Just as I headed back to the sled, the lead lunged forward without any command and we were off again.

Not more than ten minutes passed when the same thing happened, an instant stop and sit. This occurred a third time, and I observed that the lead's brother was like-minded. He sat when the lead sat. I was to be burdened for much of the trip with this stop-and-start pattern and had to slow the pace of the team to avoid the problem of harnesses getting tangled. Years later, I ran into Alex Lafferty and told him the story of the dogs I had purchased from his brother and the details about the lead's stopping and starting on the trail.

"I guess I should have told you about that," he said with a laugh and a shrug. He went on to tell me that he had borrowed the dogs from his brother to go hunting and the same thing happened to him, forcing him to give up the hunt.

"Why were the two dogs behaving like that?" I said, asking the obvious question.

"That lead dog," he said, "was about nine years old. It spent its life working on my brother's trap line. Every winter, my brother traveled about two hours out from town to get to his trap line. When he got there, he followed the same routine, stopping at frequent intervals to check his traps. Old habits are hard to break."

This simple explanation of ingrained, trap line dog behaviour brought to mind a story I had heard from my father many years ago. It was about a milkman in his hometown of Dublin, Ireland, in the 1930s. This milkman had a lucrative delivery route in the days when milk was delivered using a horse-drawn milk wagon. The milkman was getting on and decided to sell his milk route and retire. A young lad who delivered milk in a nearby neighbourhood got wind of this and approached the elderly milkman with a generous offer for the purchase of his milk route. He was confident he could get more than his money's worth out of the deal, as it was a shorter route than his and had more customers to the mile.

The milkman accepted the young man's offer. When the day came for him to take over the new route, he was up early, headed to the dairy, loaded his milk wagon and set out on his new route at the accustomed time and happy at the thought of the good deal he had made. He was confident that he could cover the route in much less time than the previous owner, who was known to drag himself home at all hours.

The first street of deliveries went even quicker than the young fellow anticipated. When he rounded the corner to continue his deliveries on the next street, the horse came to an unexpected stop. No matter how much coaxing or pulling on the harness the young lad did, he could not get the horse to move. So he sat back in his seat to think this out and noticed he was outside a pub. He decided to ask the publican if he would be interested becoming one of his customers. Sure enough, the publican agreed, and the young man spent a bit of time telling the publican about his good luck purchase.

Out he went, climbed onto his wagon and, without as much as a command or the flick of the whip, the horse jerked the cart into motion. Deliveries went well until they came to the next pub, where the horse stopped once again of its own accord. This was to happen again and again, in front of every pub on the route. The young lad caught on to what was happening and why. He wasn't much of a drinking man himself and likely spent some of his time, as he waited outside pubs, thinking that maybe the deal he had made wasn't such a great bargain after all.

As for my conversation with Alex, I laughed along with him when told me that his brother couldn't give the dogs away in Fort Resolution. Alex probably saw referring me to him as a way to help out a family member, and maybe help me at the same time. I wondered if he had forgotten his own experience with the dogs.

Somewhere between Hay River and Kakisa River, I headed for the shore to take a tea break. As I drew close, the dogs seemed to be unusually alert, ears straight up, like bat ears tweaking on their sonar. I opened the rifle case that lay strapped to the top of the sled as a matter of precaution. Quite unexpectedly, a large flock of snow buntings fluttered up and lit on the willow branches, looking like puffed-up Christmas ornaments. I had never seen such a large flock of these birds. The dogs came to a stop. I watched as the birds rose again in a cloud of white and settled a few feet farther on. I was about to signal the dogs to get moving when I heard the sound of tiny bells jingling. The dogs just sat there, not at all anxious or fearful.

There on the shoreline, a snow fairy came into view, bouncing around on the snow. She was at most three feet tall, dressed in fur as white as the snow around her. Her feet were clad in knee-high mukluks with strings of bells sewn on. Her head was hidden in a hood behind white fur trim, and she wore white mittens attached to a coloured cord that ran over her shoulders, the length of it decorated with white pompoms. I stood stock still, as did the dogs, until one of them gave a yelp. A pair of dark eyes squinted from within the fur hood. She ran and disappeared into the bush.

Bewildered, I staked the dogs, strapped on my snowshoes and trudged over the shoreline snow bank. I caught sight of her as she entered a small cabin partially buried in snow. Smoke rose from the chimney, and I could see movement inside though a small window. I unstrapped the snowshoes and walked over to the cabin entrance. The trapper emerged as I approached. After a short introduction, he asked how I managed to spot the only cabin on that lakeshore, behind such huge drifts. I tried to explain as best I could how I ended up there. He invited me in for tea and bannock, and there in the house stood the furred fairy.

A bush cabin and fish stage

The young family had arrived a few days earlier. The girl's mother took pride in how she had clad her child from head to foot in traditional dress. She explained that she had added the bells so that when the girl was outside playing she would be able to tell that she was still close by. The cabin was small and well-kept, a true northern trapper's abode. A few marten skins hung on drying stretchers, and a number of newly crafted stretchers stood nearby. A frozen marten was in the process of being thawed in preparation for skinning. In one corner there was a bed with a down sleeping bag, on which the little girl perched herself as she eyed me. I was as much a mystery to her as she had been to me minutes before.

This stop was a strange and unexpected experience. I had decided to make this journey to enrich my life through new experiences, and this brief encounter was one affirmation of that decision. I was still young enough to romanticize the couple's seemingly idyllic existence as they lived off the land and raised their family together in such a traditional setting.

I stayed longer than I might otherwise have, because they began telling stories. One of the stories was about a relation of theirs who was muskrat hunting in a canoe when he spotted a man waving franticly from the shoreline. The man had crashed his plane in the wilderness. He had given up hope and concluded that he would probably die out there. So upon being rescued, he believed he should do something in return for his rescuer.

"I want to do something for you by way of thanks," he said to the young man. "What is the one thing you wish for most often?"

"I'd like to be able to fly a plane," the young trapper replied.

"I'll see to it that you get your wish," the pilot told him. After the pilot returned to his home, true to his promise, he returned at a later date, flying a small bush plane. He trained the young man to fly it as he had promised, and then, to the surprise of his rescuer, he made the young man a gift of the bush plane in which he had learned to fly.

As I got ready to leave, the young trapper gave me valuable information about the location of a Renewable Resources cabin at the delta of the Kakisa River, which I could use for shelter that night. He also flagged the dangerous ice conditions in the delta and warned me to be careful there. With that, we shook hands and parted company. I left knowing I wouldn't have to struggle with tent poles on this, my first night on the trail. I headed around the point, where the huge islands of the Mackenzie Delta came into view through the ice fog. When I saw the large checkerboard markers on land that were used as navigation aids by the barges, I knew I was still on track.

I was now close to the mouth of the Kakisa River. The treeline here was set far back from the lake's edge, leaving a shoreline of tall, snow-covered grasses and willow bluffs. I got off the lake and traveled along the shoreline to increase my chances of spotting the Renewable Resources cabin. The dogs struggled to get traction in powder snow and the tall grasses, and I began to realize that I had pushed them and myself a bit too hard on this first day out. I came to a channel, steered the dogs onto it to use as my roadway inland, and shortly after spotted the cabin roof, back in the bush.

Once inside, I saw that there was no firewood. I went out scavenging and eventually found enough to get the stove going, made beds for the exhausted dogs, thawed some fish for them, and unpacked my gear. The cabin was taking a long time to warm up because of large gaps in the chinking. I used moss to fill them but had to resort to also using socks, underwear and a pair of pants.

I slept well. I had a hearty bowl of oatmeal for breakfast and pulled my clothing out of the gaps in the walls, only to find them damp or stiff with frost. I dried them out at the stove and loaded the sled. The dogs were hyper, and as soon as I had untied the sled, they took off with no need for encouragement and headed onto the trail. I recall the thrill I felt at seeing the eagerness of the dogs; they performed like veterans on the wide trail.

Wide trail leading down to Great Slave Lake

It was a bitterly cold day for travel as I traversed the delta, with its many small channels, like the one I had taken to get to the trapper's cabin. To avoid the bad ice where the Kakisa River merged with the Mackenzie, I headed far out onto the Mackenzie and then downriver. Once past the Kakisa junction, I headed back to the shoreline, my goal being to reach Burnt Point, where I intended to take a break and warm up before continuing.

I arrived at Burnt Point earlier than expected, under a clear sky. I made a fire and cooked a lunch and sat by the fire. I looked in the direction of Fort Providence and could make out the ice crossing for the Mackenzie Highway that led to Yellowknife. I could see some eighteen-wheeler trucks in the distance, leaving clouds of grey exhaust hanging in the air as they crossed the ice bridge.

As I sat by the fire, gazing in the direction of the ice road crossing, I could also see in the vapour clouds rising from the rapids. I knew that there were cabins belonging to people from Fort Providence in the area ahead, close to the winter road. I hoped they might have fish I could purchase. Disappointment followed when I arrived at the cabins. There were no fish stages anywhere, and the cabins had the appearance of having been long abandoned. This was just one more sign of the changing times.

I headed for the truck stop further up the highway, where I hoped to rest, eat dinner and set up camp somewhere nearby. I made good time as I traveled the hard-packed snow on the shoulder of the highway. I reached the truck stop, pulled up to the wooden stair and tied the sled to it. There were no vehicles around and just two people inside having coffee. One of them was the owner, a Mr. Arychuck, who took stock of what had come through the door, with hood up and ice-covered scarf around my frostbitten face.

"Where the hell did you come from? Broke down on the highway? You look like you just walked from Yellowknife," he exclaimed.

"No, but close guess. Hay River. I had the help of my dog team," I replied.

"Dog team!" he exclaimed, "Haven't seen one here in years."

"Where do you want me to tie them up?" I asked. He got up and walked outside excitedly, then stood staring in amazement at the team. A dog team had become an oddity, even here at this remote northern outpost. Then he gave me an invitation.

"Tie them up by the motel, and when you've had your supper, join me in the bar."

I tied up the team, cleaned up in the restaurant washroom, had a hot beef sandwich, and wandered into the bar, where the owner sat with two of his employees. He asked a few questions about my journey and then proceeded to tell me how he came to be there, along with a brief history of the area.

One thing in particular he mentioned was that, while trapping as a way of life was fading out in the Dene communities, both of his sons had a very successful trapping season the previous year. This success was driven by the demand for lynx fur in Russia. They were trapping in the area between Edzo and Fort Providence known as Nàhga country, or the land of the Boogeyman. They were unusually well-equipped, with a new Bombardier. They'd earned enough the previous season to make it possible to pay cash for it.

The area they worked had been burnt over in a forest fire eight years previously and was now covered with new-growth forest, ideal conditions for rabbits and, as a result, perfect for lynx to thrive. This had all the appearances of a great success story: two men making a living trapping in a seldom accessed wilderness and harvesting a renewable resource. However, this is one of the prime shelter and grazing areas for the woodland caribou. It is also a habitat for moose and many fur bearers: fox, fisher, lynx and marten.

This unusual geographic region is also a no-go area for the Dene. It is bordered by Great Slave Lake in the south and Great Bear Lake in the north. The area is about seventy-five miles wide by 450 miles in length, half the size of Ireland. This region overlaps several tribal areas, and these tribes have avoided travel in Nagha country for generations. Unlike the Nagha region, the lakes in the nearby Precambrian Shield hold their water and are home to many varieties of plants, marsh grasses and fur-bearing creatures like beaver and muskrat, whereas the Nagha region's ecology does not support this.

There are some unusual natural phenomena in the area, such as a ten-foot-deep pond that a rider could cross on a snowmobile, only to find that, on the return journey, it had collapsed to the lakebed at its center. These disappearing lakes and giant potholes are a dangerous characteristic of the Nagha area. Such phenomena may well have given rise to the legend of the Boogeyman, or Nagha, in the region. Given the taboos related to the area, it would have served well as a wildlife refuge and breeding ground, a stopping-off point for wildlife to refresh and rebuild before moving on, much like the role some national parks play today.

Unfortunately for the Nagha region, in the 1970s, the changes in the culture of the surrounding communities, plus the intrusion of snowmobiles and large Bombardiers like that belonging to the truck stop owner's sons, have all had a negative impact on the role of the Nagha region as a form of wildlife preserve. The legends are no longer a deterrent to people accessing the resources here, be they game, timber or subsurface minerals. Woodland caribou that frequent this region are now regarded as a threatened species.

As I got up and excused myself to go and feed the dogs and set up the tent, Mr. Arychuck told me to get a motel room key from the cook and that my breakfast and beer were on the house.

"It's not often we get someone traveling through here in the old-fashioned way," he said with a smile. He also mentioned that there was a fellow who was homesteading on the Horn River, a potato farmer who would be happy to have me as a visitor. This gave me peace of mind for the night and a destination for tomorrow.

The next morning, I set out after a hearty breakfast and headed along the almost deserted highway to Fort Providence, where I hoped to buy fish or get dog food from the Northern Store. When I arrived, I asked customers and employees if they knew anyone in town with fish for sale. Nobody knew of anyone, so I went to plan B, store-bought dog food. All the store had was a fifteen-pound bag, which I purchased, and then I headed off to continue my 300-mile trek, expecting, like Alexie, to live off the land. This was taking a risk, but I pressed on in the belief that it would all work out.

The road had not been plowed in quite a while and had four-foot drifts with the occasional section of flat surface. Up and down the sled went, with bone-jarring regularity. It was a painfully slow and exhausting experience for both the dogs and myself, until we reached the Horn River. I spotted signs of an old snowmobile track there and a small house with smoke rising from the chimney. This was the residence of the potato farmer I had been told about. There were no signs in the snow of anyone having come in or out of the house recently, and if it were not for the smoke I would have been convinced that no one lived there. I did the unusual thing in Dene country; I knocked on the door. No response. I knocked again; still no answer. I tried the door, but it was locked, something very unusual in the North. Finally, the door was unlocked and opened slightly. A thin-faced man peered out, looking puzzled. I introduced myself. At any other home in the North, the door would have opened and I'd have been ushered in and offered tea, but not here.

"What do you want?" he asked curtly.

I explained that I was just passing by and had been told about his place by Mr. Arychuck at the restaurant and hoped he wouldn't mind if I came in and warmed up. He apologized for keeping me at the door and explained that they had never had a visitor in wintertime. He explained that they didn't hear the knock because he and his wife were in the cellar, rotating their seed potatoes to keep them from freezing. The man was obviously ill at ease.

I entered the cabin directly into a very small kitchen. The man's wife gave me a passing glance as she poured water sparingly from a pail into a sink to wash her hands. She never made eye contact with me during the time

I was there—two nights, as it turned out. We sat at a small table while she made tea and he told me of his struggles to homestead this small delta plain close to the shores of Mills Lake. He had been fighting with the government and the local Band for the right to homestead there. Unfortunately, this was at the time when land claims were being addressed and one of the Dene alliance's preconditions for the process was that no outsiders would be allowed to stake claims or set up homesteads on lands that were part of the claims negotiations. One lone farmer up against the Indigenous land claims process was a no-win situation. I asked if he knew a spot close by where I could set up camp. He suggested that I spend the night in the cellar and be responsible for keeping the Coleman light going all night there.

"Why do you need the light on all night?" I asked.

"It keeps the potatoes from freezing," he replied. "The lantern throws enough heat to keep the frost from getting to them. We usually take turns at night refilling the lantern every few hours." He led me down the narrow, steep steps into the cellar.

There was a clear area, about a body length, where they stood to sort the potatoes, and in the middle they set up the lantern. Mounds of potatoes were spread around the walls. The man and his wife occupied their winters like coal miners, on their hands and knees, working deep into the corners of the crawl spaces, moving their potatoes about. I moved a large number of potatoes off a wooden shelf that stood a foot off the floor to lay out my five-star blanket on it. I went outside and fed the dogs. When I returned, the couple were climbing up another ladder into the attic, where they went to bed. They pulled their ladder up behind them.

I descended mine into what was probably the warmest spot in the house. In keeping with his instructions, I got up to refill the lantern every few hours. When morning came, I crawled out of the basement and checked things outside to find that a storm had blown in overnight, stranding me where I didn't particularly want to be.

I was invited to stay until the storm blew over and was told that the three of us would spend the day rotating the potatoes. So, no warm stove to sit around for a chat or to share stories, just a day's hard work moving potatoes. The man and I crawled to the farthest corners of the basement, filled baskets with cold potatoes and passed them to his wife, who, after emptying the basket in a warmer area, passed it back to us full of warm potatoes she had gathered from the potato pile behind her. All day long, this transfer of spuds went on. I know we had tea breaks and must have eaten at some point, but I have no memory of what was on the menu. To add to that, during all this time, little or nothing was said.

The following day, the storm abated. As I prepared to leave, the potato farmer sat with me over my map and explained what I could expect upriver. He explained that when I got to Wallace Creek I would be close to the highway, which would be an option for me to take if I got into any difficulty. The information he gave was sketchy, but every little thing learned from local people on a trip like this was important, so I took it all in. I was of the impression that my help had been appreciated. I expressed my thanks for the temporary shelter and left.

It felt good to be back on the trail. The snow was hard-packed and I made good time. I was about seven miles out on Mills Lake when I identified the landmark I was looking for, an abandoned Quonset hut on the Canol Trail. I continued on my way as the snow conditions began to change dramatically. The potato farmer had told me a chinook off the Yukon Mountains had blown through a while back and brought with it a mid-winter rain. I now found myself challenged by the conditions left in the wake of that chinook.

I had placed Akaitcho in the lead dog position, and he appeared to be doing a great job until we hit an unusual crust of ice on the snow surface, likely as a result of that chinook. It was a brittle coating that gave way under paw pressure in chunks the size of the dog's paw. While this interrupted the momentum of the dogs, it had another, more serious impact, as I would soon discover.

After a mile or so of this, I noticed that Akaitcho began to stop repeatedly and later began to whimper, something I had never heard him do before. I went back to help clear the snow build-up between his toes that I thought might be the problem. As I bent down to do this, I froze at what I saw. Bare flesh was exposed on both of his front paws, from his ankle upwards, for about two inches. The ice crust he had been breaking through as lead had flayed his front legs. The skin was severed around both ankles and rolled up like a sock toward the knee joints. I gently unfurled the skin back into place, went back to the sled and dug out a pair of socks, which I cut to create two sleeves. I slipped these coverings over his damaged legs and tied them in place with sinew. I unhooked his harness and placed him on top of the sled. He lay there quietly as I checked the other dogs. Thankful that they were fine, I readjusted the harness and set out again. But this time, I redirected the team into the middle of the river channel, where the snow was hard-packed and didn't present the hazard that caused the damage.

It was then I remembered the potato farmer's advice, that if I got into trouble on this stretch of river I could access the highway, which was about thirty-five miles away. The diminished dog team had to get there before nightfall. Akaitcho jumped off the sled every once in a while and ran alongside. I stopped to check his legs periodically, to rewrap them as needed, and snugged him back in the sled after each excursion. I located the cutline I was looking for just as it was getting dark.

I set up camp, gathered wood for the night, and got a small fire going to heat up food for the dogs and myself. The tent was cozy and warm, and after all the chores were done I spent time tending to Akaitcho and contemplating my next step. Considering the combination of things—the warnings I had been given about open water, the unpredictable ice conditions ahead, the shortage of dog food and Akaitcho's condition—I came to the decision to rest myself and the dogs here and make my way to the highway to hitchhike the 150 miles to Fort Simpson, to get food for myself and the dogs.

The next morning, I fed the dogs and looked up the cutline to see what I was up against. It was all uphill, with heavy snow cover. I got an early start in the hope of getting back to the dogs late that night. I placed Akaitcho inside the tent on the caribou rug, gave him a small amount of dry meat I had on hand, and with that I headed for Fort Simpson. It was about seven miles uphill in deep snow. Even though the temperature was exceedingly low, I began to overheat from the exertion and decided to hang up my down-filled jacket in a tree, to be retrieved on my return.

After hours of hard slogging, I made it to the highway, removed my snowshoes and felt the welcome relief of solid ground beneath my moccasins. With the snowshoes tied on my back and gun over my shoulder, I strode along, hopeful that a truck or car would come by shortly. Twelve or thirteen miles later, I was still going, with no sign of traffic. Fortunately, I had a muskrat hat folded over my ears and cheeks, along with a scarf, so no exposed skin. I had on layers of clothing and walked at a steady pace, all of which helped me to get by without the parka. I decided to stop, build a fire by the side of the highway and wait for a ride to come by.

The location I picked had plenty of dead wood and was on a bend in the road where the fire would be seen by oncoming traffic. I dug into the snowbank and built a fire. The heat melted a cavern in the snowbank which I lined with spruce boughs, and I settled in and fed the fire. I had set out thinking I'd be in Fort Simpson by early afternoon, be done shopping and have had dinner in town before heading back to my campsite. Night fell on that plan.

I sat there, nodding on and off and hoping to see a set of headlights shortly. A while later, I saw the movement of some kind of animal close by. I instinctively grabbed my gun and strained my eyes to make out what it was. It eventually came into range of the firelight; it was the one thing in the world that would never pose a threat to me—my dog, Akaitcho. Somehow, he had managed to get out of the tent and followed my scent all that distance. All I could think was, "How the hell did you get loose? And please tell me there aren't six more dogs trailing behind you."

He was alone. I dropped the gun, jumped up and hugged him hard. The socks were still in place, and all appeared well with him. Just having him there gave my spirits a lift. As I gathered my stuff together, getting ready to move on, I heard the distinct sound of tires crunching on snow.

I jumped out onto the highway and waved down an approaching truck. The driver drew alongside as he rolled down his window.

"Where's your vehicle?" he asked. I explained to him there was no vehicle and how I came to be there.

"How long have you been waiting here?"

"Overnight." I told him.

"Do you have any idea how lucky you are that I came along?"

"No," I said and asked, "Why?"

"The highway is closed down because it's one of the coldest days on record for this area; it close to minus sixty degrees. There isn't a vehicle coming or going anywhere for 300 miles. Lucky for you, I was ordered to do a highway check," he replied, still somewhat bewildered.

I grabbed my gear, along with Akaitcho, and got into the truck. He turned it around and headed for the Department of Highways camp, located halfway between Trout River and Red Knife River. He dropped me off there and told me I could spend the night in the trailer and, later in the morning, he would return and take me to Fort Simpson.

I had a good night's sleep. The next morning, he gave me a ride to the Hudson Bay Store in Fort Simpson, where I bought the dog food and bandages. While there, I met the manager, Dave Collie, who had also been the manager of the store in Fort Rae where I got to know him. He told me that I was welcome to stay at his place in Fort Simpson if I wished. I also talked to an elderly Slavey woman, Sara Hardisty, who, when she heard my story from the highway guy, offered to let me stay at her place in Jean Marie River on my way through to Fort Simpson. She made the unusual request that, on the unlikely chance I should come across a moose on my travels, to please shoot it for her as she needed the hide and meat. She told me that she was a widow, and if anyone complained about my shooting the moose, I was to tell them that it was for her.

I spent another night at the trailer and left Akaitcho there to rest up while I was driven back to the cutline and hiked to the campsite. The dogs showed no signs of distress at being abandoned for so long a time. I fed them, took down my tent and headed up towards the highway again. I hadn't gone far before I had the remarkable good luck to bag a three-year-old moose for Sara Hardisty. I skinned it, fed the dogs with some of the meat, and loaded the sled with the rest. I made it to the highway, but it was hard going with the top-heavy sled. A short while later, the highway guy came by once again, we loaded the bulk of the meat into his truck, and I arranged to pick it up from him later at his trailer.

While I was in Fort Simpson, I was told about a cabin located by the Red Knife River, which was my new destination. It was owned by Stan the Man, and I was told I could stop off there. Later that day I located it, a beautifully built log cabin. I sat back on the bunk bed admiring the log workmanship and the handcrafted furniture. I even gave a passing thought to staying there for the winter, an indication I was still impulse-driven. There were some marten stretchers on the wall, and in one corner there was a string of miniature stretchers. I couldn't figure out their use and even considered an off-the-wall explanation: could the trapper have become so bored that he was trapping and skinning rodents for entertainment?

Years later, I worked with Stan's son, Allen Lerocque, and told him what I had speculated about the mini stretchers. He laughed hard as he explained that they were for stretching and drying the leg hide of the marten.

The next morning, I made it to the Department of Highways trailer, where Akaitcho was resting. The highway guy helped me load the dogs, sled and moose meat onto his truck and gave us a ride to the Jean Marie winter road intersection, where we unloaded and I harnessed the team once more. I was now on a narrow road through the bush, leading to a small Slavey village at the junction of the Jean Marie and Mackenzie rivers.

I arrived at Sara Hardisty's one-room log house; she was there along with her thirteen-year-old granddaughter. She could hardly believe her eyes as I arrived, fully loaded with moose meat and a fine moose hide. She inspected the hide and admired the skinning job I had done, saying it would make a number of good moccasins to sell. I staked out the dogs and she cooked up a meal of moose.

She told me, as so many others of late had, that nobody went hunting anymore and that the last time anyone from the community had shot a moose was about five years ago. She attributed the loss of the traditional hunt to the impact of the residential schools, and also because most of the adult males were now working in oil exploration camps. While I was sharing the meal with Sara, she told me of an incident that had happened recently involving a local trapper.

The trapper had been traveling that winter on the same overland trail I intended to take. There had been a wind storm in the area, and a lot of trees had come down. One huge spruce tree had fallen across the trail the trapper was following. He went to inspect the situation, to figure out how he would get around the obstruction. Suddenly, he fell through the snow-covered branches lying on the trail into a large cavern-like hole under the tree limbs. When he hit bottom, he found to his dismay that he had landed in a bear's den. Fortunately, he managed to get out without disturbing the hibernating bear. She warned me to be careful because the tree hadn't been moved and, to the best of everyone's knowledge, the bear might still be there.

Early the following morning she asked around the community if anyone had information about sled travel conditions to Fort Simpson. The answer was bad news all round. There was no overland trail broken, and river travel this year was also bad. Nobody had been able to make it upriver this year using snowmobiles because of huge ice jams. The highway was ruled out, because it had been freshly scraped down to gravel for eighty miles or more. I harnessed up the team. The river seemed the best of the bad choices, and so the river it was. I left Sara most of the moose meat, and she provided fish for the dogs.

The river route ahead looked beautiful and tranquil. My destination was Rabbit Skin River. All went well for the first few hours as I traveled along the east shoreline in unexpectedly good snow and ice conditions, until I came up against a shattered ice field. I have never seen the likes of it before or since. The ice had formed in early fall to a thickness of about six to eight inches and had fragmented, due to changing weather and water conditions, into huge, glass-like shards standing frozen in place as high as eight feet in some areas and all close packed, at different angles. They formed a formidable barrier, with no clear path through the maze for the sled.

First, I attempted to navigate it without snowshoes. It was difficult to find good footing and I ran the constant risk of sliding into gaps between the walls of ice. On occasion, the sled ended up at a precipitous height above the dogs, putting them at risk of having it careen down onto them. I resorted to tying the sled at a distance of ten feet behind the last dog to overcome the problem. It was slow going. At times I strapped on my five-foot-long snowshoes and used them to straddle gaps, using a long pole for balance. The sharp edges of the ice slabs took their toll on the snowshoes, shredding the babiche in places. I cut the sleeves of my shirt into strips, which I used to repair the damage. It took a long time to make it through, but I managed to make it in one piece.

I got to Rabbit Skin River and crossed over to the other side of the Mackenzie, where I found a snowmobile trail to follow. Before I got going, I built a fire and made tea. As I sat there, I looked back at the river and the ice nightmare I had come through. It looked hauntingly beautiful from a distance. I went back to the sled and headed toward Fort Simpson.

The geography of the area was one of steep hills and valleys, unfolding with monotonous regularity. As I emerged out of one of the valleys, I spotted a set of snowshoe tracks and was perplexed. All I can say by way of analogy is that they were the snowshoe tracks of the Jolly Green Giant. The person's stride was enormous.

After travelling from seven in the morning to midnight, I arrived at a small cabin on the shoreline close to the highway, stopped, fed the dogs, staked and settled them down on spruce bedding, and headed to the highway. This time, I caught a ride almost right away and got dropped off at an acquaintance's place. He put me up for the night.

The next morning, when we went back to pick up the dogs, I told him about the enormous snowshoe tracks. He had a good laugh and informed me that a Mr. Mouse—yes, that was his name—owned a cabin there and was known to be a man with an extraordinary stride. He added that Mr. Mouse was probably the last full-time trapper in the area and that his family continued to live in the traditional way. I had a sense that I may have trod the trail used by one of the last of a generation of traditional trappers in the Fort Simpson area. It was another sad indication of the changing times.

My journey had been difficult and was undertaken without a schedule, pushing my limits and living on the edge. Fort Franklin was my original destination, but I could have stopped anywhere along the way, much like Alexie's whimsical traveling ways. Fort Simpson was a small town with ready access to the Nahanni region, which attracted me. So I terminated the trip in Fort Simpson and started looking for work the day I arrived.

I was soul-searching at the time, but I was also beginning to see that losing myself in the wilderness was not an answer to my quest for a sense of purpose. However, I undertook a number of journeys similar to the Hay River trek before I shook off my wandering, risk-taking ways.

FORT SIMPSON AND HAY RIVER IN 1977

Fort Simpson was of interest to me because it was a frontier town right on the edge of the Nahanni region, with access to great rivers and wild country in all directions. This was big-timber country the likes of which a log builder like myself could only dream of. If I could find work, I made up my mind to try settling in here. Unfortunately, I found out that because of the collapse of the McKenzie Valley pipeline project, there was little prospect of getting work. Even so, I decided to try it out here for a while. I got a ride back to Hay River to pick up my tools and belongings.

When I got to Hay River, I dropped in to see my friend, Dan Sonfrere, at the Hay River Reserve. My timing couldn't have been better from the work viewpoint. Dan told me he had plans to build a log community hall and asked if I would be willing to build it. The materials had already arrived in Hay River, courtesy of a government grant. Here I was, in the wrong place at the right time, with another chance to do what I did so well, log building. So, Fort Simpson went on the back burner.

I told him that I would be delighted to take on the project and took up residence in an abandoned house just outside the community that had holes in the floor and no heat, electricity or water. It was not exactly a step up from the accommodation I had in Fort Simpson. Added to that, the job was not a money maker for me. I undertook it because Dan had made the request and because of the nature of the work involved.

While visiting the Reserve to look for staff, I dropped by to ask Chief Dan if there was anyone he would recommend to serve as a role model for others on the work crew. He suggested Frank Fabian. I went to Frank's house and asked if he was interested in coming to work for me. Both he and his wife were in disbelief that someone would drop by their home with a job offer. I also asked if Frank's wife was willing to cook supper for me on a daily basis and permit me to join them for supper. I said I would pay her for her work. I told them both to take time to think about my offer and get back to me.

The next day, Frank showed up for work and, much to my delight, said he and his wife had agreed to accept both offers. It was such a welcome change for me to share supper with them, with their children laughing and playing around the place while I ate. Frank lived up to Chief Dan's description of him. He was one of the hardest working of the many dependable Dene workers I hired over the years.

I got settled in and started work on the community hall. This time I had the luxury of logs of uniform size, milled down to eight inches in diameter. I hired an entirely Indigenous crew who came from either Hay River or Fort Resolution. The work on the building went very well, largely because of people like Frank Fabian, who took pride in their work and in working together as part of a team.

Frank Fabian and family

THE HORN PLATEAU EXPERIENCE

I stayed in Fort Simpson for about a year, doing odd jobs and living in a cramped eighteen-foot camper trailer until my friend, Rene Lamothe, told me about a three-bedroom house available for rent. I rented it and moved my belongings there, looking forward to the luxury of having a house all to myself.

One of the men, who had worked with me on several jobs, was also a good friend: Allen Lerocque. He came by my place and asked if I had lined up any work yet. He was Métis, about two years younger than me, and had the wisdom of an eighty-year-old elder. He was a heavy snuff chewer and carried himself with the demeanor of a Clint Eastwood character in a spaghetti western. I told him I hadn't managed to find anything yet.

"I have this idea that I'm giving some thought to," he said. "My girlfriend's aunt, Mary Louise Norwegian, has a family trap line, and the Game Office has started a program to encourage trappers to get back into trapping. They're offering to supply the building materials to build a new or rebuild an old cabin. There's no money for labour, just a grub stake. So what do you think?"

"And where do we fit in?" I asked.

"We go to the Norwegian trap line, build the family cabin for the grubstake, and we can make some money trapping while we're there. I'm told they left all their traps behind on the line," he replied.

"I'll think about it," I said, thinking, not likely. I continued to scour the town for work for a few days but found nothing and consequently contacted Allen to get further details.

"If we decide to do this, how do I get to take my dogs?" I asked.

"They'll fly them out," he said.

"What about dog food?" I pressed further.

"I'm told the cabin is located on a lake where the fishing is good, so we can set a net there," he replied. It was sounding better now, so I began to add to the plan.

"We can use my dogs to haul the logs. I've got my chainsaw and all the tools; I even have a fish net," I said. We went to Mary Louise's house to discuss the plan. She was the sister to some prominent community members, Leo, Albert and Roderick Norwegian, the latter being a well-known Nahanni River outfitter. She told us the family history of working the area where her father's cabin and trap line were located. No one had trapped there for several years. She was a widow who lived alone with her children in Fort Simpson and was hoping to get the cabin in good enough shape to take them trapping there. She appeared to be someone who knew what she wanted and was not caught up in the partying that was going on in the community at that time. After that friendly, informative chat, Allen and I agreed to take on the project.

A day later, Mary Louise informed us that Philip Bonnetrouge, Allen's father in-law, along with his youngest son, Eric, were to come with us. Mary Louise explained that Philip had been the best trapper in Fort Simpson; he was on record for harvesting the most marten furs in the North. She explained that it was important for his son, Eric, to see his father at his best out on the land. Unfortunately, what I didn't know when I agreed to take on the project was that the grub stake package was for a single trapper and not for four people working on the cabin. The Game Department supplied the funds to Mary Louise to purchase the food.

The day before leaving, Allen and I went to see Roderick Norwegian, who had trapped in the area with his father. We hoped to pick his brain about the region and the trap line before heading out. He told us about the seismic lines running through the surrounding region, and the locations where he and his dad had hung their traps in the trees some years back. He showed us the location of the lake on the map, now known as Hay Lake, and indicated a spot on the shore where the old cabin was located.

He then provided us with an invaluable piece of information. He took a ruler, slapped it down on a map we had with us, drew three staggered lines and handed it back to me. These lines indicated the location of cutlines in the area and the directions in which they ran.

"If you choose to come back to Fort Simpson by land, you could follow these cutlines, but be warned, it would be tough going because of new-growth trees that'll be there by now." Looking back, I know I didn't grasp the implications of that piece of information.

Just before we were about to leave, he told us a story of one of his journeys up near the area we were going, to give us an idea of the linkages of the river systems. He said that he used to paddle north up the Mackenzie to the Willow River and then follow the Willow, which flowed down from the Horn Plateau. He would then wind south, parallel to the Mackenzie, and climb high into the Plateau. The Willow got smaller and smaller as they neared its source. After a short, swampy portage, they were on the divide of the Plateau and at the source of the Horn River. From there, it was all downhill to Fort Providence on the Mackenzie, and they could come full circle back to Simpson. A great muskrat spring hunt circuit.

The next morning, on the way to the plane, we picked up Eric Bonnetrouge at Albert Norwegian's house. Albert mentioned that he had a cabin on the Rabbit Skin River and that he would be trapping out of there on Mustard Lake, which was about halfway between the cabin and Fort Simpson. He suggested that we might find him there if we decided to come out by dog team before Christmas. In the event he was not there, he assured us that there was plenty of food stored at his cabin. I thanked him for the information but let him know that we had already arranged for the flight out.

We loaded the truck with all our personal gear and my tools and were ready to head to the airport. Allen Lerocque, about twenty-five years old; Eric Bonnetrouge, a youth of seventeen; and me, age twenty-seven, piled into the truck along with five dogs, a sled and my SBX-11 radio. We then headed to Simpson Island Airport, where we met Philip Bonnetrouge, our sixty-two-year-old former trapper. His son Eric was all keen and ready to work in the bush for the first time and to learn everything he could from his dad.

Mary Louise arrived at the airport as we were loading, only to tell us she hadn't had time to buy the groceries and would head back to town right away to get them. This was not a good sign, but we were very rushed getting ourselves ready. She returned with a couple of boxes of groceries, some oats and flour.

There's something not right here, I thought to myself. We're to build a cabin for a grubstake that fits into a couple of small boxes? That's it? Regrettably, I didn't act upon this or express my concern.

It was bitterly cold that day as we took off. I remember feeling discouraged rather than excited about the venture, given the way it had started. The plane climbed up beyond the Mackenzie River. I had a great view of the cutlines crisscrossing the landscape for mile upon mile, the remnants of work related to seismic lines cut about ten years previous, the lines Roderick Norwegian had described and sketched out on the map for me.

As we approached the lake, Allen asked the pilot to circle the area to see if we could spot signs of game. The only signs we saw were about fifteen miles from our lake, which was bad news as far as any hunting was concerned. As we came in close to the lake, I asked Philip to point out where the old cabin was located on the shoreline. He was unable to.

We touched down and had the pilot taxi to the middle of the lake, where we unloaded everything because we had no idea where on the lakeshore we would be working and could move the stuff once that was decided. We staked the dogs to the lumber pile, and Allen and I strapped on our snowshoes to scout the shoreline more closely for signs of a cabin, while Philip and Eric huddled for shelter beside the building materials. The shore was treed with willows poking out of heavy snowdrifts, and behind that was the remnant of a forest fire some years back.

As Allen and I tromped off towards the shoreline, the plane roared by in a flurry of snow that set the dogs howling. The sound of the plane faded to nothing as it disappeared behind the hills and the dogs settled down. A heavy silence settled over what would be our work site for many months to come.

Philip and Eric followed us and struggled to make their way in our snowshoe trail. It was curious that they had come into this white wilderness without snowshoes. When Philip caught up with us at the shoreline, he had a perplexed look on his face as he scanned the snow drifts, still looking for signs of a cabin that to all appearances wasn't there. It had been twenty or more years since he had trapped this area with the Norwegians. After scanning the shoreline he identified a stretch covered by a larger drift, likely an indication of the buried cabin.

Allen cut down four small trees. We trimmed them and made four poles about sixteen feet long to use for probing the drift. He made his way up onto the large drift and stuck one of the poles into it.

"I hope the damn cabin didn't burn to the ground in the forest fire," he mumbled. We were surprised as his pole went down to a depth of about ten feet, easily deep enough to hide a flat-roofed cabin. "This'll be an old-timer's cabin, with a flat roof covered with moss," he said, as we poled steadily in the hope of hitting some kind of resistance. Philip and Eric couldn't help with the poling very much, without snowshoes. After a while, I broke off to cut firewood and built a fire for Philip and Eric. Allen kept on poling. I got Eric to bring the dogs and tie them up close by. Then suddenly, Allen called out excitedly.

"I've hit something!"

Philip and Eric managed to scramble onto the now well-packed snowdrift to help establish where the outer walls of the cabin were. Philip indicated where the doorway was probably located. We removed our snow shoes, dug down, and located the door. It opened inward and had a large step down to floor level, below grade.

It was a very small cabin. Interestingly, it was made from eighteen-inch diameter logs, but none of the trees we could see in the area was even close to that size. It was about eight-by-twelve, with one narrow double bunk at the back, which was broken, and a small log stool. The roof was about six and a half feet high and the logs were in good shape. There was one sixteen-inch-square window. A wood stove stood against another wall, its stovepipe rusted paper thin. Fortunately, Allen had had the foresight to ensure that the stovepipe intended for the new cabin came in on our flight.

As we entered, we saw the descendants of the mice Philip had for company twenty years ago all scuttling about. We set up the stove and lit the fire.

It was getting late, so I hooked up the dogs and snowshoed with them to the other shoreline to haul some additional firewood, while Phillip and Eric cleaned up the cabin and Allen whipped together another bed and repaired the old one. When I got back, there was a roaring fire going in the stove and the lantern was lit. With all these tasks out of the way, we sorted through our gear and set up our sleeping spaces for the night.

In the meantime, Philip, who was designated cook, made some bannock with difficulty, not having a table on which to work it. As he struggled in these difficult conditions, we tried to problem-solve the rest of our situation. We rummaged through the grocery boxes and were dumbfounded at what we found there. I noted the contents: two heads of lettuce, three cartons of eggs, a quantity of flour and baking powder, rolled oats, raisins, a slab of bacon, a pail of lard, tea, coffee, sugar, and a few loaves of bread, peanut butter and jam. That was it! Allen opened the door of the cabin and climbed outside. I followed. We stood in silence for a while.

"Thanks for not saying anything, Kieran, no sense getting Eric all worried," he commented.

I understood and observed, "We're sure isolated here. There's no one for miles and miles."

"Yeah, nobody traps anymore. We'll set a net in the morning and hopefully have some fish by nightfall," Allen replied, as he tried to put a good spin on things. There was no sense bemoaning what we couldn't fix.

On the first day of our stay, the temperatures rose dramatically and the recent snow began to melt, creating overflow problems for the building materials sitting in the middle of the lake. So Eric and I used the dogs to move the lumber before the temperature dropped again and everything bonded to the ice. Meanwhile, Allen punched test holes around the lake to determine where the lake would have enough depth to set a five-foot-deep net. Having moved the lumber, I joined him. It wasn't until the following morning that we found water with a deep enough clearance to suspend the 150-foot by five-foot-deep net.

Where do we set that net?

"It'll do for now, but if we get a long cold snap, it could freeze to the bottom of the ice if we're not careful," Allen cautioned. With the help of Eric, we hacked out the series of holes required to set the net. Once finished, we cut the sticks and poles used to put the net in place. It was a complicated process requiring considerable teamwork.

We went back to the cabin with one important task on our minds: to set up the high-frequency transmitter aerial for making contact with the outside world. We stomped around in deep snow till late in the evening, trying to pick up a signal. Unfortunately, there wasn't a trace of a signal, no matter what direction we faced. This was a major concern, should we require outside help. We headed back into the cabin, exhausted and disappointed. Close to ten o'clock that night, when we were ready to snuff out the lantern, Allen suggested that we check the net.

"We owe ourselves a good meal," he said. His timing was just right, for Eric got excited at the thought of seeing the fruits of his labour setting the net. Off we trekked and full of anticipation to haul the net up for the first time. Success! What a great boost to our spirits this was. We had netted two northern pike, three or four losh or ling cod, and a trout. We fried up something considered a delicacy, the large five-by-three-inch losh livers, which were taken, believe it or not, from fish only two feet long. We fed the famished dogs after a long day of hauling wood through the overflow.

Checking the fish net

After three days of getting settled, setting the net, placing snares for rabbits and moving the lumber, we set out to find a suitable site for the new cabin. We located an appropriate spot and cleared an area about twenty feet square on which to build it. The scarcity of logs in the immediate vicinity led to difficult distance hauling for the dogs. The trees we did find were nothing like those used to build the old cabin. They were a conical shape, around seventeen inches in diameter at the bottom and two inches at the top, and grew to a height of around sixteen feet. Their lower branches were spread out and buried in deep snow, making it very difficult to get at the tree trunks to cut them down. As a result we only skidded four logs that first day of hauling.

We cut trenches through the shoreline snowdrifts to enable the dogs to haul the logs out onto the lake and up to the new cabin site without too much difficulty. We called it a day as a storm blew in. Allen and Eric hauled the net up and brought some fish back. We settled in and that night feasted on the few white fish we had netted.

White fish

By morning, the storm had abated and we had to dig ourselves out. It was cramped quarters in that tiny cabin and difficult to have a conversation, due to the clutter of garments hanging up to dry. We understood what was meant by cabin fever and tried to be fair with one another as we struggled with who got to sit where. We did manage to avoid serious disagreement, but the discomfort made for an uneasy atmosphere at times.

Over the following days, we established a routine, harvesting logs, shaping them, building the walls, and around mid-afternoon someone checked the net. By this time we had come to the conclusion that we had caught the only trout in the lake that first day. Our diet was now composed of losh, some whitefish and jackfish, morning, noon and night. We boiled, fried, and baked fish, and the stench impregnated our clothing, blankets and the very logs of the cabin itself.

As the days passed, we ran out of white gas for the lantern and primus stove. We fell back on candles for light. Allen took a day off once in a while and walked for miles in search of the traps that were supposedly hanging on trees at designated places along the cutlines. At the same time, he searched for signs of moose or woodland caribou. He inevitably returned empty-handed, and we concluded that someone must have gathered up the traps. We were nearing the stage of placing the last logs on the walls of the new cabin when we discovered that we were out of lard for cooking. We had asked Philip to ration it, because we had no idea when the plane might come.

The promised plane with the groceries and roofing supplies was overdue. We were finished the floor and the walls and were ready for the roof, and Christmas was coming. Summing up our situation, we were without lard, baking powder and oats, out of white fuel for primus and lantern, without traps, and more important, without radio contact with the outside world. All we had left was flour and the fish catch. We had not snared a rabbit in weeks.

It was the fish that kept us going. We tried to view things in a positive light by talking about moving into the new cabin when it was finished. That was the situation when we heard the drone of an approaching plane early one afternoon. We ran to the airstrip we had set up close to the new cabin. By God, were we happy!

The plane circled and landed. After quickly unloading the plywood, lumber, shingles and nails, I looked around for the groceries.

"Where are the groceries?" I asked the pilot.

"What groceries?" he asked. "I wasn't given any groceries. But I was asked to bring back any extra moose meat you might have. Do you have any?"

"No," I told him. "We don't have any moose meat, and we're virtually out of food of any kind."

"Not a thing?" he queried, showing surprise. He never followed up on that comment, as he fumbled around in his pockets for something. He remembered that he had a letter to deliver. He dug it out and gave it to Allen, who read it quickly.

"Holy shit!" he exclaimed. "My wife's been medivac'ed to Yellowknife, and she needs me back right away. She's having our baby early and there are complications. I've got to leave."

He took off to the cabin and grabbed his gear. As he boarded the plane, he yelled, "as soon as I get to Simpson, I'll tell my sister-in-law about the situation and have her send the groceries as soon as possible." Just as the door was about to close, he yelled one last thing over the roar of the engine: "I noticed the ice was getting thick and close to the top of the net; be sure to check on it regularly." With that, the door closed and, before I could take in what had just happened, the plane was gone.

Everything about this episode is a blur. Cold in body and spirit, we stood in shocked silence. The three of us trudged back to the cabin without speaking a word, trying to come to grips with the loss of our skilled work partner, the absence of groceries, and the speed with which everything had happened. We didn't go back to work that day. The cargo remained sitting on the ice. The next morning, I got a better grip on myself, knowing that Allen was on his way to Fort Simpson and would relay the state of affairs to Mary Louise.

Days passed with no contact. As it got closer to Christmas, we still maintained hope that the plane would arrive, but in the back of my mind I was beginning to worry. We agreed to ration the bannock. We continued to work on the cabin with very little enthusiasm. Our catch of fish was decreasing, and we were catching only losh or scrawny jackfish and just feeding the dogs once every second day. We rarely used them for work.

Every time we netted jackfish, I gutted them and saved the stomachs with the intention of having something special if we ended up at the cabin for Christmas. We had a small stockpile of frozen, drowned losh we used for the dogs and a few frozen fresh losh and jackfish to keep us going for a few days, but that was it. We needed a supply plane.

I skipped checking the net for a couple of days and went back to it with hopes of a larger catch. We chipped out the holes, latched onto the net and pulled. Our worst nightmare was realized. Allen's words came back to haunt me. The net was frozen to the bottom of the ice, and we couldn't pull it free.

"What am I to do?"

I was still at a loss to understand why no help had arrived, since Mary Louise, the pilot and Allen knew we were in trouble. The rest of Philip and Allen's family must know by now. I could only conclude that we had been forgotten. More than that, I now believed that we had been abandoned.

We were down to our last three days of food at best, and if we stayed where we were much longer, we soon wouldn't have the energy to cut firewood, so I made the critical decision. I told Eric and Phillip that I had to leave for Fort Simpson in the morning. There was no more conversation, just silence; wasted and worn, we went to sleep.

The following morning, we heard the drone of an airplane in the distance. We rushed out onto the ice, scanned the horizon and listened. It was circling somewhere else. The sound faded to nothing on the other side of the hills. After a short while, we heard it again as it took off, and the sound faded into the distance once again. It was now only three days till Christmas. We would later find out that he had landed at the wrong cabin with our groceries and thought we had dog-teamed out.

I took stock of our supplies. We had seven fish and a small amount of flour left to feed the three of us, plus the five dogs. Over tea, I asked Philip to make a batch of bannock and then explained my plan. I told him that we had no alternative, and I would have to go for help. I took the gun, the dog team, three of the fish for the dogs, and left the remaining fish for the others. I loaded the sled and set off in the early morning. My destination, Fort Simpson, was 80 miles away but if I saw a moose I would return with the meat.

I arrived at the first cutline that Roderick Norwegian had sketched on my map. From this point on, I had to break trail for the dogs, a couple of hundred yards at a time, through deep snow on an uphill slope and then call them forward. They struggled and at times could not break the sled loose. This meant that I had to backtrack to get the sled moving again. I was walking 300 yards for every one hundred covered by the dogs. If I were travelling without the sled, I would have been out of the valley and at the top of the Horn Plateau by now. The dog team was holding me back, not helping.

Reluctantly, I turned around and made my way back to the cabin. I arrived there disheartened at the loss of a critical day and to find both men still in a depressed state of mind. I had to come up with a different plan.

I ate my daily ration of bannock, bedded the dogs down and dug jackfish stomachs and other food scraps out of our garbage pile. I cooked the stomachs to a crisp on a stick and packaged them, fed the dogs the scraps, and met with Eric and Phillip over tea. We sat by the woodstove as I told them of my plan to make another try, but without the dogs. It was agreed that I would take the gun and they would keep what fish was left.

It was two days before Christmas. I got up early, had tea and bannock by the fire, and drank plenty of water. I pocketed hard candy that Allen had left behind and placed a can of lighter fluid and matches in a plastic bag. I was confident that I could make it in a day to Albert Norwegian's cabin at Rabbit Skin River, where he said he had food stored. He had also said he would likely be trapping out of there in the Mustard Lake area close to Christmas. I was confident that once I got to the halfway mark around Mustard Lake I would find it easier going from there.

I was ready to go at daybreak. I took the machete and left the heavy axe behind, took my gun and shells, my snowshoes, a small teapot and cup. Because I had sweated heavily inside my parka the day before, I chose instead to wear my military trench coat as a replacement, which could also serve as a blanket. Beyond that, moccasins, long underwear, blue jeans, an undershirt and shirt, a down vest and a blue jean jacket made up the rest of my travel clothing.

I stepped out the door of the cabin as well prepared as possible. Eric told me that his dad wanted to speak with me. I turned to Philip, who looked me in the eye and uttered the clearest of any expression I had heard him use since we had arrived.

"You'll never make it," he said. I was initially taken aback by the bluntness of his statement. It was such an emotional moment. I pulled myself together and hugged him.

"Thanks for the advice, Philip," I said. "You know I have to do this; it's our only chance."

It was Christmas Eve morning as I headed down the lake shoreline with one goal in mind: Fort Simpson. I traveled at a brisk pace uphill in windy conditions and found it hard slogging, even though I was following the sled trail from the day before. By noon, I was still miles away from my first goal, the intersection with the next cutline. A cross-country route, I speculated, could cut a half-day of snowshoeing out of the journey, and a glance at the map convinced me that I could do it. I was fully aware that in leaving the security of the well-defined cutline I would face some tough snowshoeing conditions, but I decided to take the chance. I took my bearings and headed into the bush with the compass in hand.

The snow began to fall thick and heavy. The bush provided shelter from the wind but was tough to navigate, and I was forced to change direction frequently. This was glacial moraine territory, littered with huge rocks and boulders, some the size of a house, with small spruce trees clustered between them as thick as quills on a porcupine. I had to remove my snowshoes at times to get through the tangle.

Around midnight, the wind abated. I was fighting fatigue by this time. The discomforting thought occurred to me, as I know it has to others who have traveled deep in unfamiliar bush alone: What if I should die out here in the middle of nowhere? My body would never be found.

In this exhausted state and in the dim light, I perceived a dark area within the thicket of spruce and willow in front of me. It was a strange-looking tree that seemed entirely out of place here. It differed from all of the other growth surrounding it, more like a large bush about eight feet high and five feet wide, with a dense structure of branches. It was odd enough to make me stop and take notice of details. It was covered with elm-like, green leaves with sawtooth edges.

In this season, in this place, a leafed tree is not possible. Am I hallucinating? I wondered. As a reality check, I picked a leaf. It had a shiny surface, was supple, and did not crumble in the hand like a dried leaf. An anomaly for sure, and I took it to be my unexpected Christmas tree. I dug into my pack for one of Allen's Christmas candies and thought, However this tree got to be here, whatever it has gone through, it has survived against the odds. That's what I'll take from this. With that, I pressed on to find the cutline that was waiting out there somewhere.

The night appeared to go on forever as I tried to pick as straight a course as possible, a difficult task without landmarks. I began to reference my compass less frequently in order to conserve my flashlight batteries. The snow stopped at about two in the morning, and I stumbled in the moonlight onto what could only be Albert Norwegian's trap line trail. I figured that he must have extended his trap line north. It was a happy moment. Once I got on his trail, the snowshoeing went easier and I knew that shortly it should merge with a well-packed snowmobile trail. I picked up my pace, and after a while of travelling on the trail, a question came to mind.

Why would Albert be snowshoeing this far from his snowmobile? Then the horrible truth hit me. Oh my God! I'm walking in circles and overlapping my own snowshoe track. I was doing what led to the death of many a person lost in the bush, losing orientation and going in circles. This dispiriting experience was also fear-inducing, because I was unsure of being able to regain my orientation to make my way out of this seemingly endless bush. I stopped, pulled myself together, referenced my compass and started walking, but this time taking compass readings at frequent intervals to maintain my line.

I nibbled on one of the crisply cooked fish stomachs every once in a while, and the odd bite of bannock, to keep my energy up. The temperature began to rise, so I took off my trench coat and tied it on like a backpack as I continued to hack my way through overhanging branches with the machete. As daybreak approached, to my great relief, I broke through to the cutline. After twenty-four hours of walking, I had put the uphill stage and the nightmare of the bush behind me.

The cutline was a welcoming, wide-open space compared to what I had just come through. It seemed to run endlessly in both directions, a path of white bordered by the darkness of the forest on both sides. I had no idea at what particular point I had entered it, and as a result I couldn't use the map to establish where I was. So I plodded on, hoping to find some kind of a landmark to help me to get my bearings, but fatigue took hold. I came to a large spruce tree in a clearing, took off the snowshoes, plunked myself down up against it, covered myself with the trench coat and surrendered to sleep.

I awoke flat on my back and surprised to find my face wet. A chinook had blown in, not unusual in some sections of the Mackenzie Valley. It had been minus forty degrees when I had left the cabin and now, on Christmas Day, it was raining.

I gathered branches, soaked some birch bark with lighter fluid and got a fire going, made tea, ate the last of the bannock and some of the jackfish stomachs. When the rain stopped and the cloud cleared, I found the landmark I was hoping to see: I was looking down towards Mustard Lake. I felt energized at the sight of it. I no longer had to fight the fear of being lost and could now follow this wide cutline northwards and take the next one west to the Mackenzie River and Fort Simpson.

I rolled the down-filled vest I was wearing into my trench coat, tied up my teapot and slung my rifle over my shoulder and headed off. The temperature continued to rise, so I traveled stripped down to my shirt for a while. I met up with the westward cutline and, true to Roderick's description, I could see that it led straight down to the mighty Mackenzie River, which showed as a strip of white twenty to thirty miles away. It was downhill all the way, and I had only about ten miles to go to get to the Mustard Lake turnoff. There, I would pick up on Albert's snowmobile trail to his cabin. Things were unfolding well. I labored to make my way through the rain-sodden snow, but at least it was all downhill.

The early part of the walk went well, but conditions changed rapidly. This cutline, which had been clear-cut about twenty years ago, was now filled with young poplar and birch saplings about a foot apart and around eight feet high. On each side of the cutline, there were walls of small spruce that had risen from the ashes of a forest fire and were clustered together as thick as whiskers. The cutline, instead of providing a clear trail through the bush to my destination, became almost impenetrable in places and rimmed by the hostile barrier of short evergreens. The terrain had changed dramatically, and the further I advanced the more difficult it became to navigate. This drastic change was caused by the cutline having been clear-cut on a steep incline, which created a pathway down the center of it for the flow of water from regular rains and melting snow.

The slope was as steep as forty-five degrees at times and in places had a fifteen-foot-deep gully gouged down its middle. The only way to navigate it was to weave from one side of the gully to the other while picking a way through the trees and struggling over or between the boulders. I cut a long pole to help me navigate the incline and to relieve the pressure on the snowshoes. It was an exhausting ordeal that strained every muscle in my body.

Finally, I broke clear of it all. I had made it to the turnoff to Mustard Lake and met up with Albert's snowmobile trail. The slope here was not as steep as that of the cutline. It was a hard-packed trail. I could see by the tracks how Albert had to weave from bank to bank to cope with the incline.

I expected to arrive at the cabin at Rabbit Skin River in good time, so I took a break and gathered kindling and birch bark, and sprayed the lighter fluid on it to ensure a quick start. As I picked the matches out of the plastic bag, I realized that all of the match heads had been dissolved by lighter fluid that had leaked out of the container inside the bag. I gathered my gear and hit the trail in utter disgust. I conjured up an image of the pilot and others sitting down to turkey dinner, with not a worry in the world.

"Damn all of you," I shouted into the emptiness. But as bad as things were navigating the torturous cutline, fortune had not finished with me yet.

As I got further down the trail, I found that the rain brought on by the chinook had softened the hard-packed snowmobile track and, when the temperatures dropped again, coated it with a layer of ice. This was the beginning of another unexpected nightmare. My snowshoes broke through the ice at unpredictable intervals, shocking my system and straining my leg muscles. The unpredictability of my footing, the pattern of two successful steps on the surface followed by breaking through and then falling forward, stretched my ankle tendons to extremes. Each plunge through the ice layer caused me to pitch forward, and only the pole I was carrying prevented me from falling. I continued on, lifting, dragging and lowering the heavily weighted snowshoes, one step at a time. The strain led to severe leg cramps, causing me to fall at times. It took everything I had to fight the overwhelming urge to just stay lying down.

I had nothing left to eat and needed water badly. The trees around were drooping with icicles as a result of the chinook rain. I broke off a few icicles and ate them like rock candy as I carried on. I paid the piper for that, with an attack of the shivers. If it wasn't one thing, it was another.

It was past midnight when I came to a turn that led south to Rabbit Skin River and Albert's cabin. His trap line ran close to the shoreline of a series of small lakes, and it seemed to go on forever. All traces of anger were gone now as I pushed on. I concentrated on Philip's and Eric's predicament and talked to myself.

Get off your ass, you self-centered shit. No damn way, Philip! I am going to make it. Eventually, I arrived where the Rabbit Skin River flowed into the Mackenzie. I climbed a large snowdrift on the shoreline and spotted the cabin in a clearing. Here was a place to rest and recover before I undertook the last leg to Fort Simpson. I pushed through the deep snow for fifty yards or so and opened the door.

The window was broken; three meatless moose bones lay scattered on the floor. There was a bed with a heavy sleeping blanket and a wood stove, but again, no firewood. I rummaged around and found a booklet of matches with three matches in it. I remembered how we used green willows to make fire in the Barrenlands, and there were plenty of those around. I slashed heaping arms full. I gathered dry moss and scavenged for pine cones and built a fire.

I searched for the food Albert said he had left there, but there was no sign of any cache. In desperation, I took the three well-gnawed moose ribs, broke them apart with the machete and boiled them to make a soup of sorts. After drinking some of the soup, I crawled into the sleeping blanket and dropped into a long-postponed sleep.

It was around ten o'clock the next morning by the time I got up. The chinook was now past, and in its place came clear skies and biting cold. I got the fire going once more, heated up the remains of the soup and conducted a fruitless search for food outside the cabin. Not a trace anywhere. I found a tube of flavoured toothpaste, washed my teeth, slipped the tube into my pocket and got back on the trail.

I headed out onto the Mackenzie River, where the lack of snow pack made for easier going for a change, and I was feeling better. As I trudged along I took an occasional squeeze of the mint-flavoured toothpaste and began to eat it freely thinking, it would give me some energy. It didn't take very long before my stomach reacted with spasms of vomiting that left me dehydrated. I needed water again.

I stumbled on and, much to my surprise, came to open water flowing fast at ice level. With my cup in hand, I got down on my belly and crawled to the water's edge, dipped the cup and drank. I eased myself backwards, stood up and shook my head at the unquestioning stupidity of the risk I had taken. It was just one more symptom of my fatigued state of my body and mind.

I kept moving as if on auto-pilot, then sat down on the ice by the shore for a brief rest. As I sat there, a flock of ptarmigan landed about twenty feet away. They dangled on the willow branches like plump fruit. I shouldered my rifle and shot. I shuffled over, picked up the shattered bird, opened the chest cavity and drank what little warm blood was there and ate the heart. I offered thanks as Jimmy Lacorde had done at another time, in another place. I gathered up my stuff and stumbled on into the night.

Eventually, I detected the glow in the sky from the lights of Fort Simpson. Everything seemed so close, yet it was hours later before I came to the confluence of the Liard and Mackenzie rivers. I stood for a short time looking at my destination, Simpson Island. There should have been joy in my heart, but there was none. I laboured on to the Liard's far shoreline, knowing I had exactly two miles left to go. I don't know if it was out of a sense of relief or utter exhaustion, but I ended up lying on my back and staring at the sky. As I lay there, I felt a curious sense of warmth down the back of my body. It didn't feel right.

"What the hell's going on?" I sat up quickly. "Good God! I'm lying in overflow." The back of my clothing was saturated from top to bottom. I struggled to my feet. I had reached the end of my tether over and over again on this journey, but this was almost too much.

I allowed the memories of the Barrenlands, with Harry Simpson and Jimmy Lacorde, to flood my mind. "What would they do in this circumstance?" I used that thought to help me gather my gear and stagger my way to the

Laird's embankment. I crawled up and over, onto the solid surface of a well-plowed roadway. I had arrived at my destination after three days and two nights of walking, a destination that at times I thought I might never see. It was three o'clock in the morning on Boxing Day, 1977.

There was a trailer close by with a light on, and I saw someone moving around inside. I knocked and the door was opened slowly. The owner stood there, somewhat dumfounded at the sight of this visitor in his doorway, looking like death warmed over. I muttered some kind of apology for bothering him so late at night.

"I need a drink badly," I told him, then quickly explained, "Not alcohol, just water." He asked me to come in and urged me to sit down as he rushed to the fridge. There were cats everywhere, and the couch was matted with their hair to the point of obscuring the fabric design. He set a jug of Tang drink on the counter with a whole container of ice cubes in it. I asked him if he wouldn't mind taking out the ice cubes. I chugged the drink down and plunked myself on the couch, saturated clothing and all. He offered to let me spend the night, but I couldn't convince myself to take him up on his offer, knowing that my three-room house, with its bathtub and bed, was just a phone call away.

I thanked him and asked if I could use his phone. I called my friend Rene Lamothe, who had the key to my place. I briefly explained that I had arrived in town after walking out from the camp. I asked him to pick me up and take me to my place, and that I would give him more details after I got some sleep. There was a momentary silence on the other end of the line before he responded.

"There's a problem, Kieran. I can't take you to your place. Someone else is living there. I'll explain when I pick you up and take you to the hostel. There's no one there for a few days because of Christmas holidays." I was at a loss for words, confused and unable or unwilling to ask for an explanation.

"I need clothes" was all I could bring myself to say. He picked me up, took me to the hostel, where I had my choice of thirty bunk beds, a poor substitute for what I had in mind.

I had great difficulty processing the circumstances surrounding my arrival and reception at the end of this harrowing journey. I felt disheartened and couldn't bring myself to talk much to Rene while he drove me to the hostel.

I had a shower and went to bed, still trying to come to terms with this anticlimactic arrival. Phillip and Eric would now be safe. I had given no consideration as to how this significant event would come to a close for me. But close it did, in a manner unanticipated.

The hostel was so hot that I just lay down on the bunk bed, wrapped in a towel. It was too late in the day to get help to Philip and Eric. I would address that in the morning.

Rene came early the following morning and brought some of my clothes. He noticed that I had difficulty walking and suggested taking me to the hospital. I told him that we could do that after I had made the arrangements to have Philip and Eric picked up. I arrived at the airport, limped through a hallway where pilots sat waiting for instructions on where they were to fly that day, and got to the main office. It was a windowed office, and I could see the owner of the airline there, talking with one of the pilots.

I walked into the office without knocking, asked the pilot to leave, closed the door behind him, turned to the owner and told him why I was there. I pointed at the pilots sitting in the hallway.

"One of your pilots, the one who dropped off the building material for the cabin I was building, was fully aware that we were out of food. We waited for close to a month for that plane to return, while living on a starvation diet." He tried to assure me that the pilot had returned to the lake, walked into the cabin but found no one there and left.

"That's not possible." I said. "We had a man at the cabin who never left it, and we were working directly across the lake within sight of the cabin and would have heard or seen the plane." I again pointed through the glass at the pilots sitting outside and told him, "Never tell me or anyone else in this community the name of the pilot that you and I are talking about, because I don't want to be responsible for what I might do if I met up with him." I was talking with a great deal of pent-up emotion. He told me he would send a Twin Otter out right away to pick up the two men.

"There's an airstrip lined with small trees and an S.O.S. sign marked in the snow that has been waiting for your plane to arrive for the past month," I said with emphasis. The owner apologized and told me that a plane had been sent out to pick us up just before Christmas, and he was informed that the pilot found an empty cabin. He said the pilot must have gone to the wrong lake. That explained the plane that came and went in the distance shortly before I set out to get help. It explained why the pilot hadn't returned, but there were many unanswered questions that could be asked of others as to why I was driven to risk my life to get help.

I left the office, my anger still pent up, but at least knowing that the help I came to get was on its way to Philip and Eric.

I went to the hospital at Rene's insistence to have my legs and feet examined, only to be told to take some aspirin and get lots of rest. Fortunately, I was only temporarily disabled. For some reason, I got a laugh out of that. I got back to the airport just in time to see the twin-engine Otter taxi up to the office building. The side doors opened and Philip and Eric emerged, smiling from ear to ear.

Phillip gave me an unexpected hug, and Eric commented, "We thought you were dead, Kieran. We had nothing left to eat. This morning we talked about having to eat one of the dogs." For these few moments, I put my anger aside and shared in the happy ending of what could have been a tragic experience. The dogs tumbled out of the aircraft one after another, tails wagging. Akaitcho and I greeted one another like the long-lost friends that we were. We had taken many a sled trek and canoe trip together and forged a bond stronger than any I had with other dogs over the years. He was my consolation in difficult times. The deep and abiding friendship we had bubbled over at the sight of him.

With Phillip and Eric back, there was still was the matter of my rented home. Rene told me that a relative of his had been hired to work at the hostel. He had brought his pregnant wife to the hostel when she arrived, but she refused to stay there, so Rene offered them the use of my place as a temporary arrangement. I told him I had no problem sharing the place under the circumstances.

"Well, there's still a problem," he replied.

"I don't understand; it's a three-bedroom house. So what's the problem?" I asked. I wasn't quite ready for the answer.

"It's tough to tell you this, Kieran, but she doesn't want to share the house with you."

"It's not up to her to decide; it's for me," I blurted out, likely yelling at this point. "What the hell is this? I just survived a life-threatening experience to come home to be treated like I don't belong here, like I don't exist."

This was so hard to take that I insisted on going to the house to talk the matter through with his relative. I knocked on the door while Rene sat in his truck. The man's wife answered the door. I told her who I was and began to explain why I was there. She blocked the doorway and told me, in no uncertain terms, that I couldn't come in, not even to get my belongings. I returned to Rene's vehicle, trying to remain calm.

I said to Rene, "Look, man, you've got to do something about this. I just don't want to lose it." He got hold of his relative, and all three of us went back to the house. The moment we stepped in the door, his wife broke into a wailing tantrum. Her husband took me outside and asked for some time to discuss the matter with his wife, who he said was having difficulties related to her pregnancy. He contacted me and said he had worked out an arrangement. The compromise was that I could stay in my basement, but on condition that if he had to leave the house at any time, I also would have to leave. Effectively, my house was no longer my home.

Many years later, in 2002, Leo Norwegian, a member of Louise's family, came to visit me. We talked about the events described in this story. He informed me that they had finished the work on the cabin and that he had traveled by snowmobile along much the same route I had taken to get help and measured the distance. He said it was around eighty miles. Then he said something I thought I would never hear.

"I'm here because I felt that I needed to thank you personally for the work you did on the cabin and, more importantly, to recognize what it must have taken for you to complete that journey to get help. You're as tough as any Dene I know."

AKAITCHO

My dog, Akaitcho

One day, while I was living in my trailer in Fort Simpson, I heard a knock at the door. I answered and was astonished to see a friend from one of the communities where I worked.

"What the heck are you doing in Fort Simpson?" I exclaimed, delighted to see him.

"I'm here to go to work with you," he replied, as he stepped in the door. We had worked together building many log structures; he was quick to learn on the job and, like myself, willing to turn his hand to any new challenge. It was flattering to know that he had traveled such a distance, wanting nothing more than to work with me. However, the timing wasn't great. I was unemployed and looking for work.

"That's okay," he said. "I'll stick around and we'll look for work together." I rearranged the trailer that night to accommodate the two of us. A few days of job hunting passed, with neither of us having any luck finding work. Then one day we went out job hunting separately. I arrived home in the evening to find him lying on his bed, covered in blood and his face hardly recognizable. His head was so battered and bruised that his eyes and nose were buried in the swelling. As I cleaned him up, I pressed him to find out what had happened.

The story, as he told it, was that while walking down the street in Fort Simpson he passed by a man and woman out walking. Without provocation, the man grabbed him from behind by the hair, threw him to the ground and had kicked the hell out of him. I tried to persuade him to let me take him to hospital and to report the incident to the police. He refused both suggestions outright.

The next day I went into town to identify and confront the man responsible for the beating. I made enquiries, got his the name and learned that the woman the man was with at the time of the assault was a local by-law enforcement officer. I also learned where he hung out for morning coffee with his girlfriend's boss, a bank manager and other people from the hamlet office.

The following day, I went into the coffee shop on the south end of the island. I entered, quickly looked around, and in a voice that everyone could hear I used the man's name as I asked the owner if he had seen this guy around. The owner read the threatening tone of voice.

"I don't want any trouble in my restaurant," he cautioned me. I spotted a table shared by a group all wearing suits except for one person, a man who sat hunched over and obviously avoiding eye contact. I walked up to the table, stood behind the man and loudly asked the question.

"Has anybody here seen an asshole by that name around anywhere?" The guy leapt up and grabbed me as I called him out for what he was and yelled to his companions, "So this is the kind of company the business community keeps in this town." With that, tables were pushed and chairs knocked over as the owner yelled at us to get out. We continued to scuffle out the door and onto the street. Once outside, the brawl between the two of us got going in earnest, punching, wrestling and rolling over vehicle hoods, while his coffee companions stood around and watched. In a short while we heard a police siren and, as quick as it started, the fight was over. The guy I was fighting hightailed it as the police pulled up and asked what was going on.

"Nothing. Whoever was causing trouble is gone," someone said.

The cops left and I headed home, having vented my anger. I was still frustrated that there appeared to me, at the time, to be no other way of addressing the situation. My friend understood that word would get around and it would make things uncomfortable for him in a small town like Fort Simpson, so he decided not to stay. I took him to my tent at Martin Lake to give him time to heal before he returned to his home community.

A few days later, the acquaintance who had earlier given me the assailant's name stopped by my trailer for tea. In the course of our chat, he asked a curious question, the underlying intent of which I didn't grasp at the time.

"What's the one thing you own and that means the most to you?" he asked.

"My dog, Akaitcho," I recall telling him. I don't recall where the conversation went from there or why I didn't ask him why he had posed that question.

A day or two later, I had gone to buy groceries and had all my dogs tied up at my trailer except for Akaitcho. I left him to run free. As I approached the trailer on my return, I noticed Akaitcho staggering along the side wall. I ran to him and saw that he had a large wound in the stomach area. It was obvious to me that he was dying. I took him in my arms, held him, and within minutes he was gone. I was overcome with grief and crying at the loss of my best friend.

I examined the wound and found a large tranquilizer dart with red bristles. The dart was of the size used to tranquilize bears. I put two and two together and resolved to speak with the by-law enforcement officer, the girlfriend of the man I'd fought with in town.

I went to the hamlet office and asked to speak with her and was told that she not working that day. I asked who had authority to approve the use of the tranquilizer gun when she wasn't there. They said no one. I asked to see the sign-out register for the gun. They gave it to me. Her boyfriend's signature was on the sign-out line. Angry at the sight of it, I demanded that the gun be signed out to me. I was not altogether in control of my emotions when the office manager came out and rightfully refused my request, as I ranted on.

"If the guy I'm looking for could sign the gun out and use it on my dog, then why not me?" I demanded. "I know where there's a sick, demented dog that I'd like to tranquilize before I bring it in here." There was no mistaking what

I meant by the rash outburst. I carried on. "Give me the usual bear dosage you so freely give to others," I added. They threatened to call the police. I stormed out.

I let everyone I knew in town know that I was looking for the guy. It took me a few days to come to my senses and realize that I needed to forget about this, or I would get myself into serious trouble. On reflection, I don't understand why I didn't take the matter to the police.

I wasn't blameless in the events that led up to the death of Akaitcho. That awareness fueled my grief, and I bottled up the pain for many years. But thankfully, I've learned to deal with it and will forever treasure the memory of my good friend, seen below in my rat canoe.

Akaitcho in my rat canoe

MY MOTHER SAVED MY LIFE

It was 1977, and I was staying in a tent alongside the Marten River about fifteen miles from Fort Simpson, where I was harvesting logs to build that elusive log house I had promised myself over a few years. When I finished cutting, hauling and stacking the logs, I packed up camp to move back into town. My truck was parked by the old Baily Bridge downriver and, to save myself the work of making two trips on foot to the truck with my gear, I decided to load up my canoe and make one run downriver to where my truck was parked.

It was in mid-spring and the river was in flood. It had been running so low in the fall that it froze right down to the river bed, where the ice formed around the boulders and rocks on the bottom, leaving the ice with the configuration of a chocolate chip cookie. The flood waters arrived before the ice on the river bed had a chance to thaw out, which meant that the flooding waters rushed over the top of the river bottom ice, a fact that was to be of some significance for me shortly.

I secured everything in the canoe in the shelter of a small back eddy, squeezed in and pushed off. No paddling was required in this current, just steering. It was an exhilarating run around a few bends, and in short order I caught sight of the Baily Bridge not far ahead. I was pleased at having come up with this labour-saving idea. I steered for the safety of shore just ahead of a set of rapids located between me and the bridge.

"It's a good thing I don't have to steer my way through that wild stretch," I thought. Suddenly, everything changed.

The water directly below the canoe heaved upward into a huge swell. A slab of translucent ice, about fifteen feet long and eight feet wide, had broken free from the bottom of the river and surfaced right below me; it created an immediately threatening situation. Instinctively, I drove my paddle into the water to try to stabilize the rocking canoe, but with the opposite effect; the paddle hit solid ice, and in the blink of an eye the canoe flipped.

I was pitched into the icy water and pushed back up to the surface by another slab of ice surfacing beneath me. This mass of ice slid out from under me and surged on ahead. Frantically, I grasped the overturned canoe, scrambled my way onto it and, straddling it, grabbed hold of the gunwales. Right up ahead of me, plumes of white water shot up two to three feet high off the protruding rocks. The canoe skirted by some of these and smashed into others, submerging me at times in the rushing waters as I hung on.

I came into an area of fast-moving but less turbulent, shallower water and decided to flip the canoe. I slid off and under the canoe in one motion, grabbed it from below, felt the river bottom beneath my feet and pushed up with all my strength, all in one motion. The canoe flipped upright, and to my amazement I was standing upright beside the canoe with my feet planted on the ice-covered river bottom.

I was also bewildered by the fact that I was being carried by the current in a standing position and sliding along the river bottom ice, as I hung onto the canoe. The canoe was swamped, yet the tethered gear was still in place, but both ends of the craft had split open like a filleted fish. I knew that getting back into it was out of the question and decided to break the cardinal rule: "Never let go of your boat; you swim it to shore." I stood there, holding on, numbed to the bone and no longer feeling the canoe I gripped so tightly. All of this was unfolding in mere seconds in time, yet my awareness of what was happening in that short time span was vivid.

In the small gap between my decision to head to shore and taking action to do just that, something unearthly happened. I felt heat deep in my very core. Never have I felt more alive and aware, yet frozen numb. I glanced skyward and had a complex vision, one that I still can't get my head around. I was far above the river, looking down on the scene of which I was a part, and saw myself, a tiny speck, looking upwards. At the same time, at river level, I saw the length and breadth of the river as I stood there, holding onto the boat. In one final overviewing image from above, I could see a raging torrent of water passing under a shelf of ice ahead.

I stood up, drew back from the canoe, let it go, and watched it surge away.

Then, all of the depressing experiences I'd had of late crowded in on me—the sense of abandonment at the Norwegians' cabin, the life-threatening trek to get help, and the death of my dog Akaitcho. Now this, and the feeling that I didn't care what happened or didn't happen. Then one saving thought came to me: "My mother would be brokenhearted if I were to die here." With that, I swam for shore.

I was being swept downstream. I have no recollection of fear; I just knew that I had to swim with everything I had if I was to survive. I thrashed frantically at the water.

Numb and exhausted, I lifted my head and saw a tree on the shore not more than six feet away. It was not moving; I was not moving. I suddenly realized that I was no longer being swept downstream, and my arms, no longer thrashing, were now under me and touching bottom. I struggled to my feet. I was standing in less than a foot of water.

I made it onto the riverbank shaking uncontrollably, collapsed on a bed of moss, struggled back to my feet, staggered through the bush and emerged within feet of my truck. I stripped down and pulled on a dry pair of coveralls. I got into the cab, started the motor, turned on the heater and pointed the truck towards home.

Once I got there, I collapsed onto the bed and wrapped myself in a sleeping bag, shivering yet feverish. I slept for the rest of that day and night and all of the following day. I went through all the stages of recovery from hypothermia, alternating between horrific sweats and shivering cold. I now know that I was fortunate to have recovered without medical help.

When I was well enough and back on my feet, I went to the bridge about a mile from where the canoe tipped to check if I could find it. Just as I had visualized while standing in mid-river, the water at the bridge surged down and under a large ice jam. At the outer edge of the ice, in an eddy, I retrieved my battered canoe, along with most of my gear.

A few days later, I contacted my mother and, with no reference to the Marten River experience, I told her I loved her.

BLACK DUCK CAMP: WHǪSÌIWEKǪ̀Ǫ̀

I took time off from my job in Hay River to attend the Caribou Carnival in Yellowknife. On the way there, I stopped in Rae Edzo to visit my friend, Eddy Rabesca, at his home. He had a lot of visitors staying there, so he arranged for me to stay at his parents' home instead. When I got there, I was astonished when I recognized his dad, Joseph, and his brother, Washen, as the two men from Rae Edzo I had caught up with on the trail while I was dog sledding from Fort Franklin to Rae Lakes a few years back. I hadn't put names to the faces at the time but immediately identified both of them the moment I entered the house. It was heartwarming to get reacquainted.

When I got up the following morning, there was a young woman with beautiful long hair washing dishes. I introduced myself. Her name was Rose Rabesca. She made tea for us and got busy around the house, and I saw no more of her before I left Rae Edzo and headed into Yellowknife for the carnival.

Later that day, on my way to the carnival, I ran into Rose on the street in Yellowknife. Coincidence? We chatted for a while and exchanged our contact information. This led to our keeping in touch after I returned to my job in Hay River. She came to visit me there and once again in Fort Simpson, shortly after the near-fatal canoe incident on the Marten River.

Following those two visits, I thought it was time to pay her a return visit in spring. I drove to Rae Edzo, hoping to catch her at home, but she had already left to help her parents on the spring hunt. They owned a log cabin on an island in Great Slave Lake. It went by the name of Blackduck Camp, and it required about a ten-mile paddle to get there. I decided to go to the camp using the rat canoe I had on top of my truck. It was

BURNT SNOW

twilight by the time I got the canoe launched in a small creek that led down to Great Slave Lake.

The creek was narrow and fast flowing, so all I had to do was steer as I went, a relaxing paddle for the most part through uninterrupted northern forest. As I wended my way downstream, the air temperature began to drop, creating a low-level fog, one that moved out from the open areas on the river into the surrounding woods, creating shifting shadows in the moonlight.

As I rounded one of the bends in the river, I came to a small logjam, grabbed a tree branch, pulled myself out and portaged the canoe around it. I sat down on the riverbank for a brief break, relaxing in the peaceful surroundings. However, I began to experience an uncomfortable feeling, an inexplicable sense of discomfort. The eerie light and shadow effects were undoubtedly contributing factors.

This is a beautiful, late evening in spring. Why the edginess? I thought to myself. I stood up, shook the feeling off and put the boat back in the water on the other side of the logjam. The stream seemed shallower on this side of the portage, and the canoe rode unusually high as I climbed in. I stuck my paddle into the water to push off. As it entered the water, I could tell that things were not as they should have been. I had done a great deal of canoeing in recent years and sensed that something was not quite right; that something triggered an unknowing fear.

Quite unexpectedly, the canoe lifted up in the water and began to rock gently, but in a totally uncharacteristic way. I pushed on the paddle. The force that had pushed the canoe up now gave resistance to the paddle as I pushed it down. The fast-flowing water carried me for about twenty feet with this continued sense of a lack of control. I plunged the paddle into the water again and struck the same pushback, a strange slipping and sliding resistance. It was certainly not river bottom. I tried to convince myself that I was imagining things, but no; this was very real, and in the fading light and forest shadow I couldn't see anything below the surface. I began to imagine a serpent-like creature of some kind squirming under the canoe and deflecting the paddle. Everything around me fed my fear—shadows, fog, the unknown river and something happening under water that I could not explain.

Whatever was there appeared to occupy the whole subsurface of the river, making it come alive in a strange way. Once again, I tried to convince myself that it was all in my head, but no, it was interfering with the canoe, the paddle and me in a way I had never experienced before. It was very real.

I plunged the paddle into the water once again, this time in a kind of panic. I pivoted it on the gunnel, levering the blade against whatever was resisting it. The paddle burst through the surface, cascading water onto me and flipping fish by me onto the river bank. I was riding on top of an enormous school of fish! It was an incredible moment, literally. My fears turned to relief—and then, a sense of awe.

That thing below was a school of sucker fish forging its way upstream to spawn. Fish filled the creek from shore to shore, riding up and over each other as they fought to make headway. Thousands of them, stalled in their migration by the logjam I had just portaged around. It was a wonder of nature, a remarkable phenomenon to come upon in the middle of the wilderness. To see and to feel it in such a direct way was a very special experience. I gathered a few fish into the canoe, with breakfast in mind, and paddled on.

I emerged from the creek into the expanse of Great Slave Lake, stopped, made a fire and slept. When I got going early the next morning, I worried about locating Blackduck Camp, given the numerous islands and bays I could see stretched out ahead of me. As I paddled along, looking for signs of any kind of settlement, I remembered that Eddy Rabesca had told me they had dog teams on the island. I began to beat my paddle on the gunnels at intervals, hoping his dogs might hear the unfamiliar noise and react. It worked after a short time, and I could hear them howl out their location.

I paddled in the direction of the sound and identified the island I sought. My arrival was quite a surprise. Rose was making tea and stoking the fire as I entered the cabin. There were muskrat and beaver skins on stretchers strung out in every available spot, a clear indication as to how this Dene family made their living. They sat me down and cooked a tasty dish of oatmeal and boiled duck as I told the story of my strange experience on the river. What had scared the living daylights out of me became one more storytelling event for the Rabesca family.

I spent an enjoyable few hours there, connecting with Rose in particular. The visit cemented my resolve to settle down and to adjust my impulse-driven ways.

I went to Fort Rae after the spring hunt to visit Rose once more, and we decided to move in together. So I packed up and moved my trailer from Fort Simpson to Fort Rae. I parked the trailer next to the Rabesca family home to begin my life as a settled resident in the Dene community of Fort Rae.

Fort Rae had the largest concentration of Dene of any town in the NWT. It sits at the end of that yellow ribbon of a road depicted on the map on my bedroom wall in Winnipeg. It was the road that I was determined to follow into my future, and follow it I did. It seemed to me that I had accumulated a lifetime of experiences along the way.

I had a place to live now, and the next thing was to find work. I went to the local Housing Maintenance Department and outlined my work experience to the manager. He told me that I was just the person they needed on an interim basis to run their maintenance program, someone who understood the culture and had some knowledge of the language. I was to work myself out of a job once a qualified Dene person was found who could take over from me. After about a year that person was found, and my position came to an end. However, I was approached by the Band Council, in collaboration with the NWT government, to oversee a housing initiative called the Housing Assistance Program, or H.A.P., which was designed to provide new homes in Fort Rae and employment opportunities.

It was remarkable how my work life had taken on a pattern of landing me in the heart of Dene communities. I was constantly stepping into employment that placed me in the forefront of initiatives designed to provide employment and improve living conditions in these Indigenous communities. The H.A.P. program, as successful as it was, slowly died as government policies changed. But, as so often was the case for me, as one opportunity passed, another was born.

There was a very successful businessman in Fort Rae, Richard Whitford, who observed our successes with H.A.P. and undertook to see that a similar program was put in place. He called a meeting of handpicked individuals and proposed forming a legally registered company made up of those invited. We were all to be equal partners in a company that would bid on new construction jobs.

"Why are you going to such lengths to help us to set up this business?" someone asked him.

"It's the right thing to do for the community. They helped me to get a start and supported my business. I live by a pay-it-forward philosophy. It makes for a better world that way," he replied.

Richard registered the company and introduced us to a lawyer and an accountant who ensured everything was done well and above-board. The company took the name Dogrib Construction. The names of some of the partners were Joe Wedzin (Fort Rae), Bernard Nedzo (Fort Franklin), Philip Antoine (Fort Simpson), Louie Zoe (Rae Lakes), and subtrades Mike Simpson as plumber and Eddy Koyena as electrician, all Dene with the exception of me, an immigrant Irishman.

We bid on many contracts, and one of these was to build houses in a seemingly bottomless creek bed in Fort Rae. We contracted a Yellowknife company to drive the piles required. This led to a strange and fitting coincidence in my life.

The contractor we hired turned out to be the first person I met when I arrived in Enterprise in the NWT in 1971. His name was Burney, owner of Burney's Restaurant at that time. He had asked me, while I stopped to have a meal there, what I was hoping to do by way of work in the NWT. I told him that I wanted to build log buildings as a career. He had laughed and tried to discourage me, because, from his point of view, there were no trees big enough in the area for that purpose. Here he was, no longer running a restaurant and owner instead of Burney's Frontier Drilling. And here I was, the log building contractor he thought I would never become.

Meeting up with him at this time was like bookends set on either side of my experiences over my years living and working with the Dene of the Northwest Territories.

Some of the Rae Edzo women elders

A TRADITIONAL MARRIAGE

I had the mistaken impression that the men in Rae Edzo made all the important decisions in the community. Not so. The women of the community presented as quiet, unassuming and always busy, and seemed to be forever in the background. Then came the day when I asked Rose Rabesca if she would marry me.

What I thought would be decided with a simple yes or no turned out to be more complicated than that. Rose said that she needed to ask her mother for permission first, then her mother needed to call a meeting with her sisters and other female elders to discuss the matter. Then they would meet with me.

A meeting of the necessary women was called, and I found myself sitting alone in the Rabescas' kitchen as the house filled with elderly women from the community. Once they had finished their meeting, I would be questioned by the group. I was more nervous about this than I had ever been at any job interviews.

The time came, and I was summoned to join them. Mrs. Elisabeth Mackenzie was the only one who spoke English, and consequently she served as translator for both me and the women. I was so nervous during this event that I recall little of the questions asked or the answers given.

"Would you raise your children in the ways of the white man or in the Dene way?" The impression they had was that white people were overly strict when disciplining children.

"Would you be fair and understanding with your wife? Would you use violence in a family dispute?" Then came the final question that all agreed was most important one.

"Will you do what most white people do, take your wife away and raise your children outside the community?"

I responded, "It's my intention to live here, raise our children in Dogrib culture, and pass on the legacy of their grandparents' way of life." With that, they whispered among themselves and then I was asked to leave. I was totally rattled as Rose joined me in the kitchen.

"When will they make a decision?" I asked her nervously.

"It's done," she said. "They didn't say no."

"That's it? You mean we can get married?" I asked.

"Yes," she replied. "They didn't say no."

The experience felt like an initiation into the Dene world.

Rose and I got married a short time later in Rae Edzo. Several family members came from Winnipeg for the occasion, attended the community reception and joined Rose, me and the community at the drum dance that was organized to celebrate the occasion.

Dene drummers in Rae Edzo

DOG ISLAND

We decided to build a home for our family when our daughter, Teya, was born. We could not afford to purchase one, and besides, the banks would not give a loan for building anything on Crown land because of the ongoing land claims negotiations. Regardless, I applied for land, explained my intention to the hamlet manager and got turned down.

However, I stayed the course, believing I would find some way to set up my home in Fort Rae. Two RCMP buildings came up for sale, a house and an old jail facility. I put in a bid and got both buildings. So I now had the makings of a home and workshop, if I could find some land on which to locate the buildings. The purchase agreement set a tight deadline for their removal from their present location.

I went to my father-in-law's house at supper time, and when I finished eating he asked if I would feed his dogs. I took some fish and headed to an island on the shores of Marion Lake, where he kept them. As it was wintertime, I crossed to it on the ice. While the dogs were busy eating, I sat down on a rock to enjoy a beautiful sunset. This small island is located outside the town boundary, on Crown land. It is surrounded on three sides by deep water and on the fourth side is linked to the mainland by a shallow marsh. I could see a horseshoe-shaped bay on it where a boat could be parked out of the wind.

It suddenly struck me that this would be the ideal location for our house. It more than met any criteria I had for a lot on which to build. I hurried back to the Rabescas' house, my mind buzzing, and, using Rose as translator, I spoke with my father-in-law.

"You know that I've been looking for a site on which to build a home. I was sitting on the island after feeding your dogs and wondered, how long have you been using that island?" I asked him.

"A long time, since before Fort Rae was Fort Rae," he replied. "We lived there in tents when the American fur traders came to trade. We called them Big Knives back then." He continued, telling me something that was very significant. "The name for the community, Behchoko, came down from those early trading days, when our family camped on the island. Everyone else camped around Bay Island. After we moved off the island to where we live now, we've continued to use it as a place to tie up our dogs there." I asked him the crucial question I had on my mind.

"Would it be okay with you if I moved the buildings I bought from the RCMP to the island to set up our home there?

"Yes," he replied without hesitation. "It would be a good place to build a house." This was his unequivocal go-ahead for me to move the two buildings onto what had become known as Dog Island.

Dog Island in Rae Edzo at the end of the road I had travelled into the North from Winnipeg

I immediately went to where my buildings were located and finished getting them ready to be moved, with the help of a local contractor. This same contractor happened to be installing a waterline for the town and laying it down on the lake bottom in an area right by the island. He had created a 100-foot-wide pathway on the ice, over which he moved his heavy excavating equipment. This was an ideal access route and wide enough for me to haul my buildings to the island.

I chose not to inform the hamlet manager of my intentions, given my experience with him, and prepared everything to be moved on a weekend, when the hamlet offices were closed. The contractor offered to undertake the move at no charge. We moved them onto the island without incident. Once they were in place, I set to work to level and do repairs to get things ready for spring.

However, the inevitable happened. The hamlet manager got word of the move. He first sent me a scathing letter, then followed that up with an official document stating that I was illegally occupying Crown land. He saw himself as a loyal servant of the Crown, the man responsible for the Crown's land assets. Ironically, it was in the Crown's name that the very land on which my house stood had been taken from the Dene without recompense in the first place. I ignored the hamlet manager's communication, hoping against hope that the issue would resolve itself in some unseen way.

Early one morning, while I was picking up the mail, I was summoned to the hamlet office. Once there, I was handed an official letter by an RCMP officer in the presence of the hamlet manager. All very formal. The letter gave me forty-eight hours to remove my buildings from the island.

"Where would you have me move them to?" I asked the manager. "Do you have a lot or location for me?" I knew full well the answer I would get.

"The answer to your question is, no! You have forty-eight hours to move the buildings, period," he responded with authority. The letter I had received earlier had raised my hackles for more than one reason. One of the thoughts that went through my mind was that, had the letter said that I was "illegally occupying Indian land," I might have been concerned, but when it stated that I was illegally occupying Crown land, that was another matter. Given my Irish immigrant background, that raised my hackles.

I stood there in the hamlet office, within an arm's reach of an RCMP officer in full regalia, and feeling intimidated, I had nothing to say. The hamlet manager was undoubtedly happy about that. I left the office feeling powerless and infuriated.

Once outside, I noticed a number of vehicles parked in the area and realized that it was Treaty Day. Then I remembered that the Band Council had called a meeting to discuss a motion that recommended Band members refuse to accept treaty money from the Queen's representative until their land claims were addressed. The five-dollar token payment and a fish net given to the Dogrib people annually wasn't going to cut it anymore. The thought came to me that maybe this was the ideal time to put my case to the Band about my home and the matter of land rights. This was not my area of expertise, but I was motivated to give it a try.

I walked over to the Band Office. The meeting was in full swing and obviously was intended for Band members only, because as I entered, the room fell silent.

"There's an important meeting going on. What is it you want?" asked the chief.

"Is this meeting dealing with the issue of land claims?" I asked.

"Yes," he replied.

"I have a piece of paper in my hand right now which implies that the land in this area is not yours," I stated as I brandished the letter from the hamlet.

"What are you talking about?" the chief asked. I walked to the front and gave him the letter. Gary Jabe, a local school teacher assisting them, read it out, and when he finished reading I offered some further detail.

"My father in-law, Joseph Rabesca, has given me permission to set up my home on the island where he keeps his dogs, and this official paper, served to me by the RCMP on behalf of the hamlet, says that the island is officially Crown land and that I've got forty-eight hours to move my home off the island. If the Band directs me to move it, I'll move it. But if you do that, then the only conclusion I can come to is that the island must be the Queen's land after all."

There was an immediate hum of voices in the room, followed by a discussion that resulted in a letter being drafted on the spot and addressed to the hamlet manager. The letter approved my father-in-law's decision to allow me to have my home located on the island. This was based on the Band's acknowledgement of the Rabesca family's continuous use of that island over generations. I returned to the hamlet office, letter in hand, and presented it to the hamlet manager. He read it and laughed.

"I'm responsible for all land matters in the hamlet, up to and until land claims are settled. This document is worthless," he declared. I heard him out and calmly turned and addressed the RCMP officer standing beside me.

"Do you have a match?" I asked. He handed me a book of matches, obviously thinking that I was a smoker. I turned back to the hamlet administrator and in a subdued tone said, "I can't move the home; it's damaged as it is, and since you say that there's nowhere for me to relocate it to, I've only one choice and that's to burn it down."

"I don't care what you do with it," he responded.

"Very well, then," I replied. "I guess you won't mind reading a report in tomorrow's Yellowknife newspaper that the hamlet manager in Fort Rae forced a local resident to burn down the resident's home, and the matches he used were provided by the RCMP."

"You can't do that!" exclaimed the now panic-stricken manager.

"Watch me," I replied.

"You can't do that," he repeated, pleadingly.

"So I take it that I can leave my home where it is, in that case?" Silence. I walked out of the office and got on with the business of establishing my home on what was known as Dog Island. I did so with the support of the Band and without any further interference from the hamlet or the RCMP.

THE EMERGENCE OF A STRONG LEADER

The youth in Rae Edzo went through a confusing time in the 1970s, when I was living there. In the past they were kept busy contributing to the family unit, cutting firewood, helping check nets, learning to run dog teams, making canoes and taking part in the traditional hunts. But times were changing as the Dene transitioned from semi-nomadic ways into settled community life. Traditional practices and cultural values were being lost in this process. Many youth succumbed to substance abuse as a way to occupy their time, with all the accompanying damage to them and their community. They were, however, fortunate that one of their number, John B. Zoe, took on a leadership role in the community at that time.

John had grown up a part of that confused generation. His youth cohort suffered the negative impact of the residential school system, plus difficulties related to widespread substance abuse. They were, in so many ways, a lost generation.

John was one of the few who managed to survive the despair created by these conditions. He quit drinking, opened his own business and focused some of his energy on helping his people. With the guidance of community elders and the assistance of people with management skills, he revived the traditional

John B. Zoe
– credit- Bertha Rabesca Zoe

canoe trip into the Barrenlands and helped to establish a school-based program that focused on Dogrib culture, its legends, hunting traditions and language.

"If we don't use it, we will lose it." was his mantra for mobilizing people when he talked about issues related to land claims. John became a chief negotiator in matters related to those land claims, but he didn't lose touch with day-to-day matters. I ran into him on one of his early-morning walks as he picked up broken glass in a children's playground. The concerns of his community were the central purpose of his life in those years.

I built his gas station and my hardware store, which were located next door to each other. We got to know one another well in those early years. He included me in his political world by inviting me to meetings at the Friendship Center and involving me in the reintroduction of the sweat lodge to the community, among other things. John realized that many of the Dogrib traditions were at risk of being lost as the elders died off, and consequently, he helped organize a group of elders to pass on their knowledge and skills, such as those needed in the building of birch-bark canoes, to the next generation.

Not long after we first met, on an early spring day John invited me to go for a walk with him. We were two young guys searching for ourselves in different ways. I suggested that we walk to Blackduck Camp by way of the old dog-team trail that my father-in-law, Joseph Rabesca, used. The next day we met at a spot halfway between Fort Rae and Yellowknife, where the trail began. He brought a .22 rifle and I brought my bow and arrows, a new hobby I was trying out. Shortly after we set out, he got around to his purpose for inviting me on this outing. He asked me a question he had on his mind.

"You're well-traveled in the Dene territory, Kieran. Of the many Dene elders you've met in the communities where you lived and worked, which of them would you recommend as being worthwhile for me to consult about traditional Dene practices and legends, someone who would be open to sharing their knowledge with me?" he asked. I was flattered to be asked such a question.

"Harry Simpson comes immediately to mind," I said. "There may be others as knowledgeable, but I would definitely recommend Harry." I went on to tell him some of Harry's legends and stories as we sauntered along through the bush for the seven-mile hike to the Rabescas' cabin on Great Slave Lake. We crossed beaver dams, bridged creeks on fallen logs and looked for ways to get onto and off of the ice floes on the small lakes. When we eventually reached Great Slave Lake, it was still largely frozen, but there was open water along the shoreline as far as we could see. This posed a problem.

"Do you want to continue on to Blackduck Camp? It's on one of the islands out there," I asked as I pointed in the direction of the camp.

"That'll be tough; there's open water all along the shoreline," he remarked.

"We'll walk through it. It's probably only a couple of feet deep. Then we can scamper onto the ice and walk the half-mile or so to get to the cabin," I explained. The gap between the shoreline and the ice was about a hundred feet of ice-cold water.

"How will we dry off?" John asked.

"When we get to the cabin, I guess," I replied. And with that, I stepped into the water and wadded quickly through it, hoping it would not get any deeper as I went. But unfortunately it did. I made it to the ice and clambered out, feeling a hell of a lot colder than I expected, and jogged towards a low rock outcrop a short distance away. Fortunately, the sun was shining that day. When I got to the outcrop, I stripped down quickly, wrung out my clothes and laid them out on the warm moss and black lichen. I danced around on the rock in an effort to warm up for a while. I looked back for John, but couldn't see him through the haze and ran back to the water's edge.

"What took you so long?" I asked when I got there.

"My body just went into shock the moment I stepped into the damn water. I froze in my tracks," he said, as he stood there shivering. We hustled over to the lichen-covered rock.

"I saw you dancing naked on a rock and wondered what the heck you were doing; it looked weird through the mist," he said, through his chattering teeth. He stripped down, wrung out his clothes and did a dance on the warm moss. We had a good laugh as we conjured up an image of some old trapper passing by and what he would be thinking at the sight of two buck-naked guys dancing around out here and in these conditions.

We dressed and continued our journey, arriving at Blackduck Camp to a warm welcome from Eddy and Madeline Rabesca. We hung up some of our clothing to dry, warmed up by the stove and drank some hot tea, followed by a trap line meal of muskrat stew.

After a few hours of visiting, and when our clothes had dried, I suggested we head back home. John said, "We can't go back the same way we came, Kieran. We'd never make it to the highway if we had to go through that again." I shivered at the thought of it myself and agreed. The island on which the camp was located was still connected to the shore by the ice. Eddy recommended an alternative route, one I had used on a previous occasion while traveling with his father, Joseph Rabesca. They gave us some dry meat and bannock as we left.

We crossed over the ice onto the mainland and followed the family's trap line trail. John was surprised at how well I managed to navigate the woods with little or no trail evidence, and I surprised myself as well. We got to one spot where the trail led onto unsafe ice. I remembered coming to this spot with Joseph and recalled a curious instruction he gave me at the time.

"If ever you pass this way in spring and can't go on the ice, look for that tree." He pointed to the top of a nearby tree and said, "Do you see the direction the bent tip of that tree points? Don't go that way. It's all sloughs and lowland. Go the other way, where there's high ground. You can use a beaver dam near the end to cross over a low-lying area there." John laughed at the idea of the tree pointing the wrong way as a guide to the right way to go. We journeyed on and arrived at the highway just feet from our vehicles.

"You do know that there's something very wrong with this picture of the two of us, don't you Kieran?" John asked as we got to the vehicles.

"What do you mean?" I asked.

"Here's this white guy guiding an Indian over Indian land without a compass or map, and he's using trail markings and landmarks passed on to him by one of my elders. And to add insult to injury, here's this Indian carrying a gun, and the white guy is armed with bow and arrows." We got a good laugh out of that, and still do.

John was rediscovering his heritage at that time and was aware of the importance of spending time on the land. One of his goals was to have all of the traditional trails in Dogrib territory mapped. He connected with Harry Simpson. They hit it off well together and mapped trails, scoured the countryside for sites of archeological significance and identified places that were referenced in Dene legends and stories. Among John's awards for his work is an honorary doctor of laws degree from the University of Alberta, conferred upon him in recognition of his work preserving the Dogrib (Tłįchǫ) culture.

John B. Zoe was the lead negotiator in the final settlement of the Dene land claims in 2005 that resulted in 39,000 square kilometers of land between Great Bear Lake and Great Slave Lake coming under Dene group ownership and control.

BROTHER GOSSELIN

Brother Gosselin lived in the mission house in Fort Rae. He was a lay brother, belonging to a religious order but not a priest, who became a very close friend. He was a widely admired man and one whose life's work in the Dene community deserves to be remembered here. He was born Leonide Gosselin, in 1906, on a small subsistence farm in Quebec. When he turned seventeen, he joined the Oblate missionary order as a lay brother and was sent north to assist the missionaries in the NWT. He spent the next sixty-nine years in service, working 365 days a year.

Paying the rock in Old Fort Rae

After serving a few years in Fort Resolution, he was sent to Old Fort Rae. It was a fur trading post that no longer exists, but the place is still visited as people stop by the site to "pay" the large rock there, a tradition in Dene culture of leaving tokens behind before carrying on with a journey. It could be anything from a coin to a bullet.

Brother's job was to start a garden there for the priest at the church. He cut the trees, yanked tree stumps out using oxen, and proceeded to plow the rock-filled land. He tried to grow potatoes there, but when they grew no bigger than a golf ball he realized that he needed to enrich the soil.

To do that, he netted huge quantities of fish from Lake Marion, which he then piled to a depth of almost three feet over the entire garden area. He harvested water weeds from a nearby bay and moss from the surrounding area and spread these on top of the fish. This foul-smelling compost was left to rot and mingle over a few years. He then planted his garden and harvested healthy crops of many kinds of vegetables.

I had started a vegetable garden around the time I first met Brother Gosselin and wasn't having much luck. He told me how he fertilized his field and about his seeding and watering techniques, and I set to work to replicate what he had done. I obtained horse manure from Lloyd Taylor, and Joe Migwi supplied me with fish, and I applied these with amazing results. The relationship between Brother Gosselin and me flourished, as did the garden.

While Brother's primary job was to keep the church-run hospital heated, he took on many other tasks, one of which was building a well to provide a clean water supply. The lake water, murky and silted all year round, was impossible to filter effectively using the available systems. So it was decided a well needed to be dug. They dug it offshore in about two feet of water, behind a berm built to hold the lake water back. They used rocks and mortar to build the wall as they dug down into the sandy bed of the lake, to use it as a natural filter for the water entering the well. A Briggs and Stratton pump was used to keep the digging area free of water as they worked.

Father Amourous assisted in the digging when he could, and on the last day of the dig, when the others had left, he went down the well by himself to put the last few rocks in place. He started the pump, which resulted in a buildup of carbon monoxide as he worked, and he passed out. Fortunately, Brother Gosselin came by, knowing Father Amourous was there, and noticed the priest unconscious at the bottom of the well. Being a strong man, he carried Father up the ladder and onto the shoreline, where he managed to revive him.

Another of his tasks was to supply the hospital with fish, rabbits and ptarmigan to feed the many patients there. The ptarmigan he caught in fish nets strung out in the willows during the winter months. He was also the one solely responsible for stoking the fires required to heat the church and residences all year long. He cut, split and stacked over 800 cords of wood per year.

He was the coffin builder, a responsibility he passed on to me in later years. He built them in his workshop, where he puttered away on various projects for the benefit of his Tłı̨chǫ neighbors. One such project was that, as the church building aged, the wooden steps in the stairs required replacing. Brother used the discarded steps to make small stools for the women to use as they sat at their sewing machines or outside their front doors on summer evenings. They became treasured heirlooms in the Dene community. No store-bought stool could match these gifts for their embedded history and nostalgic value. Another article of unique value to the community emerged from the workshop, and that was knives.

Brother knew that the people's lifestyle required knives for a great many uses, particularly when out hunting. He had salvaged a number of old eight-foot-long pit saws. He scratched the shape of the various knives on the saw blades and, using an electric grinder, cut a groove along the line he had drawn. He placed the saw blade in a vice and hit it with a hammer in a particular way, snapping out the basic shape for the knife blade with the skill of a glazer. He ground, shaped and sharpened the form into a perfect knife blade. He had the children drop off broken hockey sticks so that he would have seasoned wood to make knife handles. Many of the households throughout the Tłı̨chǫ nation had at least one of these knives and they cherished them as a household or hunting item to be passed on in the family.

I sat down to have tea with him one day and he insisted I try some moldy looking cheese he had. I lacked the sophistication to recognize a good cheese when I saw one.

"Now there's the vow of poverty being taken to its limits. The man is eating cheese riddled with mold." I thought. Just to be polite, I took a nibble and with great difficulty, swallowed it. Not long after, I approached Father Pochat and expressed my concern that Brother was reduced to the point of eating moldy cheese. I knew I had gotten something wrong when Father laughed his heart out and he proceeded to enlighten me about the process of making blue cheese. I smiled at my own ignorance and, as time passed, I acquired a taste for this cheese. For years after that it became one of the highlights of my visits with Brother to share not only his company, but also a slice of his moldy, blue cheese.

The vow of poverty he had taken, he lived to the letter. He had just one set of clothes for his daily wear. This did not go unnoticed in the community. I was there on one occasion when an elder dropped by to bring him a pair of new socks. Brother accepted them with expressions of gratitude. As soon as the elder had left, Brother turned to me and offered me the socks. I respectfully declined the offer and suggested that he should keep them.

"That's all right," he said. "I know someone who could use them."

When the nuns, priests and hospital staff sat down to eat, he occasionally joined them. After they had eaten and left, he went around the dining area and, if people had left behind the customary orange that was provided, he would collect these oranges. Then, following Sunday mass each week, he walked around Bay Island passing the oranges out to the children he met on his route. He told me that this was the highlight of his day. The children called him, "yahtı jìek'oo," the orange priest.

As age caught up with him, Father Pochat searched for a relative of Brother's. He located a nephew who was about forty years of age at the time. Father told him of Brother's condition and asked if he would consider coming to visit his aging uncle. He agreed to come. Brother was not informed about the upcoming visit of his nephew. I found out much later what had transpired.

Brother was out on one of his walks around the island handing out oranges and, as he crossed the bridge on his way home, he froze in disbelief at what he saw standing in front of him on the bridge. To his eye, he believed he was looking at his own father as he remembered him when Brother left to join the Oblates at age seventeen. For a brief moment he wondered if he himself had just died and was experiencing a vision. The man on the bridge, who of course was his nephew, bore a strong resemblance to the dad. Brother was overcome with emotion and wept. His nephew stayed the day, the only few hours Brother had ever shared with a family member since the day he joined the Oblate Order.

Unable to get around very well, he ended up confined to his upstairs room. I continued to share his company and his blue cheese. He was aware that the end was near. I went to the pet shop to buy bird seed for a cockatiel I had at home. As I looked at the budgies there, I thought of a way to improve Brother's quality of life in the limited time he had left. I bought a budgie and offered it to him.

"Thanks Kieran," he said. "But no. I wouldn't know what to do with a bird." He was obviously not all that enthusiastic about the offer. I had anticipated that something like this might happen.

"Okay Brother," I responded. "Don't worry about it. I'll bring it back to the store, but I need you to look after it just for the weekend while I'm away in Edmonton with my family."

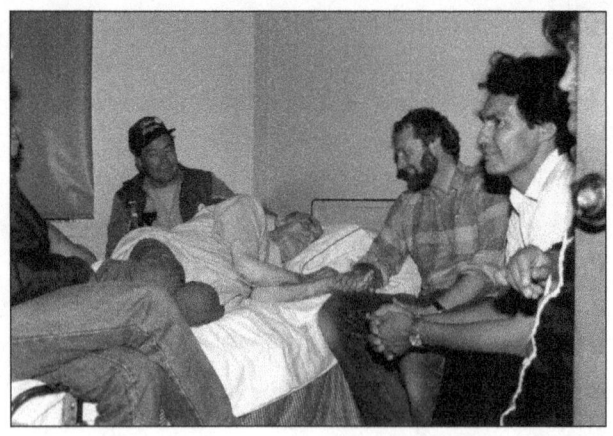

L.to R. Joe Erasmus, Rose Moore, Ernie Camsel, Brother Gosselin, Kieran Moore, Joe Rabesca, and Madeline Rabesca

When I returned to his place after the weekend, I found him sitting in his smoke filled room, grinning from ear to ear with the budgie sitting on his finger. The matter of returning the bird to the store was never mentioned. He and the bird watched the coming and going of life in Rae Edzo together from the upstairs window of his residence. Brother was never more than an arm's length away from his newfound friend. Time caught up with Brother. He had a strong heart and, as a result, his body hung on for quite a while.

"It's like he wants to keep on going; he doesn't want to quit," I told Father Pochat.

"That's exactly what he's doing." Father responded. "He's holding out for Sunday. Brother said he wanted to die on Sunday." I got a phone call at four o'clock Sunday morning from one of the nuns.

"He's going Kieran!" she said simply.

I rushed over to his place, sat with him as his breathing became erratic, then it slowed down as if he were sleeping. As I held his hand, he turned his head, appeared to look at me and was gone. It was a moving experience to be with this kind and humble man at the end of his life.

"What do you expect to see when you get to heaven?" I asked him a few weeks before he died. I was surprised by his answer.

"I don't know what it will be like, but I do expect to see everything I ever did for the church there before me," he said.

"What's that? I asked.

"Cord wood and more cordwood. Every stick I cut in my lifetime," he said with a grin. "If you were to put it all in one pile, I know it would stretch as far as the eye can see in both directions and as high as the sky. You'd see no end to it," he laughed as he made a promise. "I'll keep heaven warm for everyone." I took the budgie home. Brother's little friend followed him within two days.

JOSEPH RABESCA: K'AADEE SUSIE

Joseph and Josephine Rabesca

Joseph Rabesca spoke very little English, had never attended school or visited a hospital or dentist. He had never worked for a wage nor collected social assistance. He maintained his culture and language and lived life without compromising his values. Joseph abstained from alcohol with the exception of New Year's Day, when he drank with his best friend, Jimmy Lacorde, as they played cards. He earned his living over a lifetime trapping some three hundred miles from his home.

This role model and elder told me many stories, one of which was about hunting in the Coppermine River area in the Barrenlands. He made this particular journey in the company of three other trappers. Unfortunately, on this particular trip they ran into an unusually bad snow storm that lasted a week and as a result, they ran out of firewood and food for both themselves and their dogs.

Just prior to the storm, one of their hunting party had spotted an Inuit camp nearby. Things were so bad for Joseph and his men that he decided they pay a visit to the Inuit camp to see if they had any extra food that they would be willing to share. He reassured his companions it would be safe to visit with the Inuit.

When they arrived at the camp and were invited in, Joseph's companions continued to be nervous and concerned for their safety. Joseph had been in Inuit country along with his father, spoke a little Inuktitut and was familiar with their customs, but that was not the case with the others. When they sat down to eat, they were handed slices of raw meat which was a common part of the Inuit diet. One of the men began to complain.

"What do they think we are, feeding us this, dogs?" he muttered. Joseph quietly informed the man that this was the Inuit way and that he needed to stop his complaining or he might have reason to be afraid if he continued to make insulting comments about their hosts. Things quieted down and the Inuit hunters provided them with plenty of food for themselves and their dogs for their return journey. The old fear of the Inuit, harbored by Joseph's Dogrib companions, was replaced by feelings of gratitude and respect.

Many years later, at age of eighty three, Joseph had a heart attack and ended up in hospital. While there, he shared a room with an Inuk who was around the same age as Joseph. As they exchanged stories, it wasn't long before they realized that they had met before and they ended up talking about that fateful day on the Barrenlands when a helping hand was extended. He took the opportunity once again to thank his roommate for the help he and his fellow hunters had provided at a critical time.

On another occasion, Joseph went hunting for muskrat one early spring in his rat canoe when he was in his late seventies. He was dropped off at the Stag River to begin his hunt. A blizzard blew in that night and lasted for two days. It had winds strong enough to cause the breakup of the ice on Marion Lake creating crushing ice flows that pushed through the narrows of the Frank Channel. The storm abated and the family were contemplating going in search of him if he didn't show up that day.

I was on my way to work at the time and, as I looked out onto Marion Lake, in the distance I saw Joseph making his way through the ice flows. A short while later, he pulled up to the shore close to Dog Island having navigated his way through all that heaving ice with no damage to the canoe. But the real wonder of it was that the craft didn't end up foundering, it had so little clearance above the water. It was filled to the gunnel from stem to stern with fish, muskrat and beaver, a bounty of impressive proportions for two days of work in the middle of a blizzard. He climbed out of the canoe, stiff from his arthritis, steadied himself on shore, lit his pipe and indicated to me to attend to the canoe and its payload. He then strolled down the road to his home located one hundred and fifty yards away as if he were coming home from a mornings' walk.

On another occasion, I visited my father-in-law in the bush as he worked on his traps. He was a very private man and didn't share a lot, so I took the opportunity to ask him a few questions.

"Did they ever build sweat lodges in this area when you were young?" I asked.

"Yes, they did use them, but it was a very long time ago," was his brief response. So I let that topic drop.

"How did the people treat the dead in the past; did they bury them?" His answer this time was more detailed.

"No," he said. "They looked for a large tree, one hollowed out at the base, if possible. The body was placed in the cavity, legs folded up as if sitting by the fire. Over time, the body settled into the earth and, as it decayed, was absorbed by the roots and fed the tree. The seeds of the tree fed the birds and the fox or wolf might feed on the bones. In this way, a person goes on living in nature." Then he added somewhat sheepishly, "The priests who first came north told us that our old beliefs were evil and that even to speak about them might cause us to burn in hell. That's why we never talk much about the old beliefs."

In later years I travelled with both Joseph and Josephine to the grave sites of his mother in Rae and of his father at the village at the top of Marion Lake. In both locations the graveyards were cleared of brush every year and, within the customary fence that surrounded each of those graves, there was a wooden cross. Also however, on each of those two grave sites there was a small tree growing. I suspect that this was their subtle way of living within the parameters of their two spiritual traditions.

Joseph told me of a trip he made to the Barrenlands with another hunter, one that illustrates how they went out of their way at times to maintain contact with Dene people they knew in other communities. The story he told also contained elements of the Dene belief in medicine power or ɪk'ǫ̀ǫ̀.

Joseph and a companion spent a winter trapping in the Barrenlands from Christmas until spring and headed for home just before the spring melt, taking the long way back via the Mackenzie River. They planned to stop off at some of the small settlements along the way and visit friends and relatives they hadn't seen for quite some time. They planned to stop at Fort Providence before the last leg of their journey across Great Slave Lake back to Fort Rae.

The further south they travelled, the less snow cover there was, and to make matters more difficult for them, the Mackenzie was showing a lot of open water. By the time they got close to Fort Providence, they found themselves facing open water between them and the town. They looked across the Mackenzie and wondered how they might get to the other side. It looked pretty hopeless. As they sat by the fire that night, Joseph's travelling partner made a pronouncement.

"Don't worry Joseph, I'll use ɪk'ǫ̀ǫ̀ and we'll cross tomorrow." Joseph then described how his partner walked over to the river, turned his back to it, took a handful of salt and threw it over his shoulder as he chanted. They went to bed and in the morning, when they got up, the entire Mackenzie River between the camp and Fort Providence was covered with ice strong enough to walk on.

This was one of a number of times for me hearing someone telling of their experience with ɪk'ǫ̀ǫ̀, but it was the first I was to hear one told by Joseph. I'd heard of medicine power being used for good and for bad. It was a form of old belief that had survived the Christian teachings and the discouragement by the local clergy of what they considered superstitious practices.

Joseph continued. "After we ate breakfast that morning, we broke camp and crossed on the ice. We visited friends at Fort Providence and by the time we got up the next day the whole river was open water once again.

From there we traveled over Great Slave Lake where the ice was still thick and strong." Although he laughed at the part where his friend throws the salt over his shoulder, I was left feeling that he believed in the idea of medicine power.

It was rumoured that Joseph also possessed strong medicine power handed down to him from his father. He never claimed that and I saw no evidence of this. His son, Moise, believed his father had the power, but never witnessed any examples of him putting it to use. He told me that he didn't know why his father didn't use his gift and also wondered why he didn't pass the gift along to any member of the family.

Two other men, whose last names were, Wedzin and Wetrade, were known in the community as medicine men. One was reputed to have the power to become a changeling. The other was believed capable of travelling through the roots in the ground and, if his name was uttered, he could be in your presence in moments and could hear everything you said.

I had an interesting exchange with Joseph while visiting him on his trap line one day. I happened to mention that when we got back to Rae-Edzo, I was going up north to Inuvik for a meeting. He looked puzzled for a moment.

"What do white people mean when they say, up north?" he asked.

"When we head towards the North Pole, we say we're heading up north." I responded in a matter of fact way. That seemed fairly straightforward to me. He hesitated and then responded.

"In our culture we say that we go down north and up south. All of our largest rivers flow down towards the north. When we travel down the Mackenzie as it flows to the Arctic Ocean, we are travelling down north. When we travel up the Mackenzie towards Edmonton we say we are going up south." He went with the flow of the water, while I went by the points of the compass. I noticed, as time passed, that I could generally tell whether a person was born in the North or not, when they gave me directions.

This small difference, in the way Joseph and I referenced directions, was an indication of a difference of perspective rooted in culture and language among the Dene. It was one of many things I was to learn from him about the way of life and the alternate way of thinking practiced by him and other elders throughout the Dene homeland. I learned that they often shared a different world view from the one I held upon my arrival in their territory and I am the richer for that awareness.

Joseph and Josephine Rabesca lived the traditional way and were, by example, role models. While embracing their tradition in every corner of their lives, they respected the ways of non-Indigenous people like me. We lived in mutual respect of one another as members of one large, embracing family.

Josephine Rabesca

When I stayed with my in-laws at Blackduck Camp around the time of the spring muskrat hunt, we sat around the wood stove in the evenings skinning muskrat and listening to old stories. The following story was told by my mother-in-law, Josephine Rabesca.

She began, "At the time of the fall hunt one year, when I was a young mother, we packed up our stuff and set out with our children for the Barrenlands. We got as far as Faber Lake, which is located close to the place where the village of Rae Lakes was set up years later. It was from here that the hunting party chose one of the two main routes to get to the Barrenlands.

Fall had come earlier than usual that year. It was decided that the women and children would stay behind at Faber Lake where the fishing was supposed to be good. The men felt that they needed to move fast to catch up with the caribou herd that had migrated earlier than usual. As we later learned, by the time they got to the Barrenlands, the caribou were gone and the hunters were forced to paddle far beyond the tree line towards the Coppermine River to find them. This meant that they were late in returning and we were left to look after ourselves as far as food was concerned.

There were very few rabbits around that year, the ducks were overflying us and we were catching very few fish. We were running out of food. Early one morning, while the men were away, Julie, my eldest daughter, went to the lake to get water and saw a moose swimming towards one of the islands. She hurried back and told me. I quickly grabbed a skinning knife and some strips of hide and told her to bring one of the tipi poles with her as we rushed to the shoreline.

We jumped into the canoe with Julie in the front and me at the stern and pushed off. I paddled as hard as I could keeping the moose in sight, while Julie followed my instructions and tied the knife to the end of the tipi pole with the strips of hide. We caught up to the moose as it neared the shore of one of the islands. If its feet had touched bottom, we would have missed our chance. Julie got ready with the homemade spear in her hands as I steered the canoe as close to the moose as possible. She plunged the spear into the moose and killed it. Chance that brought that moose to us; it was quick thinking and team work that got him," she said, as she concluded the story.

Josephine, along with carrying out her daily household functions, collected herbs and made traditional medicines. I showed up one day with a strange root I had collected from the lake. It had bobbed up from the lake bottom and gave me a scare as it broke through the surface with its roots spread out from it like an octopus's tentacles. I cut a chunk off and brought it to Josephine. When I described my reaction to its sudden appearance, she laughed and said she was happy I had brought it back because it was a traditional medicine, a form of laxative. It was the large root of the water lily plant.

On another occasion, I was all set to head out to the Barrenlands on a fall hunt when she dug into her bag of extraordinary odds and ends. She pulled out a piece of birch tree fungus.

"Two things I have to tell you about this," she said. "Whenever possible, make sure not to hunt alone on the Barrenlands. This is the most important rule, because there are grizzly bears all over the Barrenlands. But if you do find yourself alone, be sure to carry this strong medicine, 'k'I ti'ehte', with you. It keeps the bears away after you kill a caribou. The bears can smell blood for many miles and will come looking. If your back is turned to them, they will attack. This fungus will protect you." Then she handed it to me.

"How does it work?" I asked.

"You light it, then you blow it out and it will smolder, giving off steady smoke, much like incense does," she answered. "Place it behind you while you're skinning the animal. If bears are around, they'll smell strong medicine and leave you alone." From then on, I always brought this fungus with me on the hunts I undertook in the Barrenlands.

When I first had reason to use the fungus in the Barrenlands, I was acutely aware that I was in the grizzly bears' pantry and acted on Josephine's advice. I lit the fungus before I got to work skinning the caribou. Why or how works, I don't know. But I had learned to respect this kind of traditional Dene knowledge passed on by those who held it.

Another incident involving Josephine had to do with a sweat lodge ceremony. The tradition of the sweat lodge was not practiced among the Dene for generations because the Church actively discouraged it. My good friend, John B. Zoe, was working with the local Friendship Center in Rae Edzo exploring ways to address the loss of traditions and cultural practices in the community. John had heard of the success that other Dene tribes in the south had with reviving the sweat lodge ceremony. He decided to bring in a medicine man from Sioux Valley, Alden Pompana, to re-introduce the sweat lodge tradition to the community.

Upon Alden's arrival, a meeting was held with the male elders. John and Alden wanted the elders to decide where the sweat lodge would be best located. There was surprisingly strong resistance from the elders to the very idea of a sweat lodge and they told John and Alden that they would have nothing to do with it and refused to allow it to be set up in town. John approached me and asked if I would allow it to set it up on Dog Island where I had my home, a location not officially part of the town. I promptly agreed. However, after agreeing I had second thoughts about going against the wishes of the elders in the community. In order to settle the issue in my mind, I visited my in-laws, Joseph and Josephine Rabesca, to sound them out on the idea of the sweat being set up on Dog Island.

I went to their house and told them about the sweat, the proposed location and the resistance of the elders. Josephine quietly listened and my father-in-law sat by stolidly as I talked, not saying a word. I asked Josephine if she was familiar with the sweat lodge tradition.

"Yes," she responded. "I attended one a long time ago." There was a visitor at the house, a Mrs. Charlo, and they began to chat about the sweat lodge and the taboos related to it since the arrival of the missionaries. I didn't follow all of what they said, but after their exchange, Josephine turned to me, looked me in the eye and made a comment that caught us all off guard.

"Build it and I'll be there," she said. Mrs. Charlo agreed to join her in supporting the sweat. Having heard her decision, I felt comfortable going ahead with helping to set up the sweat lodge on the island.

The women at the Friendship Center became more accepting of the idea of a sweat after hearing the positive results it had in places like Hobbema where Rae Edzo people sometimes went to Pow Wows. When I met with Alden and he explained what needed to be done and what materials were required. John B. Zoe and a couple of young people assisted us in harvesting the willows around Russell Lake. We then set up the lodge on Dog Island about thirty feet from our home. When the lodge was, a special ceremony was held to prepare the it for use.

The lodge was the talk of the town with mutterings about it being an outrage, an evil, shamanic temple. But the town was also abuzz with the fact that Josephine was going to attend the sweat. That evening the sweat was made ready. Some Dene from Yellowknife and Charlie Mantla assisted at the sweat doing fire keeping and other duties. Josephine arrived and entered the sweat along with other elderly women from the community. It was a momentous occasion. They sat huddled together there in the spirit of their ancestors and at the same time, some of them gave thanks in the Christian tradition. They knew how to be strong in two traditions, one new and one very old and neither one nor the other were denied in the lodge. While in the lodge, Josephine spoke with pride about that first sweat she had attended as a young girl at a time when the church was urging the Dene to shun such practices. She was now leading a return to the tradition of her youth. It was a proud moment for all of us.

The sweat continued for about a week and many people participated. It was the very thing John B. Zoe had wanted, a landmark symbol of the beginning of a cultural revival in the community and one in which Josephine Rabesca had played a key role.

A NEW BEGINNING

It was nineteen eighty six and I was in the finishing stages of installing a metal roof on a two story building in Fort Rae in a temperature of around minus forty degrees. I was short of some minor materials to finish the work. I knelt there frustrated as a raven dropped by and stood on the metal roof a few feet away. As I observed him, I reflected on my work situation.

"Do I want to do this kind of work in these conditions for the rest of my working life and to continue to be like this raven, clinging to a metal roof in bone chilling winter and doing the same in the sweltering heat of summer?" I was facing a one hundred and forty mile round trip to Yellowknife and back to purchase the materials I needed to finish this job. I was cold, frustrated and not keen on making the trip. I concluded, "No this is not what I want."

The thought came to me. "If there was a building supplier in town, there would be no travelling involved and I could wrap up this job right away." It was just a passing thought at that moment, but it quickly morphed into a concrete idea. "There should be a building supply store in this community." I'd hit on a life altering idea. "I'll set up a hardware store in Fort Rae."

It seemed so logical. That thought became a firm decision there and then. I didn't know how I would do it, but knew that I would. I thanked the raven for dropping by and headed for out to get the supplies I needed, but in a better frame of mind.

Soon after, I set to work on my plan to build the hardware store I had envisioned. John B. Zoe, planned to build a service-station in the community around the same time. A segment of land had been allocated to serve as an Industrial Estate in Fort Rae and both John and I got the sites we needed there to construct our buildings on adjoining properties. I received help from my brother Pat when it came to applications for funding supports for the building supply store and John gave me the contract to build his gas station. Everything was falling into place. I set to work on both buildings and had a crew of two working with me, Charlie Mantla and George Koyena. They were great tradesmen; we worked well as a team and had both buildings up in short order.

I was pleased with how well the work had gone and wanted to show my appreciation to Charlie and George. I made two replicas of the toolbox my father had helped me to make when I first started to work in Winnipeg. I filled the toolboxes with a wide selection of tools from my newly stocked store and delivered them to their homes. I felt it would be an unexpected and practical gift for both of them and I was not disappointed at their reaction on receiving them.

The building supply store was a dream business, not a great money maker, but one that provided me with a fulfilling occupation and an opportunity to be a contributing member of my community. Everything I had done since first coming to north had prepared me for this eventuality. My acquired knowledge and skills in the building industry, the strong personal and community relationships I had formed while living and working with the Dene throughout the NWT, all contributed to this moment. I was living life with a sense of purpose and in a place where I wanted to be.

My business was located in the community of Rae Edzo. My home sat nearby on Dog Island which was separated from the mainland by a one hundred foot gap. I backfilled that gap to link my island home to the yellow ribbon of road I had travelled from Winnipeg to the land of the Dene in the NWT. I came to find purpose in my life, and find it I did.

ACKNOWLEDGEMENTS

Many people are referenced in this memoir, people who shaped not only the stories, but had an impact on my life's direction. My thanks to all of you for the time we shared and for enriching the experience of the years I lived and worked in the Dene communities of the NWT.

My special thanks to:

My eldest brother, Gerry Moore, for your tireless efforts working on the manuscript and for encouraging me in my early years to keep a journal of my experiences.

My copy editors, Kim Harkness and brother Raymond, for your assistance in tidying up the text in so many ways.

My wife, Cynthia, for her help, encouragement and patience as I struggled to bring the book to completion. Especially for helping me paddle this part of this journey through life. Without her encouragement this book would never have been possible.

GLOSSARY

Translations

Nahga (nàhgą):	Bushman
Gots oka:	a muskeg berry
Dzehkwii:	the Joker
Gohzii:	handball game
Ik'oo':	medicine power
Ne kaowo:	not the boss
Soomba kaowo:	money's the boss
Dedii:	moose
Naedzo:	elder/prophet
Sih nek'e:	wind between the hills
Da'at'e:	how are you?
Ohchi:	carrying bag made of hide
Tlicho:	Dogrib
yahtı jìek'oo:	the orange priest

other northern Canadiana from HANCOCK HOUSE

Bush & Arctic Pilot
9780888391674
Authors life as an aviator in the north.
$17.95

New Exploration of the Canadian Arctic
9780888395221
Documents the nickel company's grassroots exploration of the Canadian Arctic in the 1960 field season.
$17.95

Fire into Ice
9781551923345
True Story of Charles Fipke, the mining exploration geologist who discovered some of the largest diamond deposits in Canada.
$24.95

Back to the Barrens
9780888396426
Adventures through the northern wilderness.
$17.95

Bush Flying
9780888391667
A kaleidoscope of aviation stories from a former bush pilot.
$16.95

Frontier Forts & Posts of the Hudson's Bay Company
9780888395986
A historical account of fur-trading outposts in the Pacific Northwest. Non-fiction, history guidebook.
$16.95

Wing of the North
9780888390608
This is a true story about bush pilots flying in Northern British Columbia.
$14.95

Outposts & Bushplanes
9780888395566
Describes the vital role played by new light aircraft of the day and the skill of their capable pilots and engineers. Adventure-lovers and outdoors people will enjoy reading about the fine folk of the Northwest and their often-daunting exploits as they settled this isolated region during the middle of the last century
$17.95

Wing Over the Wilderness
9780888395955
Tells the story of the secret WW II airway that arched across 8,000 miles of sub-Arctic wilderness and the adventures of the men that flew it. Non-fiction, WW II history, aviation
$39.95

Hancock House Publishers
19313 0 Ave, Surrey, BC V3Z 9R9
www.hancockhouse.com
sales@hancockhouse.com
1-800-938-1114

www.ingramcontent.com/pod-product-compliance
Lightning Source LLC
Chambersburg PA
CBHW022109150426
43195CB00008B/328